A+

100 % ALGEBRA READINESS

MASTERING ESSENTIAL CONCEPTS & SKILLS

MATHEMATICS FLUENCY BOOK

GRADE 6-8

- 120 Math Concepts & Skills
- Topics Explanations
- Full Solutions
- Pre-Post & Benchmark Tests
- **1200 Practice Problems**

ZAFER BUBER Ph.D.(c)
MATHEMATICS EDUCATION

MATH TOPIA
PRESS

SINAN KANBIR, Ph.D.
MATHEMATICS EDUCATION

Paper Book

978-1-7356252-9-4

Graphic Designer - Typesetting

cemnilsen@gmail.com

Copyright © 2023 MathTopia Academy LLC.

All rights of this book and system are reserved. The text cannot be reproduced or published by electronic, mechanical, photocopy, or any recording system without the permission of MathTopia Press.

What is Math Fluency Book and what makes this book special and unique?

This book grew from working with middle school and Algebra 1 students. It covers essential math concepts and skills that all algebra students need to succeed in their coursework. This book also covers Pre-Algebra, basic geometry, and some algebra topics. Each chapter has topic explanations, notes, examples, and problems with solutions. Students will expand their understanding and develop more than 100 essential concepts and skills by completing each chapter's problem sets and understanding their solutions. Pre, post, and benchmark tests help measure students' development of math fluency. Students will also enjoy and engage in mathematical puzzles they can find at the end of some chapters.

Target audiences of this book

- Grade 5-8 students.
- Middle school mathematics teachers using the supplement to the math course book.
- Pre-Algebra and Algebra 1 students.
- Parents who want to study to help improve their kids' math skills.
- Participants in mathematics contests such as AMC 8, MathCON, Math Kangaroo, Math Counts, and Math League.

Acknowledgments

We would like to thank MathTopia Academy teaching assistant Andrew Carratu, Sarah Zuge, Busra Sahin Celik, and Ava Kumar for holding problem-solving sessions, reading the draft of this book, and proving valuable comments. We are also thankful to the University of Wisconsin- Stevens Point elementary and middle school teacher candidates and particularly Bailey Crowell and Maycie Navis for putting valuable feedback and contributions. Lastly, we would like to mention and thank to MathTopia Academy middle grade students who joined weekly sessions and gained great math fluency by completing the draft version of this book.

TABLE OF CONTENTS

PRE-TEST
Math Fluency Pre-Test & Evaluation 1

CHAPTER 01
Whole Numbers & Operations 5
Problem Set 1 7
Problem Set 2 9

CHAPTER 02
Integers & Operations 11
Problem Set 1 15
Problem Set 2 17

CHAPTER 03
Primes & Divisibility 19
Problem Set 1 23
Problem Set 2 25

CHAPTER 04
Least Common Multiple(LCM) & Greatest Common Divisor (GCD) 27
Problem Set 1 29

CHAPTER 05
Fractions & Operations 31
Problem Set 1 35
Problem Set 2 37

CHAPTER 06
Decimals/Percents & Operations 39
Problem Set 1 43
Problem Set 2 45

CHAPTER 07
Evaluations & Expressions 47
Problem Set 1 49
Problem Set 2 51

CHAPTER 08
Equations 53
Problem Set 1 55
Problem Set 2 57

CHAPTER 09
Algebra & Geometry - 1 59
Problem Set 1 61

CHAPTER 10
BENCHMARK [Chapter 1-9] 63

CHAPTER 11
Equations & Inequalities 65
Problem Set 1 69
Problem Set 2 71

CHAPTER 12
Ratios & Proportions	73
Problem Set 1	75
Problem Set 2	77

CHAPTER 13
Operations & Functions	79
Problem Set 1	83
Problem Set 2	85

CHAPTER 14
Exponents & Radicals	87
Problem Set 1	91
Problem Set 2	93
Problem Set 3	95

CHAPTER 15
Geometry Basics	97
Problem Set 1	101
Problem Set 2	103

CHAPTER 16
Coordinate Geometry	105
Problem Set 1	109
Problem Set 2	111

CHAPTER 17
Geometry 3-D	113
Problem Set 1	117

CHAPTER 18
Linear Equations	119
Problem Set 1	123
Problem Set 2	125

CHAPTER 19
Number Systems	127
Problem Set 1	131
Problem Set 2	133

CHAPTER 20
Data & Statistics	135
Problem Set 1	139
Problem Set 2	141

CHAPTER 21
Sets	143
Problem Set 1	147

CHAPTER 22
BENCHMARK [Chapter 11-21]	149

POST-TEST
Math Fluency Post-Test & Evaluation	151

SOLUTIONS
Solutions	155

ANSWER KEYS
Chapter 01-22	199

BOOK'S TARGET CONCEPTS AND SKILLS

This Math Fluency book contains Pre & Post tests, two benchmark tests, 22 chapters with topic explanations, 200 examples and problems, and 40 problem sets with 1000 problems. Overall it covers the following list of concepts and skills essential for success in middle school mathematics and algebra courses.

Chapter 1
- Skill 1 Positive and negative integers
- Skill 2 Odd and even numbers
- Skill 3 Order of operations
- Skill 4 Associative property
- Skill 5 Distributive property

Chapter 2
- Skill 6 Negative and positive integers
- Skill 7 Integer operations
- Skill 8 Odd and even numbers
- Skill 9 Evaluating expressions
- Skill 10 Additive and multiplicative inverses
- Skill 11 Consecutive numbers and sums

Chapter 3
- Skill 12 Prime numbers & composite numbers
- Skill 13 Prime factorizations
- Skill 14 Divisors & Factors
- Skill 15 Perfect squares & perfect cubes
- Skill 16 Divisibility Rules

Chapter 4
- Skill 17 Divisors / factors of numbers
- Skill 18 Multiples of numbers
- Skill 19 Least Common Multiple (LCM)
- Skill 20 Greatest Common Divisors (GCD)

Chapter 5
- Skill 21 Equal fractions and fraction types
- Skill 22 Comparing fractions
- Skill 23 Adding and subtracting fractions
- Skill 24 Multiplying fractions
- Skill 25 Dividing fractions

Chapter 6
- Skill 26 Defining the percent and percentage of a number.
- Skill 27 Defining decimal numbers.
- Skill 28 Conversion between decimals, fractions, and percents.

Chapter 7
- Skill 29 Variables
- Skill 30 Evaluating an expression
- Skill 31 Adding and subtracting expressions
- Skill 32 Combining complex expressions
- Skill 33 Simplifying rational expressions

Chapter 8
- Skill 34 Setting up an equation
- Skill 35 Solving simple equations
- Skill 36 Solving multi steps equations
- Skill 37 Solving simple rational equations

Chapter 9
- Skill 38 Angles
- Skill 39 Areas of basic polygons
- Skill 40 Perimeters of basic polygons
- Skill 41 Volumes of basic 3-D shapes
- Skill 42 Setting equations by using geometric figures

Chapter 11
- Skill 43 Solving equations involving decimals
- Skill 44 Solving equations involving rational expressions
- Skill 45 Holistic equation solving- Cover-up method
- Skill 46 Absolute values
- Skill 47 Solving absolute value equations
- Skill 48 Inequalities
- Skill 49 Solving linear inequalities

Chapter 12
- **Skill 50** Defining ratios and proportions
- **Skill 51** Solving proportion equations
- **Skill 52** Solving real-life problems with ratios and proportions
- **Skill 53** Applying ratios & proportions to similar figures

Chapter 13
- **Skill 54** Defining functions & binary operations.
- **Skill 55** Representing linear functions in various forms.
- **Skill 56** Solving equations involving functions & binary operations.
- **Skill 57** Applying linear equations to real-life situations.

Chapter 14
- **Skill 58** Defining exponential numbers.
- **Skill 59** Defining the square root of a number.
- **Skill 60** Using the rules of exponents and square roots for simplifying expressions.
- **Skill 61** Using the rules of exponents and square roots for solving equations.

Chapter 15
- **Skill 62** Basic properties of rectangle and square
- **Skill 63** Angle properties of a triangle
- **Skill 64** Side properties of a triangle
- **Skill 65** Special right triangles
- **Skill 66** The Pythagorean Theorem
- **Skill 67** Triangle similarities

Chapter 16
- **Skill 68** Defining the coordinate plane.
- **Skill 69** Applying the Distance & Midpoint Formulas in the coordinate plane.
- **Skill 70** Applying the rules of reflection in the coordinate plane.
- **Skill 71** Area & Perimeter in the coordinate plane

Chapter 17
- **Skill 72** Defining prisms.
- **Skill 73** Finding the surface area and volume of prisms.
- **Skill 74** Finding the circumference, area, arc length, and sector area of a circle.
- **Skill 75** Finding the surface area and volume of a cylinder.

Chapter 18
- **Skill 76** Defining linear equations in one/two variables.
- **Skill 77** Solving linear equations.
- **Skill 78** Defining linear functions.
- **Skill 79** Graphing linear functions.

Chapter 19
- **Skill 80** Defining the decimal system.
- **Skill 81** Defining number sets and their connections.
- **Skill 82** Prime numbers and prime factorization.
- **Skill 83** Converting a repeating decimal to a fraction.
- **Skill 84** Rationalizing a denominator

Chapter 20
- **Skill 85** Defining main measures of central tendency.
- **Skill 86** Finding main measures of central tendency for a given data set.
- **Skill 87** Using various frequency charts to represent different data types.

Chapter 21
- **Skill 88** Defining sets and subsets.
- **Skill 89** Defining union and intersection of sets.
- **Skill 90** Defining the difference set.
- **Skill 91** Applying the Inclusion-Exclusion Principle to real-life situations.

What is Procedural Fluency?
NCTM Position

Procedural fluency is a critical component of mathematical proficiency. Procedural fluency is the ability to apply procedures accurately, efficiently, and flexibly; to transfer procedures to different problems and contexts; to build or modify procedures from other procedures; and to recognize when one strategy or procedure is more appropriate to apply than another. To develop procedural fluency, students need experience in integrating concepts and procedures and building on familiar procedures as they create their own informal strategies and procedures. Students need opportunities to justify both informal strategies and commonly used procedures mathematically, to support and justify their choices of appropriate procedures, and to strengthen their understanding and skill through distributed practice (National Council of Teachers of Mathematics (NCTM), 2014).

Procedural fluency is more than memorizing facts or procedures, and it is more than understanding and being able to use one procedure for a given situation. Procedural fluency builds on a foundation of conceptual understanding, strategic reasoning, and problem solving.

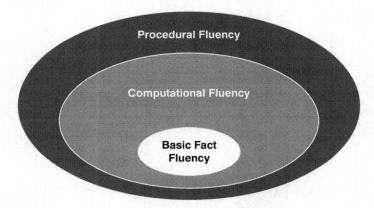

Procedural fluency encompasses both basic fact fluency and computational fluency.
This figure is adapted from (Bay-William et.al 2022).

Three components of procedural fluency defined by NCTM (2014) are as follows:

1. Efficiency
2. Flexibility
3. Accuracy

Principles and Standards for School Mathematics states, "Computational fluency refers to having efficient and accurate methods for computing. Students exhibit computational fluency when they demonstrate *flexibility* in the computational methods they choose, *understand* and can explain these methods, and produce accurate answers efficiently. The computational methods that a student uses should be based on mathematical ideas that the student understands well, including the structure of the baseten number system, properties of multiplication and division, and number relationships" (p. 152).

Math Fluency Pre-Test & Evaluation

1. Compute: $86 - 72 \div 8 \times 3$

2. What is the sum of the quotient and remainder when you divide 7550 by 15?

3. What number should go in the blank so that the equation below will be true?

   _____ $\times 90 = 30$

4. What number should go in the blank so that the equation below will be true?

   $8 \div$ _____ $= 40$

5. What is 15% of 40?

6. Find an integer between 100 and 150 that is divisible by 7.

7. Find the greatest common factor of 28, 42, and 56.

8. Find the largest prime factor of 72.

9. Solve for x: $(x - 9) \div 4 = 12$

10. Evaluate $14 \times 8.9 + 86 \times 8.9$

Math Fluency

11. Let a, b, and c be integers satisfying
    $5 < a < b < c < 10$ and $a + b = 14$.
    What is b?

12. Two fractions are equally spaced between $\frac{5}{12}$ and $\frac{2}{3}$. What is the larger of the two fractions?

13. If $b = 15 - \frac{15}{3a + 1}$
    What is the value of b when $a = \frac{4}{3}$?

14. If $\frac{1 + 3x}{2} = \frac{5 - x}{2}$,
    What is x?

15. The perimeter of the figure is 18 cm, what is a?

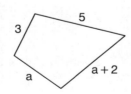

16. What is the perimeter of a regular hexagon with side length $4\frac{3}{4}$ ft?
    Express your answer as lowest term?

17. $\frac{x}{y} \div \frac{2}{3} = \frac{5}{6}$ is given. What is $\frac{y}{x}$?
    Express your answer as lowest term?

18.
    If the marking on the number line are equally spaced, what is A?

19. What is the sum of the possible values of a if the number below is divisible by 3?

    354 a 1

20. Suppose f is a linear function and $f(x) = 4x + 6$
    What is the value of $f(-2) + f(4)$?

Math Fluency Pre-Test — PRE-TEST

21. The perimeter of a triangle is 36 feet. If the sides are in the ratio of 2 : 3 : 4, find the length of the longest side?

22. What is the largest integer value of a:
    $6 \times (a + 5) < 48$.

23. If $n(A) = 40$, $n(B) = 48$, and $n(A \cup B) = 70$. What is $n(A \cap B)$?

24. Triangle ABC has its vertices at A(4, 2), B(10, 2), and C(7, 8). What is the area of the triangle?

25. What is the sum of the mean, median, and mode of the numbers 4, 6, 2, 6, 3, 5, 0, 6 ?

26. What is the value of n if $\sqrt{9 + \sqrt{n}} = 4$?

27. The prime factorization of
    $8! = 8 \times 7 \times 6 \times 5 \times 4 \times 3 \times 2 \times 1$ is the form of
    $2^a \times 3^b \times 5^c \times 7^d$
    What is $a + b + c + d$?

28. Determine the quotient when you divide $4\frac{5}{6}$ by $\frac{2}{3}$. Express your answer as a mixed number.

29. If $6 + \dfrac{12}{6 - \dfrac{12}{5x + 1}} = 9$,

    what is x?

30. Note: The volume of a cylinder is $\pi r^2 h$. The circumference of a circle is $2\pi r$.

    If the circumference of the circle is 16π and height of the cylinder is 8, then find the volume.

Math Fluency Pre-Test & Evaluation

Problem	Topic	My Answer	Correct Answer	Notes
1	Order of operations			
2	Long division			
3	Multiplication			
4	Division			
5	Percent			
6	Divisibility			
7	GCD/LCM			
8	Prime factors			
9	Equations			
10	Distributive property			
11	Integers			
12	Fractions			
13	Arithmetic manipulations			
14	Equations			
15	Geometric equations			
16	Fraction multiplications			
17	Fraction Divisions			
18	Number Lines			
19	Divisibility			
20	Functions			
21	Ratios and Proportions			
22	Inequalities			
23	Sets			
24	Coordinate Geometry			
25	Statistics and Data			
26	Radicals			
27	Prime factorizations			
28	Fraction Divisions			
29	Complex Equations			
30	Geometry			

CHAPTER 1
Whole Numbers & Operations

✓ Target Concepts and Skills

- ☐ Positive and negative integers
- ☐ Odd and even numbers
- ☐ Order of operations
- ☐ Associative property
- ☐ Distributive property

Definition 1.1 – Natural Numbers.

$\mathbb{N} = \{1, 2, 3, 4, 5, ...\}$ The natural numbers are also called the counting numbers.

Definition 1.2 – Whole Numbers.

Whole numbers are positive numbers, including zero, without any decimal or fractional parts. They are numbers that represent whole things without pieces. The set of whole numbers is represented mathematically by the set
$\mathbb{W} = \{0, 1, 2, 3, 4, 5 ...\}$

Definition 1.3 – Integers.

Any number that is not a fraction or decimal.
- Positive integers, $\mathbb{Z}^+ = \{1, 2, 3, ...\}$,
- Negative integers, $\mathbb{Z}^- = \{..... , -3, -2, -1\}$,
- Integers, $\mathbb{Z} = \mathbb{Z}^- \cup \{0\} \cup \mathbb{Z}^+$, 0 has no sign.

Definition 1.4 – Odd and Even Numbers

An odd number is an integer which is not a multiple of two. An integer that is not an odd number is an even number.

Example 1.1

- $2c + 3$ is always odd.
- If $2a + b$ is odd, then b is odd.

Definition 1.5

A digit is a written symbol for any of the ten numbers from 0 to 9.

Problem 1.1

If a and b are distinct digits, then what is the maximum value of 5a + 6b?

Solution 1.1

In order to create the largest value we replace 9 with b and 8 with a. So,
$5(8) + 6(9) = 40 + 54 = 94$.

Remark 1.1 – Order of Operations

First of all, parentheses must be performed (but some exceptions) and exponents are next. Division or multiplication have the same priority, and addition or subtraction have the same priority. Again, we need to use the following conventions on order of operations.

- All powers (exponents) are considered first
- Multiplication and division are considered from left to right.
- Addition and subtraction are considered from left to right.

Problem 1.2

Evaluate $5 - 8 \div 4 \times (3 - 1)$

Solution 1.2

By the order of operations
$5 - \underbrace{8 \div 4}_{\text{even}} \times (2)$
$= 5 - 2 \times 2$ (from left to right)
$= 5 - 4 = 1$

Math Fluency

CHAPTER 1

Whole Numbers & Operations

Problem 1.3

Evaluate

$35 - 10 \div 2 \times 5 + 3$

Solution 1.3

$35 - 10 \div 2 \times 5 + 3$

$= 35 - 5 \times 5 + 3$

{division and multiplication working from left}

$= 35 - 25 + 3$

{subtraction and addition working from left}

$= 10 + 3 = 13$

Remark 1.2 – PEMDAS - Distributive & Associative Prop

For example, $24 \times 12 - 23 \times 12$, we see that students just memorize the PEMDAS mnemonic they learned. They could start with multiplication and then subtraction which takes additional step. Instead, knowing appropriate number properties such as the associative property of multiplication or, the distributive property of multiplication over addition subtraction would be more efficent.

Problem 1.4

Simplify the following:

a) $3 \times \left(128 \times \dfrac{1}{3}\right)$

b) $81 \times 52 - 71 \times 52$

c) $25 \times (13 \times 4)$

Solution 1.4

a) Using associative and commutative properties of multiplication,

$3 \times \left(128 \times \dfrac{1}{3}\right) = 3 \times \left(\dfrac{1}{3} \times 128\right)$

$\phantom{3 \times \left(128 \times \dfrac{1}{3}\right)} = \left(3 \times \dfrac{1}{3}\right) \times 128$

$\phantom{3 \times \left(128 \times \dfrac{1}{3}\right)} = 1 \times 128$

$\phantom{3 \times \left(128 \times \dfrac{1}{3}\right)} = 128$

b) Using the distributive property of multiplication over subtraction

$81 \times 52 - 71 \times 52 = (81 - 71) \times 52$

$ = 10 \times 52$

$ = 520$

c) Using associative and commutative properties of multiplication

$25 \times (13 \times 4) = 25 \times (4 \times 13)$

$ = (25 \times 4) \times 13$

$ = 100 \times 13$

$ = 1300$

Problem 1.5

Compute $61 \cdot 9 + 61 \cdot 91$

Solution 1.5

Instead of separately computing $61 \cdot 9$ and $61 \cdot 91$, we can use the distributive property:

$61 \cdot 9 + 61 \cdot 91 = 61 \cdot (9 + 91)$

$= 61 \cdot 100 = 6100.$

Problem 1.6

What is $24 \cdot 16 \cdot 28 \div (12 \cdot 8 \cdot 14)$?

Solution 1.6

Instead of multiplying first top and bottom number, we can bring similar number together

$\left(24 \cdot \dfrac{1}{12}\right)\left(16 \cdot \dfrac{1}{8}\right)\left(28 \cdot \dfrac{1}{14}\right) = \left(\dfrac{24}{12}\right) \cdot \left(\dfrac{16}{8}\right) \cdot \left(\dfrac{28}{14}\right)$

Problem 1.7

Compute $(128 \cdot 4) \div (128 \cdot 32)$

Solution 1.7

We convert the division to multiplication

$128 \cdot 64 \cdot \dfrac{1}{128 \cdot 32} = \left(128 \cdot \dfrac{1}{128}\right) \cdot \left(64 \cdot \dfrac{1}{32}\right)$

$= \left(\dfrac{128}{128}\right) \cdot \left(\dfrac{64}{32}\right) = 1 \cdot 2 = 2$

Problem Set 1 — Whole Numbers & Operations — CHAPTER 1

1. $2 \times 4^2 - (8 \div 2)$

2. What is the value of
   $2 \times 0 \times 1 + 1$?

3. Compute:
   $2 + 2 \times 2 - 2 \div 2 + 2$

4. Compute:
   $-2 \times (6 \div 3)^2$

5. Which of the following is a multiple of 5?

   a) $1 \times 2 + 3 + 4$ b) $1 + 2 \times 3 + 4$
   c) $1 + 2 \times 3 \times 4$ d) $1 \times 2 \times 3 \times 4$

6. If $\dfrac{8 + a}{20} = \dfrac{1}{2}$
   What is a?

7. Which of the following is correct?

   a) $1 \times 8 + 8 \times 1 = 18$
   b) $0 \times 9 + 9 \times 0 = 18$
   c) $2 \times 7 + 7 \times 2 = 28$
   d) $3 \times 6 + 6 \times 3 = 18$

8. Evaluate
   $25 \times (13 \times 4)$.

9. Evaluate
   $5 - 3 \times 4^3 \div (7 - 1)$

10. Compute:
    $76 - 72 \div 8 \times 3$

CHAPTER 1 — Whole Numbers & Operations — Problem Set 1

11. What is the remainder when 493573 is divided by 7?

12. Simplify

    $6 + 3 \times (8 - 3) \div 5$

13. Simplify

    $16 - 4 \div (1 \div 4) + 1$

14. Simplify

    $80 - 64 \div 8 \times 4$

15. What number goes in the box so that

    $10 \times 20 \times 30 \times 40 \times 50 = 100 \times 4 \times 300 \times \square$

16. How many even whole numbers between 1 and 99 are multiples of 5?

17. Simplify

    $81 \times 5^2 + 19 \times 5^2$

18. Evaluate:

    $-12^2 + 5[8 \div (3 - 1)]$

19. If $3 \times 3 \times 5 \times 5 \times 7 \times 9 = 3 \times 3 \times 7 \times m \times m$
    What is a possible value of m?

20. Which of the following expression is equal to an odd integer for every integer n?
    a) 2023 − 3n   b) 2023 + n
    c) 2023n   d) 2023 + 2n

Problem Set 2 — Whole Numbers & Operations — CHAPTER 1

1. Evaluate $(-2.5 \times 0.73) \times 4$.

2. Evaluate $14 \times 8.9 + 86 \times 8.9$.

3. Evaluate $1513 \times 692 - 1513 \times 691$.

4. What is the value of 123,123 divided by 1001?

5.
```
      8 7 9
    x 4 9 2
    x 7 5 8
    7 y 1 1
    3 5 z 6
```
What is $x + y + z$?

6. $21 \times 31 = 651$.
   Use this to help you calculate 22×32.

7. Compute
   $4 \times 99 + 3 \times 99 + 2 \times 99 + 99$

8. What is the value of
   $(175 + 278 + 479) - (75 + 78 + 279)$

9. How many perfect squares are less than 1000?

10. What is the sum
    $5 + 10 + 15 + \ldots + 95 + 100$?

CHAPTER 1 — Whole Numbers & Operations — Problem Set 2

11. What is the sum of all two-digit multiples of 9?

12. Compute

    $4(101 + 103 + 105 + 107 + 109 + 111 + 113 + 117 + 119)$

13. Which of the following is the sum of three consecutive integers?

    A) 14 B) 7 C) 26 D) 27 E) 38

14. Let n be a positive integer.

    If $(1 + 2 + 3 + 4 + 5)^2 = 1^3 + 2^3 + ... + n^3$

    What is n?

15. What is the digit in the ones place of the result of multiplying?

    $1 \times 2 \times 3 \times 4 \times 5 \times 6 \times 7 \times 8 \times 9$

16. What is the largest value of $a \times b^c$.

    When we replace 2, 3, and 4 with a, b, and c once.

17. Compute:

    $(3^3 - 3) \div 4 \times 6 \div 1$

18. To make the statement $(10 \,?\, 5) + 4 - (10 - 9) = 5$ true, what operation should be replaced for?

19. If a, b are distinct digits, then what is the maximum value of 7a + 5b?

20. A = 26 × 301.

    B = 13 × 601.

    Without calculating B or A, find B − A.

CHAPTER 2
Integers & Operations

✓ Target Concepts and Skills

- ☐ Negative and positive integers
- ☐ Integer operations
- ☐ Odd and even numbers
- ☐ Evaluating expressions
- ☐ Additive and multiplicative inverses
- ☐ Consecutive numbers and sums

Definition 2.1

Any naural number is positive. The set {1, 2, 3, 4, 5, ...} is called the set of positive integers.

Given a natural number n, we define its opposite $-n$ as the unique number $-n$ such that.

$n + (-n) = (-n) + n = 0$.

The collection $\{-1, -2, -3, -4, -5, ...\}$ of all the opposites of the natural numbers is called the set of negative integers.

Example 2.1

We have, $(+19) + (-21) = -2$, since the loss of 21 is larger than the gain of 19 and so we obtain a loss.

Example 2.2

We have, $(-10) + (+21) = +11$, since the loss of 10 is smaller than the gain of 21 and so we obtain a gain.

Example 2.3

- We have, $(+8) - (+5) = (+8) + (-5) = 3$.
- We have, $(-8) - (-5) = (-8) + (+5) = -3$.
- We have, $(+8) - (-5) = (+8) + (+5) = 13$.
- We have, $(-8) - (+5) = (-8) + (-5) = -13$.

Remark 2.1

Order of Operations

1. Groupings (parenthesis) $10^2 - (8 + 4) + 5 \times 2$
                                  $10^2 - 12 + 5 \times 2$
2. Exponents $100 - 12 + 5 \times 2$
3. Multiplication and/or $100 - 12 + 10$
   Division left → right $88 + 10$
4. Addition and/or 98
   Subtraction left → right

Problem 2.1

Evaluate: $\dfrac{16 - (4 - 2)}{14 \div (3 + 4)}$

Solution 2.1

$\dfrac{16 - (4 - 2)}{14 \div (3 + 4)}$ {parenthesis first}

{evaluate numerator, denominator}

$= \dfrac{16 - 2}{14 \div 7}$

{do the division}

$= \dfrac{14}{2}$

$= 7$

Math Fluency

CHAPTER 2 — Integers & Operations

Problem 2.2
Evaluate $8 + 2^3 \div 4 - 5 + 3 \cdot 4$

Solution 2.2
$8 + 2^3 \div 4 - 5 + 3 \cdot 4$
$= 8 + 8 \div 4 - 5 + 3 \cdot 4$ (evaluate exponent)
$= 8 + 2 - 5 + 12$ (multiply and divide)
$= 10 - 5 + 12$ (add and subtract)
$= 5 + 12$
$= 17$

Remark 2.2
Negative bases-odd and even power

A negative base raised to an even power is positive
A negative base raised to an odd power is negative.

Example:
$(-1)^2 = -1 \times -1 = 1$
$(-1)^3 = -1 \times -1 \times -1 = -1$
$(-1)^4 = -1 \times -1 \times -1 \times -1 = 1$
$(-2)^2 = -2 \times -2 = 4$
$(-2)^3 = -2 \times -2 \times -2 = -8$
$(-2)^4 = -2 \times -2 \times -2 \times -2 = 16$

Problem 2.3
Evaluate
a. $(-3)^2$ c. $(-3)^3$ e. $-(-3)^3$
b. -3^2 d. $-(-3)^4$

Solution 2.3
a. $(-3)^2 = 9$
b. $-3^2 = -1 \times 3^2 = -9$
c. $(-3)^3 = -27$
d. $-(-3)^4 = -81$
e. $-(-3)^3 = -1 \times (-3)^3 = -1 \times -27 = 27$

Definition 2.2
A whole number is even if it has 2 as a factor and thus is divisible by 2.

A whole number is odd if it is not divisible by 2.

Remark 2.2
O : Odd number   E : Even number

Addition & Subtraction			Multiplication		
±	O	E	×	O	E
O	E	O	O	O	E
E	O	E	E	E	E

Example 2.4
a. The sum of two even numbers is always even
b. The sum of two odd numbers is always even
c. The sum of an odd number and an even number is always odd
d. The sum of three odd numbers is always odd

Remark 2.3
Numbers of numbers

If a and b are natural numbers with a > b, then there are (a − b) − 1 natural numbers between a and b.

If a and b are natural numbers with a > b, then there are (a − b) +1 natural numbers between a and b (a and b are included)

Example 2.5
What is the sum
$1 + 2 + 3 + \cdots + 99 + 100$
of all the positive integers from 1 to 100?
We can pair up the numbers into the fifty pairs
$(100 + 1) = (99 + 2) = (98 + 3) = \cdots = (50 + 51)$.
Thus we have 50 pairs that add up to 101 and the sum is $50 \times 101 = 5050$.

Integers & Operations   CHAPTER 2

Problem 2.4
Find the sum of
$2 + 4 + 6 + 8 + \ldots + 48 + 50$.

Solution 2.4
$2 + 4 + 6 + 8 + \ldots + 48 + 50$
$= (2 \cdot 1) + (2 \cdot 2) + (2 \cdot 3) + \ldots + (2 \cdot 24) + (2 \cdot 25)$
$= 2 \cdot (1 + 2 + 3 + \ldots + 24 + 25)$
$= 2 \cdot \dfrac{25 \cdot (25 + 1)}{2} = 25 \cdot 26 = 650$.

Remark 2.4
If x is the larger between x and y, the difference between x and y is $x - y$. However, if y is the larger between x and y, the difference between x and y is $y - x$.

Remark 2.5
If n is an integer, its predecessor is $n - 1$ and its successor is $n + 1$. So, the sum of three consecutive numbers is $n - 1 + n + n + 1 = 3n$.

Definition 2.3 – Additive and Multiplicative inverses
For each Real number of a, the equations $a + x = 0$ and $x + a = 0$ have a solution called the **additive inverse** of a, and denoted by $-a$.

For each Real number of a, **except for 0**, the equations $a \times x = 1$ and $x \times a = 1$ have a solution called the **multiplicative inverse** of a, and denoted by a^{-1} (and often written as $1/a$ or $\dfrac{1}{a}$).

Example 2.7
The additive inverse of $2/3$ is $-2/3$.
The multiplicative inverse of $2/3$ is $3/2$.

Problem 2.5
If $a + \dfrac{8}{3} = 0$ and $b \times \dfrac{3}{2} = 1$,
What is $a + b = ?$

Solution 2.5
a is an additive inverse of $\dfrac{8}{3}$.
So, $a = -\dfrac{8}{3}$.
b is a multiplicative inverse of $\dfrac{3}{2}$.
So, $b = \dfrac{2}{3}$.
$a + b = -\dfrac{8}{3} + \dfrac{2}{3} = -\dfrac{6}{3} = 2$.

Definition 2.1 – Consecutive Numbers
Consecutive numbers are numbers that follow each other in order. They have a difference of 1 between every two numbers. If n is a number, then n, $n + 1$, and $n + 2$ would be consecutive numbers

Example 2.8
The consecutive odd integers between 1 and 15 are 1, 3, 5, 7, 9, 11, 13, and 15.
The consecutive odd integers between –11 and –1 are –11, –9, –7, –5, –3, and –1.

Remark 2.6
The sum of n consecutive numbers is divisible by n if n is an odd number. For example, let us consider a consecutive odd number sequence 5, 7, 9, 11, 13, 15, 17 which has 7 numbers in the sequence. So according to the property, the sum of this consecutive odd number sequence should be divisible by 7.
$5 + 7 + 9 + 11 + 13 + 15 + 17 = 77$.
$77 / 7 = 11$ which satisfies this property.

CHAPTER 2

Integers & Operations

Problem 2.6

If $a < b < c < d$ and a, b, c, and d are consecutive odd numbers what is $(b - a)(d - a)$?

Solution 2.6

Let a be n then $b = a + b$, $c = a + 4$, and
$d = a + 2$, $c = a + 4$, and $d = a + 6$
$b - a = \cancel{a} + 2 - \cancel{a} = 2$, and $d - a = (\cancel{a} + 6) - (\cancel{a})$
So, $(b - c)(d - a) = 2 \cdot 6 = 12$

The First 4 to 25

Using each of the digits 1, 2, 3, and 4, once and only once, with the basic rules of arithmetic (+, −, ×, ÷, and parenthesis), express all of the integers from 1 to 25. For example, $1 = 2 \times 3 - (1 + 4)$

Answer	Solution 1	Solution 2
1		
2		
3		
4		
5		
6		
7		
8		
9		

Answer	Solution 1	Solution 2
10		
11		
12		
13		
14		
15		
16		
17		
18		
19		
20		
21		
22		
23		
24		
25		

Problem Set 1 — Integers & Operations — CHAPTER 2

1. If $9210 - 9124 = 210 - \square$, the value represented by the $\square$ is

2. Operations are placed in each $\bigcirc$ so that
   $3 \bigcirc 5 \bigcirc 7 \bigcirc 9 = 78$.
   Listed from left to right, the operations are

3. When two numbers are added, the result is -26. If one of the numbers is 11, what is the other number?

4. If $y = 3$, the value of $\dfrac{y^3 + y}{y^2 - y}$ is

5. In the addition shown, P and Q each represent single digits, and the sum is 1PP7.

   ```
       7 7 P
       6 Q P
   +   Q Q P
       1 P P 7
   ```
   What is P + Q?

6. If a, b and c are positive with
   $a \times b = 13$, $b \times c = 52$, and $c \times a = 4$,
   the value of $a \times b \times c$ is

7. If a is an even integer and b is an odd integer, which of the following could represent an odd integer?
   A) ab   B) a + 2b   C) 2a − 2b
   D) a + b + 1   E) a − b

8. In the addition of three-digit numbers shown, the letters x and y represent different digits.

   ```
       3 x y
   +   y x 3
       1 x 1 x
   ```
   What is y − x?

9. The sum of the first 100 positive integers (that is, $1 + 2 + 3 + \ldots + 99 + 100$) equal 5050.
   The sum of the first 100 positive multiples (that is, $10 + 20 + 30 + \ldots + 990 + 1000$) equals.

10. The sum of three consecutive integers is 153. The largest of these three integers is

CHAPTER 2 — Integers & Operations — Problem Set 1

11. To win a skateboard, the skill testing question is $5 \times (10 - 6) \div 2$. The correct answer is

12. What value goes in the box to make the equation $5 + \square = 10 + 20$ true?

13. What is A + B + C?

    ```
      A B 3
    + 4 A 2
    -------
      C C A
    ```

14. What is $\square + \triangle + \smiley$?

    ```
      □ ☺ ☺ △
    + □ ☺ □ □
    ---------
      2 0 1 3
    ```

15. In the morning, the temperature was –3°C. In the afternoon, the temperature was 5°C. By how many degrees Celsius did the temperature increase?

16. Evaluate $(-22) - (+32) + (+10)$.

17. What is the difference between –11 and 9?

18. Which of the following statements is false?

    A) The opposite of 7 is –7.

    B) The opposite of –13 is –13.

    C) The additive inverse of 0 is zero 0.

    D) If $a + b = 0$, then a is the additive inverse of b.

19. A is the additive inverse of –3.5 and B is the additive inverse of 5.3.

    What is A + B?

20. Find the value of

    $50 - 48 + 46 - 44 + 42 - 40 + \ldots + 8 - 6 + 4 - 2$.

Problem Set 2 — Integers & Operations — CHAPTER 2

1. Evaluate
   $4 - 8\left((-1)^2 - 4(-3)\right)$

2. Evaluate
   $5 + (-6)^2 \div (2 \cdot 3^2)$

3. What is the value of $x^4 - 2x$ when $x = 2$?

4. What is the value of $x^2 - 4x$ when $x = -2$?

5. Evaluate $3a^b + 4b^a$ when $a = 2$ and $b = 3$.

6. Compute:
   $(-3) - (3 \times (-4) + 7)$.

7. If $x = 2$ then
   $\dfrac{5x + 2}{x + 2} = ?$

8. Evaluate $3x^2 - xy^2$ when $x = 2$ and $y = 3$.

9. Evaluate $7 \times a + 18 \div (a + b)$ when $a = 2$ and $b = 4$.

10. Evaluate $10 - 5 \times b \times (10 - a)$ when $a = 2$ and $b = 4$.

CHAPTER 2 — Integers & Operations — Problem Set 2

11. If $12 \times \square = 360$
    What is $\square$?

12. How many different numbers can we create by replacing parenthesis to the expression
    $4 \times 4 + 4 \times 4$?

13. I'm thinking of two whole numbers. Their product is 36 and their sum is 13. What is the larger number?

14. How many perfect squares are less than 1000?

15. What is the tens digits of the product
    $5 \times 6 \times 7 \times 8 \times 9$?

16. $4^3 + 6^2 = 10^x$
    What is x?

17. If $a < b < c < d$ and a, b, and c, are consecutive odd numbers what is $(c - b)(d - a)$?

18. $-3(5 - 6) - 4(2 - 3) = ?$

19. If x and y are integers and $x = \dfrac{15}{y}$.
    How many distinct values of x can be found?

20. What number increases by 16 when tripled?

CHAPTER 3
Primes & Divisibility

Target Concepts and Skills

- [ ] Prime numbers & composite numbers
- [ ] Prime factorizations
- [ ] Divisors & Factors
- [ ] Perfect squares & perfect cubes
- [ ] Divisibility Rules

Definition 3.1
Primes and Composite Numbers

A prime number is a whole number greater than 1 that has exactly two factors, 1 and itself. Any number with more than two factors is a composite number. For example, 13 is prime since 1 and 13 are its only factors; 10 is composite since it has factors of 1, 2, 5, and 10.

Remark 3.1
The unique even prime number is 2. All other primes are odd primes.

Problem 3.1
Determine whether each number is prime or composite:

a. 20   b. 29   c. 121   d. 91

Solution 3.1
a. 20 is composite, because 20 can be written as $20 = 4 \times 5$ or 2×10.
b. 29 is prime, because 29 can only be factored as $29 = 1 \times 29$, which means the only positive divisors of 29 are 1 and 29.
c. 121 is composite, because $121 = 11 \times 11$.
d. 91 is composite, because $91 = 7 \times 13$

Remark 3.2 – Primes less than 100. The Sieve of Eratosthenes.

One method for finding the prime numbers is by using the Sieve of Eratosthenes.

Here are the steps to this algorithm, using the following table:

1. Cross out 1 (it is not prime)
2. Circle 2 (it is prime) and then cross out all multiples of 2
3. Circle 3 (it is prime) and then cross out all multiples of 3
4. Circle 5, then cross out all multiples of 5
5. Circle 7, then cross out all multiples of 7
6. Continue by circling the next number not crossed out, then cross out all of its multiples

The circled numbers are all the prime numbers less than 100.

1	2	3	4	5	6	7	8	9	10
11	12	13	14	15	16	17	18	19	20
21	22	23	24	25	26	27	28	29	30
31	32	33	34	35	36	37	38	39	40
41	42	43	44	45	46	47	48	49	50
51	52	53	54	55	56	57	58	59	60
61	62	63	64	65	66	67	68	69	70
71	72	73	74	75	76	77	78	79	80
81	82	83	84	85	86	87	88	89	90
91	92	93	94	95	96	97	98	99	100

Math Fluency

CHAPTER 3 — Primes & Divisibility

Definition 3.2 – Exponents

Applying an exponent to a number means to multiply the number by itself the amount of times equal to the exponent. For example:

$$\text{power} \rightarrow 2^3 = 2 \times 2 \times 2 = 8$$

where 3 is the exponent and 2 is the base.

The exponent 3 is applied to the base 2. This means to evaluate 2^3 we calculate the **base number** multiplied by itself **exponent** times. In this case 2 multiplied by itself 3 times or $2 \times 2 \times 2 = 8$.

Definition 3.3 – The Fundamental Theorem of Arithmetic

Every composite number may be uniquely expressed as a product of primes if the order is ignored. For example, 12 may be written as the product: $2 \times 2 \times 3$. This is called the prime factorization of 12.

The most commonly used method in elementary school to find the prime factorization of a number is the factor tree. Two factor trees for 190 are shown below. Both show that the prime factorization of 190 is $2 \times 5 \times 19$.

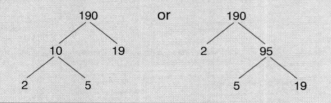

Example 3.1

Here is a factor tree of 100:

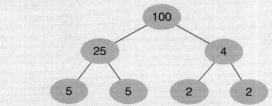

Definition 3.4 – Perfect Squares

A perfect square is the number that you get when you square another number. Some examples of perfect squares are 1, 4, 9, 16 and 25.

Example 3.2 – Perfect Squares List

The perfect squares table is given below in terms of squares of numbers from 1 to 15

Positive Integer	Integer Squared =	Perfect Squares List
1	$1^2 =$	1
2	$2^2 =$	4
3	$3^2 =$	9
4	$4^2 =$	16
5	$5^2 =$	25
6	$6^2 =$	36
7	$7^2 =$	49
8	$8^2 =$	64
9	$9^2 =$	81
10	$10^2 =$	100
11	$11^2 =$	121
12	$12^2 =$	144
13	$13^2 =$	169
14	$14^2 =$	196
15	$15^2 =$	225

Definition 3.5 – Perfect Cubes

A **perfect cube of a number** is a number that is equal to the number, multiplied by itself, three times.

Primes & Divisibility

CHAPTER 3

Example 3.3

List of Perfect Cubes 1 to 10

Number (x)	Multiplied Three times by itself	Cubes (x^3)
1	$1 \times 1 \times 1$	1
2	$2 \times 2 \times 2$	8
3	$3 \times 3 \times 3$	27
4	$4 \times 4 \times 4$	64
5	$5 \times 5 \times 5$	125
6	$6 \times 6 \times 6$	216
7	$7 \times 7 \times 7$	243
8	$8 \times 8 \times 8$	512
9	$9 \times 9 \times 9$	729
10	$10 \times 10 \times 10$	1000

Definition 3.7 – Divisibility Rules

Divisibility by 2: Every even number is divisible by 2.

Divisibility by 3: A number is divisible by 3 if the sum of its digits is divisible by 3.

Divisibility by 4: A number is divisible by 4 if its last two digits are divisible by 4.

Divisibility by 5: A number is divisible by 5 if its last digit is 0 or 5.

Divisibility by 6: A number is divisible by 6 if it is divisible by 2 and 3.

Divisibility by 8: A number is divisible by 8 if the number formed by the last three digits is divisible by 8.

Divisibility by 9: A number is divisible by 9 is the sum of its digits is divisible by 9.

Divisibility by 10: A number is divisible by 10 if its last digit is 0.

Definition 3.6 – Divisibility

If a is a whole number and b is a non-zero whole number, we say that a is divisible by b, or b divides a if and only if the remainder is 0 when a is divided by b.

Example 3.4

- Determine whether 97,128 is divisible by 2, 4, and 8.

    2|97,128 because 2|8.
    4|97,128 because 4|28.
    8|97,128 because 8|128.

Example 3.3

- 24 is a multiple of 8.
- 16 divides 32. This can be shown 16|32 (16 divides 32)
- 5 is a factor of 70. This can be shown 5|70 (5 divides 70)
- 7 is a divisor of 49.

Example 3.5

- Determine whether 83,026 is divisible by 2, 4, and 8.

    2|83,026 because 2|6.
    4 ∤ 83,026 because 4 ∤ 26.
    8 ∤ 83,026 because 8 ∤ 026.

CHAPTER 3 — Primes & Divisibility

Example 3.6

- Determine whether 1002 is divisible by 3 and 9.
  Because $1 + 0 + 0 + 2 = 3$ and $3 \mid 3$, $3 \mid 1002$.
  Because $9 \nmid 3$, $9 \nmid 1002$.

- Determine whether 14,238 is divisible by 3 and 9.
  Because $1 + 4 + 2 + 3 + 8 = 18$ and $3 \mid 18$, $3 \mid 14,238$.
  Because $9 \mid 18$, $9 \mid 14,238$.

Example 3.7

Fill the following spaces and determine divisibility.

No	Divisible by 3?	Divisible by 9?	Sum of digits	Sum of divisible by 3?	Sum of divisible by 9?
456	yes	no	4+5+6=15	yes	no
891					
892					
514					
37					
78					
79					

Problem 3.2

The five-digit 3M8M5 is divisible by 9. What is M?

Solution 3.2

Let's add the digits
$3+M+8+M+5 = 16 + 2M$ has to be multiple of 9.
Which is 18 or 27.
So, M equals 1 since 27 cannot be the sum of digits.

Problem 3.3

5m3 is a three-digit number where m is a digit.
If 5m3 is divisible by 3, find all the possible values of m.

Solution 3.3

Since 5m3 is divisible by 3, $5 + m + 3 = 8 + m$ must be divisible by 3. Let us find the possible values of m.
If $8 + m = 9$ then $m = 1$.
If $8 + m = 12$ then $m = 4$.
If $8 + m = 15$ then $m = 7$.
If $8 + m = 18$, then $m = 10$.
However, this is not possible because m must be a digit. Therefore, the only possible values of m are 1, 4, and 7.

Problem 3.4

The sum of the three digit number 2A3 and 326 is 5T9.
If 5T9 is divisible by 9, find the value of A + T.

Solution 3.4

For the number 5T9 to be divisible by 9, the sum of its digits must also be divisible by 9.
i.e. $5 + T + 9 = T + 14$ must be divisible by 9.
Since $0 \leq T \leq 9$, the only possible value of T is 4.
Also, $A + 2 = T$, which means that $A + 2 = 4$.
Therefore, $A = 2$.
The sum $A + T = 2 + 4 = 6$.

```
  2 A 3
  3 2 6
  -----
  5 T 9
```

Problem Set 1 — Primes & Divisibility — CHAPTER 3

1. The number 6 has exactly four positive divisors: 1, 2, 3, and 6. How many positive divisors does 15 have?

2. What is the smallest prime bigger than 17?

3. How many primes are between 40 and 50?

4. Express 91 as the sum of two positive perfect cubes.

5. How many integers are less than 600 but greater than 500?

6. How many whole numbers are there between 342 and 537 inclusive?

7. How many numbers between 32 and 104 (inclusive) are even?

8. Explain, in a way that your students could understand, why the formula $n_2 - n_1 + 1$ provides the answers to the questions 6 and 9.

9. How many numbers between 33 and 97 (inclusive) are even?

10. The prime factorization of 28 is?

CHAPTER 3 — Primes & Divisibility — Problem Set 1

11. A two-digit number is divisible by 8, 12 and 18. The number is between.
    A. 10 and 80
    B. 80 and 90

12. How many positive integers between 10 and 2016 are divisible by 3 and have all of their digits the same?

13. The sum of two primes is 21. What is their product?

14. What is the sum of the prime factors of 2010?

15. What number should go in the blank so that the equation below will be true?

    $8 \div \underline{} = 32$

16. Find an integer between 100 and 150 that is divisible by 8.

17. Find an integer greater than 200 and less than 300 that is divisible by both 16 and 20.

18. Find the largest prime factor of 144.

19. Find an integer between 10 and 20 divides both 48 and 72.

20. I am a multiple of 3, 4, and 5 and I am between 1 and 100. What number am I?

Problem Set 2 — Primes & Divisibility — CHAPTER 3

1. Find the remainder when 2003 × 2004 × 2005 divided by 10.

2. What is the sum of the factors of 24?

3. What is the sum of all prime divisors of 90?

4. If x is divisible by 3 and 10. Which of the following could be true or cannot be true?
   i. x is divisible by 2
   ii. x is divisible by 15
   iii. x is divisible by 30
   iv. x is divisible by 45

5. 5m6 is a three-digit number where m is a digit. If 5m6 is divisible by 3, find the sum of all the possible values of m.

6. m235m is a five-digit number where m is a digit. If m235m is divisible by 5, find the sum of all the possible values of m.

7. The 5-digit number 3A26B is a multiple of 4. What is the minimum possible value of A+B?

8. The 4-digit number ab4c is multiple of 18. Which of the following cannot be equal to a + b?
   5, 9, 10, 12, 17

9. The 6 digit number ababab is a multiple of 9. Find the sum of all possible values of a + b?

10. How many zeros are at the end of the product 25 × 25 × 8 × 8?

CHAPTER 3 — Primes & Divisibility — Problem Set 2

11. When A and B are divided by 6 the remainders are 4 and 5 respectively. Find the remainder when A + B is divided by 6.

12. 5m432n is a six-digit number where m and n are digits. If 5m432n is divisible by 9, find all the possible values of m + n.

13. For how many positive integer values of x is $\frac{60}{x}$ an integer?

14. How many ways can 2023 be written as the sum of two primes?

15. What perfect square is represented by $2^4 5^2$?

16. How many perfect squares less than 300 have three factors?

17. The sum of two prime numbers is 61. What is the product of these two prime numbers?

18. What is M if 52M2 is divisible by both 3 and 4?

19. The 5-digit number 3A26B is multiple of 20. What is the minimum value of A+B?

20. The four digit number 53xy is divisible by 3, 4, and 5. What is the sum of all possible x values?

CHAPTER 4
Least Common Multiple (LCM) & Greatest Common Divisor (GCD)

✓ Target Concepts and Skills

- ☐ Divisors / factors of numbers
- ☐ Multiples of numbers
- ☐ Least Common Multiple (LCM)
- ☐ Greatest Common Divisors (GCD)

Definition 4.1 – Factors/Divisors

A factor or divisor of a number is a whole number that divides evenly into the other number. So, when you divide by the factor/divisor, the remainder is zero.

Example 4.1

Is 4 a factor of 24?

Yes, 36 divided by 4 gives us an answer of 9 with no remainder.

Is 3 a factor of 49?

No, 49 divided by 3 gives us an answer of 15 with a remainder of 4.

Definition 4.2

Prime factorization is breaking down a number into the product of its prime factors.

- Every positive number can be prime factored
- The prime factorization of a prime number is the number itself
- Prime factorizations are unique, meaning every number has only one prime factorization

Example 4.2

Composite numbers can be broken down into their prime factors.

- $6 = 2 \times 3$
- $12 = 2 \times 2 \times 3$
- $40 = 2 \times 2 \times 2 \times 5$

An easy way to do this is to construct a factor tree.

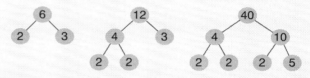

Definition 4.3 – The Greatest Common Factor (GCF)

The factors that are same for two or more natural numbers are called the common factors of the numbers.

The greatest common factor (GCF) of two or more natural numbers is the greatest element in the set of common factors. We write GCF(a, b) to mean the greatest common factor of a and b.

We can use prime factorization as a short way to find the greatest common factor of two or more numbers.

To find the greatest common factor of two numbers, follow the steps.

1. Write the prime factorization of each number.
2. Draw a circle round each common factor.
3. Multiply the common factors.

Example 4.3

The set of common factors of 24 and 30 is {1, 2, 3, 6}.

For example, GCF(24, 30) = 6.

Math Fluency

CHAPTER 4 — Least Common Multiple (LCM) & Greatest Common Divisor (GCD)

Example 4.4

If we know the prime factorizations of 40 and 60, we can just write them and the common factors.

$40 = 2 \cdot 2 \cdot 2 \cdot 5$
$60 = 2 \cdot 2 \cdot 3 \cdot 5$

Multiply the circled numbers: $2 \cdot 2 \cdot 5 = 20$.

Therefore, the greatest common factor of 40 and 60 is 20. We can write GCF(40, 60) = 20.

Definition 4.4 – The Least Common Multiple (LCM)

A multiple of a number is the product of that number and any other whole number.

The least common multiple (LCM) of two or more natural numbers is the smallest element in the set of common multiples of the numbers. We write LCM(a, b) to mean the least common multiple of a and b.

Example 4.5

36 is a multiple of 4 since $4 \times 9 = 36$.

In looking for a multiple of a number, we usually begin with the number and generate multiples of it. The positive multiples of 4 are 4, 8, 12, 16, 20, 24, 28, ...

Example 4.6

For example, let us find the least common multiple of 6 and 8.

The multiples of 6 are
{6, 12, 18, 24, 30, 36, 42, 48, ...}.

The multiples of 8 are
{8, 16, 24, 32, 40, 48, 56 ...}.

The common multiples of 6 and 8 are {24, 48, ...}.

Therefore, the least common multiple of 6 and 8 is 24. We can write LCM(6, 8) = 24.

Example 4.7

For example, let us LCM(10, 12). Look at the result of the division method. The prime factors are 2, 2, 3, and 5. Therefore,
LCM(10, 12) = $2 \cdot 2 \cdot 3 \cdot 5 = 60$.

```
10  12 | 2
 5   6 | 2
 5   3 | 3
 5   1 | 5
 1
```

Example 4.8

Find the GCD of 480 and 1800

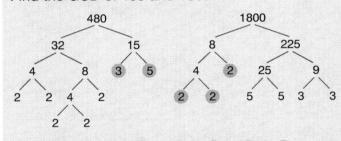

GCD(480, 1800) = $2 \times 2 \times 2 \times 3 \times 5 = 120$

Remark 4.1

LCM (m, m + 1) for any positive integer m is the product of m and m + 1.

Remark 4.2

GCD (m, m + 1) for any positive integer is m is 1.

Remark 4.3

Let a and b be two natural numbers, then
GCD(a, b) · LCM(a, b) = a · b.

Problem 4.1

Find n if GCD(n, 18) = 6 and LCM(n, 18) = 36

Solution 4.1

Using the property, GCD(n, 18) = n · 18.

Therefore, $6 \cdot 36 = n \cdot 18$, and

so $n = \dfrac{6 \cdot 36}{18} = 6 \cdot 2 = 12$

Problem Set 1 — Least Common Multiple (LCM) & Greatest Common Divisor (GCD) — CHAPTER 4

1. All numbers divisible by both 15 and 12 are also divisible by which of the following?

   A) 35   B) 41   C) 30   D) 41   E) 60

2. All numbers divisible by both 14 and 10 are also divisible by which of the following?

   A) 10   B) 42   C) 50   D) 28

3. Find the GCD and LCM of 24 and 40. Then multiply the GCD by the LCM. What do you notice?

4. How many distinct prime factors does 60 have?

5. LCM(12, 18, 24) = ?

6. GCD(72, 80) = ?

7. What is the least common multiple of 24, 30, 36?

8. Find the least common multiple of 4, 12, and 18.

9. Find the greatest common factor of 32, 48, and 64.

10. Let A, B, and a be natural number with
    A = GCD(a, 12) and B = LCM(a, 12).
    If A · B = 216, find a.

CHAPTER 4 — Least Common Multiple(LCM) & Greatest Common Divisor (GCD) — Problem Set 1

11. How many common positive divisors do 24 and 30 have?

12. How many three-digit numbers is a multiple of 12 and 15?

13. How many natural numbers are there between 1 and 110 which are divisible by 6 and 9?

14. Find the value of the single fraction (in its lowest terms) equal to $\dfrac{17}{80} - \dfrac{7}{160} + \dfrac{13}{320}$

15. Find the LCM(m, m + 1) for any positive integer m.

16. x is an integer

    $\dfrac{210}{x}$, $\dfrac{300}{x}$ and $\dfrac{360}{x}$ are also integers.

    What is the greatest value of x?

17. x is a positive number with

    GCF(x, 36) = 9 and LCM(x, 36) = 108. Find x.

18. The least common multiple of 16 and 20 is k. What is the least common multiple of 12 and k?

19. What is the least common multiple of the first 6 positive integers?

20. A builder has bricks with dimensions 3 cm · 4 cm · 6 cm.

    What is the least number of bricks the builder needs to make a cube?

CHAPTER 5
Fractions & Operations

✓ Target Concepts and Skills

- ☐ Equal fractions and fraction types
- ☐ Comparing fractions
- ☐ Adding and subtracting fractions
- ☐ Multiplying fractions
- ☐ Dividing fractions

Definition 5.1 – Meaning of a/b

The part-whole meaning of the fraction $\frac{a}{b}$ has these three elements:

- The unit, or whole, is clearly in mind.
- The denominator, b, tells how many pieces of equal size the unit is cut into (or thought of as being cut into).
- The numerator, a, tells how many such pieces are being considered.

Definition 5.2 – Equal fraction

Two fractions that look different, but have the same value, are equivalent or equal fractions.

Example 5.1 – Three equal fractions

$$\frac{3}{4} = \frac{6}{8} = \frac{9}{12}$$

We can also make sense of and visualize equal fractions, as shown below.

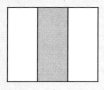
$\frac{1}{3}$

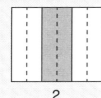
$\frac{2}{6}$

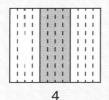
$\frac{4}{12}$

$$\frac{1}{3} = \frac{2}{6} = \frac{4}{12}$$

Example 5.2

We can create equal fractions by multiplying a numerator and a denominator with the same quantity, as shown below.

$$\frac{1}{2} \times \frac{3}{3} = \frac{3}{6} \qquad \frac{1}{4} \times \frac{2}{2} = \frac{2}{8}$$

$$\frac{1}{3} \times \frac{4}{4} = \frac{4}{12} \qquad \frac{1}{4} \times \frac{4}{4} = \frac{4}{16}$$

Definition 5.3 – Simplest Terms

A fraction in simplest terms means that the numerator and denominator have no common whole-number factors.

Example 5.3

Simpler terms →

$$\frac{8}{12} = \frac{2 \times 4}{3 \times 4} = \frac{2}{3}$$

← Higher terms

Definition 5.4 – Mixed-Fraction

A number which consists of a whole number and a proper fraction is called a mixed number.

$$a\frac{b}{c} = a + \frac{b}{c} = \frac{a \cdot c + b}{c}$$

Example 5.4 – Conversion from a mixed fraction to an improper fraction

$$7\frac{1}{3} = \frac{7}{1} + \frac{1}{3} \qquad \text{(Step 1)}$$

$$= \frac{(7 \times 3) + 1}{3} \qquad \text{(Step 2)}$$

$$= \frac{21 + 1}{3} \qquad \text{(Step 3)}$$

$$= \frac{22}{3} \qquad \text{(Step 4)}$$

Math Fluency

CHAPTER 5 — Fractions & Operations

Definition 5.5 – Reciprocals

The reciprocal of a number is 1 divided by that number. For example, the reciprocal of 5 is $\frac{1}{5}$. Note that $5 \times \frac{1}{5} = 1$. The product of a number and its reciprocal is always 1.

Example 5.5

The reciprocal of $\frac{2}{3}$ is 1 divided by $\frac{2}{3}$, which is equal to $\frac{3}{2}$.

Note that you can find the reciprocal of any nonzero fraction by switching its *numerator* and *denominator*.

Problem 5.1

How do you find the reciprocal of $2\frac{1}{3}$?

Solution 5.1

We can first convert the fraction as $2\frac{1}{3} = \frac{7}{3}$.

Then we can take its reciprocal as $\frac{3}{7}$

Remark 5.1

Ways that the fractions could have been compared:

- Same-size denominator: Fractions with larger numerator is bigger.
- Same numerator: Fractions with larger denominator is smaller.
- More than/less than benchmark

Example 5.6

Compare the two fractions by using two different ways. $\frac{9}{20}$ and $\frac{19}{36}$

We can make a common denominator. So, LCM (20, 36) is 180. The first fraction is 81/180, and the second is 95/180. Therefore, 19/36 is bigger than 9/20.

We can use ½ benchmark. So, 9/20 is less than 10/20 and 19/36 is bigger than 18/36. Therefore, 19/36 is bigger than 9/20.

Definition 5.6 – Adding and Subtracting Fractions

Adding or Subtracting rational numbers with different denominators, first we equalize the denominators by enlarging each rational number by the lowest common denominator (LCD). Then we add or subtract the numerators.

Example 5.7

Add $\frac{3}{5} + \frac{4}{7}$.

We first find the LCD.

A common denominator is $5 \cdot 7 = 35$.

We thus find

$$\frac{3}{5} + \frac{4}{7} + \frac{3 \cdot 7}{5 \cdot 7} + \frac{4 \cdot 5}{7 \cdot 5} = \frac{21}{35} + \frac{20}{35} = \frac{41}{35}$$

Example 5.8

$$\frac{2}{3} + \frac{5}{4} + \frac{8}{12} + \frac{15}{12} = \frac{23}{12}$$

Remark 5.2

Why we don't add numerators and denominators?

Plotting fractions on the number line, it becomes clear why $\frac{1}{2} + \frac{1}{4} \neq \frac{2}{6}$ since the line segments formed (shown in red) don't add up.

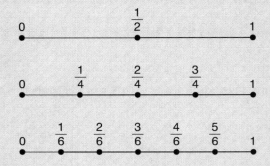

Definition 5.7 – Multiplying fractions

Let a, b, c, d be natural numbers with $b \neq 0$ and $d \neq 0$. Then, $\frac{a}{b} \cdot \frac{c}{d} = \frac{ac}{bd}$.

Fractions & Operations

CHAPTER 5

Example 5.9

$$\frac{2}{3} \cdot \frac{3}{7} = \frac{6}{21} = \frac{2}{7}$$

Alternatively we could have cancelled the common factors, as follows.

$$\frac{2}{\cancel{3}} \cdot \frac{\cancel{3}}{7} = \frac{2}{7}.$$

Definition 5.8 – Dividing Fractions

Let a, b, c, d be natural numbers with $b \neq 0$, $c \neq 0$, $d \neq 0$. Then

$$\frac{a}{b} \div \frac{c}{d} = \frac{a}{b} \cdot \frac{d}{c} = \frac{ad}{bc},$$

Example 5.10

We have,

$$\frac{24}{35} \div \frac{20}{7} = \frac{24}{35} \cdot \frac{7}{20} = \frac{4 \cdot 6}{7 \cdot 5} \cdot \frac{7 \cdot 1}{4 \cdot 5} = \frac{6 \cdot 1}{5 \cdot 5} \cdot \frac{6}{25}.$$

Problem 5.2

Find the exact value of the product

$$\left(1 - \frac{2}{5}\right)\left(1 - \frac{2}{7}\right)\left(1 - \frac{2}{9}\right) \cdots \left(1 - \frac{2}{99}\right)\left(1 - \frac{2}{101}\right).$$

Solution 5.2

$$\left(1 - \frac{2}{5}\right)\left(1 - \frac{2}{7}\right)\left(1 - \frac{2}{9}\right) \cdots \left(1 - \frac{2}{99}\right)\left(1 - \frac{2}{101}\right)$$

$$= \frac{3}{5} \cdot \frac{5}{7} \cdot \frac{7}{9} \cdot \frac{9}{11} \cdots \frac{97}{99} \cdot \frac{99}{101} = \frac{3}{101}.$$

Problem 5.3

What is the value of

$$\frac{1}{2}x + \frac{3}{2}(x + 1) - \frac{1}{4} \quad \text{if x is } \frac{5}{2}?$$

Solution 5.3

If we replace 5/2 with x

$$\frac{1}{2}\left(\frac{5}{2}\right) + \frac{3}{2}\left(\frac{5}{2} + 1\right) - \frac{1}{4}$$

$$\frac{5}{4} + \frac{3}{2}\left(\frac{7}{2}\right) - \frac{1}{4} = \frac{5}{4} + \frac{21}{4} - \frac{1}{4} = \frac{25}{4}$$

Problem 5.4

Find $\frac{x + y}{z}$ where x, y, and z are the midpoints of the given intervals.

Solution 5.4

In the given line, $x = \frac{3}{2}$, $y = \frac{1}{2}$, and $z = -\frac{1}{2}$

Therefore, $\frac{x + y}{z} = -4$

Problem 5.5

Compare and order the rational numbers.

$$\frac{3}{4}, \frac{2}{3}, \frac{5}{6}, \frac{7}{12}$$

Solution 5.5

1. Find the lowest common denominator:

   $$\text{LCD}\left(\frac{3}{4}, \frac{2}{3}, \frac{5}{6}, \frac{5}{7}\right) = \text{LCM}(4, 3, 6, 12) = 12.$$

2. Equalize the denominators:

   $$\frac{3 \cdot 3}{4 \cdot 3} = \frac{9}{12}, \frac{2 \cdot 4}{3 \cdot 4} = \frac{8}{12}, \frac{5 \cdot 2}{6 \cdot 2} = \frac{10}{12} \text{ and}$$

   $$\frac{7 \cdot 1}{12 \cdot 1} = \frac{7}{12}$$

3. Now compare the numbers:

   $$\frac{10}{12} > \frac{9}{12} > \frac{8}{12} > \frac{7}{12}, \text{ so } \frac{5}{6} > \frac{3}{4} > \frac{2}{3} > \frac{7}{12}.$$

Problem 5.6

If a and b are positive integers and $1 + \dfrac{1}{1 + \dfrac{1}{2}} = \dfrac{10}{7}$, What is the least possible value of a + b ?

Solution 5.6

$\frac{10}{7}$ can be written as

$$\frac{10}{7} = 1 + \frac{3}{7} = 1 + \frac{1}{\frac{7}{3}} = 1 + \frac{1}{2 + \frac{1}{3}}$$

Therefore minimum a + b = 1 + 3 = 4

Math Fluency

CHAPTER 5 — GAME 24 — Puzzle

Make the number 24 from the four numbers shown. You can add, subtract, multiply and divide. Use all four numbers on the card, but use each number only once. You do not have to use all four operations.

1. a)

   b)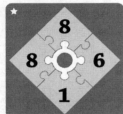

   c)

2. a)

   b)

   c)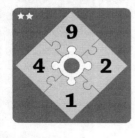

3. a)

   b)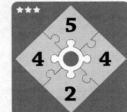

   c)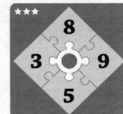

4. a)

   b)

   c)

Problem Set 1 — Fractions & Operations — CHAPTER 5

1. Which one is closest to 0?
   a) 1/2   b) 1/8   c) 1/3   d) 1/9

2. If $\dfrac{1}{15} = \dfrac{x}{60} = \dfrac{y}{30}$
   What is x + y?

3. Which one's reciprocal is bigger?
   A) –2   B) –1

4. $(6 \div -3)(4 - 12) = ?$

5. Which one is bigger?
   A) $\dfrac{1}{2} \times \dfrac{1}{4}$ B) $\dfrac{1}{2} \div \dfrac{1}{4}$

6. Which one is smaller?
   A) $\dfrac{1}{3} - \dfrac{1}{5}$ B) $\dfrac{1}{4} - \dfrac{1}{5}$

7. $\dfrac{1}{2} \cdot \dfrac{2}{3} \cdot \dfrac{3}{4} = ?$

8. $4\dfrac{3}{45} + 1\dfrac{4}{15} = ?$

9. What is x?
   $\dfrac{3}{7} = \dfrac{x}{63}$

10. If $\dfrac{3}{4} + \dfrac{4}{x} = 1$
    What is x?

CHAPTER 5 — Fractions & Operations — Problem Set 1

11. The smallest in the set $\{\frac{1}{2}, \frac{2}{3}, \frac{5}{6}, \frac{7}{12}\}$ is

12. $\frac{7}{12} - \frac{2}{3} + \frac{1}{4} = ?$

13. $\frac{3}{14} - \frac{5}{7} + \frac{1}{21} = ?$

14. If $a \div \frac{1}{5}$ is $\frac{3}{25}$

    What is $a \times 25$?

15. The number between $\frac{17}{4}$ and $\frac{25}{2}$ is

    a) 4 b) 5 c) 6 d) 8

16. Fractions $\frac{63}{13} = 4 + \frac{x}{13}$

    What is x?

17. If $\frac{1}{9} + \frac{1}{18} = \frac{1}{x}$

    What is x?

18. $(7 + 7)\left(7 + \frac{1}{7}\right) = ?$

19. Which one lies between 3 and 4?

    a) $\frac{11}{4}$ b) $\frac{11}{5}$ c) $\frac{13}{4}$ d) $\frac{13}{5}$

20. $\left(\frac{4}{10} + 2\right) \times 10 = ?$

Problem Set 2 — Fractions & Operations — CHAPTER 5

1. What is the lowest common denominator?
   $\frac{1}{6}, \frac{1}{4}, \frac{1}{15}$

2. Compute $\frac{1}{2} \div \frac{1}{6}$

3. Compute $(3 \cdot 4) \div \left(\frac{1}{5} \cdot \frac{1}{4}\right)$

4. $\frac{6}{8} \cdot \frac{4}{6} \cdot \frac{7}{14} = ?$

5. $\frac{5}{49} + \frac{3}{98} = ?$

6. If $a = 5 + \frac{1}{5}$, then $\frac{1}{a}$ is

7. $1 + \dfrac{1}{2 + \frac{1}{2}} = ?$

8. $\frac{3}{19} \cdot 100 - \frac{3}{19} \cdot 81 = ?$

9. What is $\frac{1}{2} \cdot 4 \cdot \frac{1}{8} \cdot 16 \cdot \frac{1}{32} \cdot 64$?

10. What is the reciprocal of $2 \cdot 3 \cdot \frac{1}{4} \cdot \frac{1}{9}$

Math Fluency

CHAPTER 5 — Fractions & Operations — Problem Set 2

11. If $\dfrac{1}{2} + \dfrac{1}{4} = \dfrac{x}{12}$
    What is x?

12. $40 \cdot \dfrac{1}{8} + 40 \cdot \dfrac{1}{5} = ?$

13. $-\dfrac{1}{9} \div \left(\dfrac{-5}{18}\right) = ?$

14. Find the product of the multiplicative inverses of $-\dfrac{3}{4}$ and $\dfrac{4}{3}$.

15. Which one is bigger?
    A) $4 \div \left(2 + \dfrac{1}{4}\right)$
    B) $4 \div \left(2 + \dfrac{1}{3}\right)$

16. $\dfrac{11}{23} \div \left(\dfrac{12}{23} + \dfrac{1}{230}\right) = ?$

17. $3\dfrac{1}{2} \times \left(\dfrac{3}{8} - \dfrac{3}{4}\right) = ?$

18. $\dfrac{3}{4} - 1\dfrac{1}{2} - \left(-\dfrac{1}{8}\right) = ?$

19. $3\dfrac{5}{6} - \left(-1\dfrac{1}{6}\right) = ?$

20. If a and b are positive integers and
    $$1 + \dfrac{1}{1 + \dfrac{a}{b}} = \dfrac{20}{19},$$
    what is the least possible value of a + b?

CHAPTER 6
Decimals/Percents & Operations

✓ Target Concepts and Skills

☐ Defining the percent and percentage of a number.
☐ Defining decimal numbers.
☐ Conversion between decimals, fractions, and percents.

Definition 6.1 – Percent & Percentage

Percent means per hundred. A percentage is a number expressed as a fraction of 100. It is denoted using the percent sign "%".

For example, one percent = $1\% = \frac{1}{100}$, five percent = $5\% = \frac{5}{100}$, fifty-seven percent = $57\% = \frac{57}{100}$

Example 6.1

Let's find the following

a) Fifty percent of 200. Without even thinking, we can say that it is equal to 100.

Algebraically, we **multiply** 50% or $\frac{50}{100}$ by 200.

That is, $\frac{50}{100} \cdot 200 = \frac{50}{100} \cdot \frac{200}{1} = \frac{1}{2} \cdot \frac{200}{1}$

$= \frac{1 \cdot 200}{2 \cdot 1} = \frac{200}{2} = 100.$

b) 25% of 200.

By the reasoning in part (a), $\frac{25}{100} \cdot 200$

$= \frac{25}{100} \cdot \frac{200}{1} = \frac{1}{4} \cdot \frac{200}{1} = \frac{1 \cdot 200}{4 \cdot 1} = \frac{200}{4} = 50.$

c) 55% of 300.

$\frac{55}{100} \cdot 300 = \frac{55}{100} \cdot \frac{300}{1} = \frac{11}{20} \cdot \frac{300}{1} = \frac{11 \cdot 300}{20 \cdot 1}$

$= \frac{11 \cdot 15}{1 \cdot 1} = 165.$

d) 27% of 45.

$\frac{27}{100} \cdot 45 = \frac{27}{100} \cdot \frac{45}{1} = \frac{27 \cdot 45}{100 \cdot 1} = \frac{27 \cdot 9}{20 \cdot 1}$

$= \frac{243}{20} = 12\frac{3}{20}.$

Definition 6.2 – Decimal Number

A decimal number (decimal numeral) is a number with whole and decimal parts. Between these two parts, there is a separator, which is a point. Depending upon the position, each digit takes different place values.

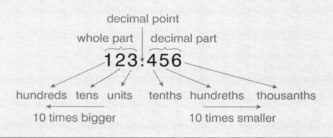

Example 6.2

Let's expand the decimal number 123.456.

123.456 = 1 hundreds + 2 tens + 3 units + 4 tenths + 5 hundreths + 6 thousanths

$123.456 = 1 \cdot 100 + 2 \cdot 10 + 3 \cdot 1 + 4 \cdot \frac{1}{10} + 5 \cdot \frac{1}{100} + 6 \cdot \frac{1}{1000}.$

Remark 6.1

Notice that 4.5 = 4.50 = 4.500 = ...

Math Fluency

CHAPTER 6

Decimals/Percents & Operations

Example 6.2 – Converting a Fraction to a Decimal Number

When we need to convert a fraction to a decimal number, dividing the numerator by the denominator results in the corresponding decimal value of the given fraction. If the denominator can be written as a power of 10, then you can find the decimal number by hand. Otherwise, you can use a calculator if allowed, or you can do a long division of the numerator by the denominator.

Example 6.3

Convert the following fractions to decimal numbers.

a) $\dfrac{50}{100} = 0.50 = 0.5$.

b) $\dfrac{2}{10} = 0.2$.

c) $\dfrac{12}{25} = \dfrac{12 \cdot 4}{25 \cdot 4} = \dfrac{48}{100} = 0.48$.

d) $\dfrac{12}{30} = \dfrac{3 \cdot 4}{2 \cdot 10} = \dfrac{4}{10} = 0.4$.

e) $\dfrac{15}{24} = \dfrac{5}{8} = 0.625$.

f) $\dfrac{40}{15} = \dfrac{8}{3} = 2.\overline{6}$.

Problem 6.1

Complete the table.

	Fraction	Percent	Decimal
a)		30%	
b)	2/5		
c)			0.27

Solution 6.1

a) $30\% = \dfrac{30}{100} = \dfrac{3}{10}$ and $30\% = \dfrac{30}{100} = 0.30 = 0.3$

b) $\dfrac{2}{5} = \dfrac{40}{100} = 40\%$ and $\dfrac{2}{5} = \dfrac{4}{10} = 0.4$

c) $0.27 = \dfrac{27}{100} = 27\%$

Thus,

	Fraction	Percent	Decimal
a)	3/10	30%	0.3
b)	2/5	40%	0.4
c)	27/100	27%	0.27

Notice that the fractions are written in **simplest** form, and the decimal point is carried to the right by two digits to get the percent.

Problem 6.2

Find the following.

a) 40% of 80 is what?
b) What percent of 35 is 8?
c) 45% of what is 20?

Solution 6.2

Let's translate each sentence into mathematical language.

a) 40% of 80 is what? : $\dfrac{40}{100} \cdot 80 = x$,
$\dfrac{2}{5} \cdot 80 = x$, $\dfrac{160}{5} = x$, $x = 32$.

b) What percent of 35 is 8? : $\dfrac{x}{100} \cdot 35 = 8$,
$\dfrac{x \cdot 35}{100} = 8$, $\dfrac{x \cdot 7}{20} = 8$, $x = \dfrac{160}{7}$, $x = 22.86$.

c) 45% of what is 20? : $\dfrac{45}{100} \cdot x = 20$,
$\dfrac{9}{20} \cdot x = 20$, $x = \dfrac{400}{9}$, : $x = 44.44$.

Notice that "of" is translated as "**multiplication**", "what" as "**x**", and "**is**" as "**=**".

Problem 6.3

What percent of 20 is equal to 25% of 40?

Solution 6.3

Let's translate it into mathematical language.

$\dfrac{x}{100} \cdot 20 = \dfrac{25}{100} \cdot 40$

$\dfrac{x \cdot 20}{100} = \dfrac{25 \cdot 40}{100}$, $\dfrac{x \cdot 1}{5} = \dfrac{25 \cdot 2}{5}$, $x = 50$.

Decimals/Percents & Operations

CHAPTER 6

Problem 6.4

a) Find the percent increase if the original number 60 is increased to 70.

b) Find the percent decrease if the original number 70 is decreased to 60.

Solution 6.4

$\dfrac{\text{Difference}}{\text{original numbers}}$ is used to find the percent increase or decrease. So,

a) Difference = 10 and percent increase $= \dfrac{10}{60} = 0.17 = 17\%$.

b) Difference = 10 and percent decrease $= \dfrac{10}{70} = 0.14 = 14\%$.

Problem 6.5

a) Find the new price if a 15% discount is applied to an item of $120?

b) Find the total amount of payment if the 6% tax rate is applied to an item of $120?

Solution 6.5

a) $120 - 120 \cdot \dfrac{15}{100} = 120 \cdot (1 - 0.15) = 120 \cdot 0.85 = 102$.

b) By the same reasoning, we can directly find the resulting number:
$120 \cdot (1 + 0.06) = 120 \cdot 1.06 = 127.2$.

Problem 6.6

Simplify the following expressions
a) $3.5 + 2.4$ b) $3.5 + 2.61$ c) $3.51 + 22.39$

Solution 6.6

a) $3.5 + 2.4 = 5.9$
(First, decimal part to decimal part is added and then whole part to whole part)

b) $3.5 + 2.61 = 3.50 + 2.61 = 6.11$
(The sum of the tenths digit is 11, which is more than 10. So, 10 is carried to the units digit and added as 1.)

c) $3.51 + 22.39 = 25.90$
We can add them in a vertical way, also. Pay attention to how decimal points are lined up.

$$\begin{array}{r} 3.51 \\ + 22.39 \\ \hline 25.90 \end{array}$$

Problem 6.7

Simplify the following expressions
a) $3.5 - 2.4$
b) $3.5 - 2.61$
c) $3.51 - 22.39$

Solution 6.7

a) $3.5 - 2.4 = 1.1$
(Whole part form whole part and decimal part form decimal is subtracted)

b) $3.5 - 2.61 = 3.50 - 2.61 = 0.89$
Also, we can line up the decimal points. Notice how we borrow from the left digit when the number on the bottom is greater than the number on the top. After borrowing, 0 becomes 10, 5 becomes 4, 4 becomes 14, and 3 becomes 2.

$$\begin{array}{r} 2\ 4 \\ 3.\cancel{5}0 \\ - 2.61 \\ \hline 0.89 \end{array}$$

c) $22.39 + 3.4 = 22.39 - 3.40 = 18.99$,
or we can line up the decimal points

$$\begin{array}{r} 1\ 1 \\ \cancel{2}2.39 \\ - \ \ 3.40 \\ \hline 18.99 \end{array}$$

Math Fluency

CHAPTER 6 — Decimals/Percents & Operations

Problem 6.8

Simplify the following expressions
a) 2.4×3
b) 3.6×2.4

Solution 6.8

To multiply decimal numbers, implement the following steps:

1. Line up the decimal points vertically.
2. Ignore the decimal points and multiply as if there are no points.
3. The sum of the number of decimal places of the given numbers determines the number of decimal places in the result.

a)
```
    2.4
  ×   3
  -----
    7.2
```

b)
```
     2.4
  ×  3.6
  ------
     144
  +  72
  ------
    8.64
```

Problem 6.9

Simplify the following expressions
a) $2.4 \div 0.3$ b) $3.6 \div 2.4$ c) $4.26 \div 2.4$

Solution 6.9

a) Notice that $2.4 \div 0.3$ is equivalent to $24 \div 3$ since $\dfrac{2.4}{0.3} = \dfrac{2.4 \times 10}{0.3 \times 10} = \dfrac{24}{3}$

So, you can shift the decimal point to the right by the same number of digits in both given numbers. Thus, $2.4 \div 0.3 = 24 \div 3 = 8$.

b) By the same reasoning in part (a), $3.6 \div 2.4 = 36 \div 24 = \dfrac{36}{24} = \dfrac{3}{2} = 1.5$.

c) $4.26 \div 2.4 = 426 \div 240 = \dfrac{426}{240} = \dfrac{71}{40} = 71 \div 40$.

After getting an easier equivalent form of the given division, we can use long division to get the result:

```
       1.775
    _____
 40 ) 71
     -40
     ----
      310
     -280
     ----
      300
     -280
     ----
      200
     -200
     ----
        0
```

So, $4.26 \div 2.4 = 1.775$

Problem 6.10

Simplify the following expressions.
a) $40 \div 0.5$
b) $\dfrac{30}{2.4} + \dfrac{20}{3.6}$
c) $(4.05 - 2.3 \times 4) + \dfrac{3}{4}$

Solution 6.10

a) $40 \div 0.5 = 400 \div 5 = 80$.

Alternatively, we could convert the given decimal number to a fraction:

$40 \div 0.5 = 40 \div \dfrac{1}{2} = 40 \cdot \dfrac{2}{1} = 80$

b) $\dfrac{30}{2.4} + \dfrac{20}{3.6} = \dfrac{300}{24} + \dfrac{200}{36} = \dfrac{900}{72} + \dfrac{400}{72}$

$= \dfrac{1300}{72} = \dfrac{325}{18} = 18\dfrac{1}{18}$.

c) $(4.05 - 2.3 \times 4) + \dfrac{3}{4} = (4.05 - 9.2) + \dfrac{3}{4}$

$= (4.05 - 9.20) + \dfrac{3}{4} = -5.15 + \dfrac{3}{4}$

$= -5.15 + 0.75 = -4.40 = -4.4$

Problem Set 1 — Decimals/Percents & Operations — CHAPTER 6

1. $5.2 \div 0.4 = ?$

2. $36 \div 1.2 = ?$

3. $100 \div 0.4 = ?$

4. If $0.75 + 1.6 = \dfrac{x}{20}$, what is x?

5. What is the difference between 10.8 and –9.7?

6. Three tenths plus four thousandths is equal to

7. How much does 2.5 exceed its reciprocal?

8. Where the do decimal points go?
   a) $124.6 + 35.35 = 15995$
   b) $12.48 + 78.15 = 9063$
   c) $377.78 + 23.441 = 361221$

9. $45 + \dfrac{3}{10} + \dfrac{4}{100} + \dfrac{7}{1000} = ?$

10. If $8 + \dfrac{7}{a} + \dfrac{3}{1000} = 8.073$
    What is a?

CHAPTER 6 — Decimals/Percents & Operations — Problem Set 1

11. $\dfrac{6}{0.3} + \dfrac{2}{0.1} = ?$

12. $-0.2 - (-1.6) + \dfrac{25}{8} = ?$

13. $\dfrac{3}{2} \div (-1.8) = ?$

14. $\dfrac{7}{40}$ is equal to

15. Express the sum $\dfrac{1}{2} + \dfrac{0.1}{2}$ as a decimal.

16. $(36 \div (1.2)) \times 0.04$

17. $3.25 - 3\dfrac{5}{8} - (1.75)$

18. $0.15 \times 0.3 \div \left(\dfrac{9}{10}\right) \times \left(\dfrac{5}{4}\right)$

19. $\dfrac{3(-0.75 + 0.05)}{1.2}$

20. $0.6 + \dfrac{1}{0 \cdot 5 + \dfrac{1}{0.5}} = ?$

Problem Set 2 — Decimals/Percents & Operations — CHAPTER 6

1. 2.5 pounds of oranges costs $7.5. How much does 1.5 pounds costs?

2. What is the value of
   $0.1 + 0.2 + 0.3 \times 0.4$

3. What is 80% of 800?

4. 15 is what percent of 5?

5. 16 is 8% of what number?

6. What is 110% of 500?

7. 10% of 10 multiplied by 20% of 20 equals

8. $4 + \dfrac{3}{10} + \dfrac{9}{1000} = ?$

9. James earns $13.25 per hour working at a store. How much does he earn in 4 hours?

10. On the number line, point B and C divide AD into three equal parts..

    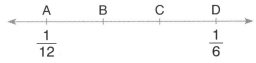

    What is the value at B?

CHAPTER 6 — Decimals/Percents & Operations — Problem Set 2

11. It costs 2.5¢ to copy a page. How many pages can you copy for $15?

12. x is 20% of 50. 40 is 20% of Y. What is x + y?

13. What percent of 40 is 25?

14. $0.02 \times 1.25 = ?$

15. If 18% of 60 is equal to 27% of x, what is x?

16. If 10% of a number is 5, what is 25% of the same number?

17. If 10% of 200 is decreased by 25, the result is

18. If 60% of a number is 30, what is 50% of the same number?

19. A is 80% of B and C is 120% of B. What is $\frac{A}{B}$?

20. If 20% of a number is 20 less than the number. What is the number?

CHAPTER 7
Evaluations & Expressions

Target Concepts and Skills

- [ ] Variables
- [ ] Evaluating an expression
- [ ] Adding and subtracting expressions
- [ ] Combining complex expressions
- [ ] Simplifying rational expressions

Definition 7.1

A variable is a symbol used to stand for a value from a particular set of values.

A variable is a symbol, often a letter of the alphabet, that represents a numerical value.

Example 7.1

We have the problem "a + a + a + b + b". What is the simplest way to express this statement? Just as "3 + 3" is equivalent to saying, "2 × 3", "a + a" is equivalent to saying "2 × a", or just "2a".

Thus, a + a + a + b + b = 3a + 2b

Definition 7.2 – Distributive Property

This property states that multiplying the sum of two numbers by one number will give the same result as multiplying the one number by both numbers individually and then adding them together.

Example 7.2

- 3 × 18 = 3(10 + 8) = 30 + 24 = 54
- x(y + z) = xy + xz
- 3(n + 4) = 3n + 12

Example 7.3

Replace the appropriate mathematical terms in the following spaces.

1. variable 2. expressions 3. operations 4. expression
5. formula 6. equation 7. numbers

An .... is a mathematical phrase that combines .... and/or variables using mathematical ....

An .... is a mathematical statement that two things are equal. It consists of two .... , one on each side of an equals sign.

A .... is a special type of equation that shows the relationship between different ....

4 - 7 - 3 - 6 - 2 - 5 - 1

Example 7.4

When matching these terms, we match the expression with exactly how we say it.

2x + 4	Four more than twice x.
2x – 4	Four less than twice x.
2(x + 2)	Twice the sum of x and two.
2(x + 4)	Twice the sum of x and four.
2(x – 4)	Twice the difference of x and four.

Example 7.5

Who Am !? With a check mark in the appropriate column, classify each of the following as an expression, equation, or formula.

	Expression	Equation	Formula
3a + 2b	✓		
x + 5 = 29		✓	
A = lw			✓
12x – 6 = 18		✓	
3n + 12 – 3m	✓		
F = ma			✓

Math Fluency

CHAPTER 7

Evaluations & Expressions

Example 7.6

Think of a whole number less than 10.	6	x
Multiply it by 4	$6 \times 4 = 24$	$4x$
Add 12.	$24 + 12 = 36$	$4x + 12$
Divide by 2.	$36 \div 2 = 18$	$\frac{4x + 12}{2} = 2x + 6$
Subtract 6.	$18 - 6 = 12$	$3a + 2b$
Divide by the number you first thought of	$12 \div 6 = 2$	$3a + 2b$

Problem 7.1

Choose any number then add 12 to your original number. Multiply by 6. Divide by 3 subtract 4. Divide by 2 subtract 7. Your number you picked was ...

Solution 7.1

We are going to use algebra to create a general solution of this number puzzle.

x	Choose any number
$x + 12$	Add 12
$6(x + 12) = 6x + 72$	Multiply by 6, simplify
$(6x + 72) \div 3 = 2x + 24$	Divide by 3, simplify
$2x + 20$	Substract 4
$(2x + 20) \div 2 = x + 10$	Divide by 2, simplify
$x + 3$	Subtract 7

Notice that our answer is 3 more than the number picked.

Problem 7.2

Write that in the simplest form
$$2(n - 1) + 2(n + 1)$$
Write that in the simplest form
$$3n + 3(n - 1) - (2n - 2)$$

Solution 7.2

When simplifying it is important to remember that we must remove grouping symbols like parentheses through the distribution propertiy. From there we combine all like terms.

$2(n - 1) + 2(n + 1)$
$\quad 2n - 2 + 2n + 2$ — Distribute into the parenthesis.
$\quad\quad\quad 4n$ — Combine like terms.
$3n + 3(n - 1) - (2n - 2)$
$\quad 3n + 3n - 3 - 2n + 2$ — Distribute into the parentheses.
$\quad\quad\quad 4n - 1$ — Combine like terms.

Notice that our answer is 3 more than the number picked.

Problem 7.3

Which expresion correctly represents the area of the figure below?

a. $b(a + 3) + 2a$
b. $a(b + 2) + 3b$
c. $ab + 2a + 3b$

Solution 7.3

$ab + 3b + 2a \quad ab + 2a + 3b \quad ab + 2a + 3b$
$b(a + 3) + 2a \quad a(b + 2) + 3b$

All of the options are correct responses for an expression that represents the area of the figure.

Problem 7.4

$(9m - 4n) - (2n - 5m)$ is equivalent to:

Solution 7.4

We can distribute –1 to the second promtesis.
$= 9m - 4n - 2n - 5m \quad (-(-5m) = 5m)$
$= 9m + 5m - 4n + 2n \quad$ (combine like terms)
$= 14m - 6n$

Problem Set 1 — Evaluations & Expressions — CHAPTER 7

1. If $x = 4$ and $y = 3x$, the value of y is

2. If $x = 2$ then $\dfrac{2 + 5x}{2 + x} = ?$

3. Simplify the expression by collecting like terms.
   $4x + 3x - 2x$

4. Simplify the expression by collecting like terms.
   $5c + 3c + 2d + 8d$

5. What is the value of $x^5 - 2x$ when $x = 3$?

6. Evaluate $3x^y + 4y^x$ when $x = 3$ and $y = 4$.

7. When $x = 3$,
   the value of $x(x - 1)(x - 2)(x - 3)(x - 4)$ is

8. If $x = 12$ and $y = -6$, then the value of $\dfrac{3x + y}{x - y}$ is

9. If $a + b = 12$, $b + c = 16$, and $c = 7$, what is the value of a?

10. If $x = 3$, which of the following is true?
    A) $2x = 5$ B) $3x - 1 = 8$ C) $x + 5 = 3$
    D) $7 - x = 2$ E) $6 + 2x = 14$

CHAPTER 7 — Evaluations & Expressions — Problem Set 1

11. Evaluate the expression

    $x^2 - xy + 2y^2$

    when $x = 1$ and $y = -2$

12. If the symbol $\begin{array}{|c|c|} \hline p & q \\ \hline r & s \\ \hline \end{array}$ is defined by $p \times s - q \times r$,

    then the value of $\begin{array}{|c|c|} \hline 4 & 5 \\ \hline 2 & 3 \\ \hline \end{array}$ is

13. Evaluate each expression

    if $k = -3$, $m = 4$ and $n = -6$.

    a) $k - m$

    b) $m - n$

14. Evaluate each expression

    if $k = -3$, $m = 4$ and $n = -6$.

    $n + m - k$

    $n - k - m$

15. What is the value of the expression

    $2x^2 + 3xy - 4y^2$ when $x = 2$ and $y = -4$

16. If $x = -4$, what is the value of $-2x^2 - 3x^2$?

17. What is the value of $\dfrac{x-2}{2x+7}$ when $x = -3$?

18. What is the value of $\dfrac{x-2}{2x+7}$ when $x = \dfrac{1}{2}$?

19. Express $\dfrac{7}{16x} - \dfrac{3}{10x}$ as a single fraction.

20. In the table, what number should be placed in the box?

n	$n^3 + n - 1$
1	1
2	9
3	29
4	67
5	☐

Problem Set 2 — Evaluations & Expressions — CHAPTER 7

1. Simplify: $5(2 - x)$

2. Which expression is equivalent to $3 - (x - 2)$?
   A) $1 - x$
   B) $5 - x$

3. Let a, b, and c be numbers. Simplify the expression $\bigl(a - (b - c)\bigr) - \bigl((a - b) - c\bigr)$.

4. Simplify: $4(2 + 3r) - \dfrac{1}{2}(4 + 24r)$

5. $3y + \dfrac{y - 8}{2} + \dfrac{6y}{4}$

6. Combine like terms: $2(a - 2b) + 3(-a + 2b)$.

7. Simplify: $r - 3(s - r) + 2s =$

8. Simplify: $3(x - y) - 5(y - x) =$

9. Simplify: $\dfrac{p}{2q} + \dfrac{p}{3q} =$

10. Simplify: $3a + 4b - (-6a - 3b)$

CHAPTER 7 — Evaluations & Expressions — Problem Set 2

11. If $x = 2y$ and $y \neq 0$, then $(x + 2y) - (2x + y)$ equals

12. Simplify: $4[x + 3(2x + 1)]$

13. Simplify: $9 + 3[x + (3x + 2)] + 4$

14. Simplify: $4 + 10[x + (2x + 3)] + 12x$

15. Simplify: $5 + 2[3 + (2x + 1) + x] - 2$

16. Expand and simplify:
    $2(a + b - 2c) - 3(a - b - c)$.

17. What is $a - (a - b - a - c + a) - b + c$?

18. $(-8a) + 9a + (-15a) + 4a$

19. Which of the following expressions is not equivalent to $3x + 6$?

    A) $3(x + 2)$

    B) $\dfrac{-9x - 18}{-3}$

    C) $\dfrac{1}{3}(3x) + \dfrac{2}{3}(9)$

    D) $\dfrac{1}{3}(9x + 18)$

    E) $3x - 2(-3)$

20. If x, y and z are positive integers with $xy = 18$, $xz = 3$ and $yz = 6$, what is the value of $x + y + z$?

CHAPTER 8

Equations

✓ Target Concepts and Skills

- ☐ Setting up an equation
- ☐ Solving simple equations
- ☐ Solving multi step equations
- ☐ Solving simple rational equations

Definition 8.1

When given an equation we always have a goal in mind that goal is to find what the missing value equals. We can try to demonstrate how to do this using a balance scale to visualize what this looks like.

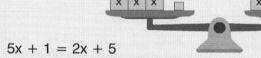

$5x + 1 = 2x + 5$

Steps for solving an equation

1. Determine the variable / figure out what you're trying to solve
2. Combine / eliminate like-terms to simplify the equation
3. Get the variable by itself by performing opposite operations that are show in the equation.
4. Collect like-terms after performing operations as well.
5. What you do to one side of the equation, you must do to the other.

Example 8.1

How would you write "six less than x is equal to 57"?

"Six less than x" indicates that six is being subtracted from x, and this whole thing equals 57, so the equation would look like this: $x - 6 = 57$

Example 8.2

The perimeter of an isosceles triangle is 78 cm. The two equal sides are each x cm and the other side is 6 cm more than x. Write an equation for the perimeter using these values.

The first thing to remember is that both sides of the equation must be equal. This is always true. We know that two sides of the triangle have length x cm, and the third one has length x + 6 cm. Therefore, since the perimeter is the sum of all the sides, our equation will look like this: $x + x + x + 6 = 78$

Example 8.3

Let's figure out the value of one square on the following balance.

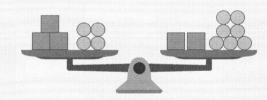

Step 1: $b + b + b + 4 = b + b + 7$. Solve for b, which is how many lines make up one block

Step 2: When simplified, this equation would look like this: $3b + 4 = 2b + 7$

Step 3: We can subtract or take away 2b from both sides, which would mean taking away two blocks from each side in order to obtain the equation $b + 4 = 7$

Step 4: Then we can subtract four from each side, which would mean taking away four lines from each side in order to obtain: $b = 3$

Math Fluency

CHAPTER 8 — Equations

Problem 8.1
Create an equation that could be used to solve for the angle with measure x.
When placed together, these 5 angles form a straight line:

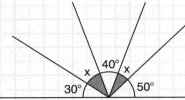

Solution 8.1
Step 1: We know that a straight line has an angle measure of 180 degrees.
Step 2: Therefore, since the five angles together form a straight line, then their sum must be 180 degrees.
Step 3: Thus, the equation would be:
$30 + x + 40 + x + 50 = 180$
Step 4: $2x + 120 = 180 \Rightarrow 2x = 60 \Rightarrow x = 30$

Problem 8.2
If the three angles of a triangle are 40, $(x + 5)$, $(2x + 15)$, then what is the value of x?

Solution 8.2
The sum of all the angles in a triangle always is 180 degrees.

$180 = 40 + x + 5 + 2x + 15$	Set up equation
$180 = 60 + 3x$	Combine like terms
$120 = 3x$	Substract 60 from each side
$40 = x$	Divide by 3

Problem 8.3
When the sum of x and 8 is divided by 2, the result is the same as when the product of x and 4 is decreased by 3. What is the value of x?

Solution 8.3
Before solving, we must set up what the number sentence will look like.

$\frac{x + 8}{2} = 4x - 3$	
$x + 8 = 8x - 6$	Multiply both sides by 2
$8 = 7x - 6$	Substract x from both sides
$14 = 7x$	Add 6 to both sides
$2 = x$	Divide both sides by 7

Problem 8.4
Solve for x: $4(2x + 5) - 3(x - 2) = 16$

Solution 8.4

$4(2x + 5) - 3(x - 2) = 16$	{distrubiting 4}
$8x + 20 - 3x + 6 = 16$	{distrubiting −3}
$5x + 26 = 16$	{collecting like terms}
$5x + 26 - 26 = 16 - 26$	{subtracting 26 from both sides}
$5x = -10$	
$x = -2$	{dividing both sides by 15}

Problem 8.5
Solve for x: $\frac{3x + 2}{1 - 2x} = \frac{1}{6}$

Solution 8.5

$6(3x + 2) = 1 - 2x$	{distrubiting 6}
$18x + 12 = 1 - 2x$	
$18x + 12 + 2x = 1 - 2x + 2x$	{adding 2x to both sides}
$20x + 12 = 1$	
$20x + 12 - 12 = 1 - 12$	{subtracting 12 from both sides}
$20x = -11$	
$\frac{20x}{20} = \frac{-11}{20}$	{dividing both sides by 20}
$x = -\frac{11}{20}$	

Problem Set 1 — Equations — CHAPTER 8

1. Evaluate the expression below for given values
   $3(2x + 1)$ for $x = -8$

2. Evaluate the expression below for given values
   $\dfrac{x - 6}{4} - 4$ for $x = -14$

3. Evaluate the expression below for given values
   $-2m^2 + 10$ for $m = -6$

4. Evaluate the expression below for given values
   $6m^2 + 2n^2$ for $m = 7$ and $n = 3$

5. Evaluate the expression below for given values
   $(6x)^2 - \left(\dfrac{x}{5}\right)$ for $x = 5$

6. Evaluate the expression below for given values
   $ab + bc + ac$ for $a = 2$, $b = 5$, and $c = -2$

7. Solve
   $2x - 7 = -2x + 1$

8. Solve
   $3x + 4 = x + 8$

9. Solve
   $5x + 4 - 2x = -(x + 8)$

10. Solve
    $-2m + 8 + m + 1 = 0$

11. Solve

$-(y^2 - 2) = y^2 - 5 - 2y^2$

12. Solve for p

$m = 8 - 2(p - m)$

13. Solve

$8(3m - 2) - 7m = 0$

14. Solve for x

$\dfrac{6}{x + 2} = \dfrac{3}{4}$

15. Solve for x.

$(x - 3)(x + 4) = x^2 + 4$

16. Solve for x

$4 - 2(3x + 2) = 4x - 10$

17. Solve for x

$9x - 21 + 9 = 2(5 - x)$

18. Solve for x

$\dfrac{4}{3x + 2} = \dfrac{2}{x + 3}$

19. If $\dfrac{1}{4}$ of x is 16, what is $\dfrac{3}{4}$ of x?

20. Solve for x

$\dfrac{1}{4}x + \dfrac{7}{16} = 11\dfrac{7}{16}$

Problem Set 2 — **Equations** — **CHAPTER 8**

1. If 4x + 12 = 48, the value of x is

2. The symbol $\begin{array}{|c|c|}\hline 3 & 4 \\\hline 5 & 6 \\\hline\end{array}$ is evaluated as $3 \times 6 + 4 \times 5 = 38$.

   If $\begin{array}{|c|c|}\hline 2 & 6 \\\hline 1 & \\\hline\end{array}$ is evaluated as 16, then the number that should be placed in the empty space is

3. If 3 + 5x = 28, the value of x is

4. If x = 11, y = 8, and 2x − 3z = 5y, what is the value of z?

5. If x is a real number that satisfies $\frac{48}{x} = 16$, find the value of x.

6. Solve: $\frac{1}{2}x - 6 = 4$.

7. Solve: $\frac{w}{5} - 1 = 15$.

8. What is the value of x: 24 = x − 18?

9. If 2t = s + 4 and t = 3, then s =

10. If 2x − 3(x + 4) = −5, then x =

Math Fluency — **Equations**

CHAPTER 8 — Equations — Problem Set 2

11. An integer n is decreased by 2 and then multiplied by 5. If the result is 85, the value of n is

12. If $4x + 14 = 8x - 48$, what is the value of $2x$?

13. Solve: $7 + 6x = 13 + 9x$.

14. $5\frac{2}{3} \times a = \frac{3}{5} \times 5\frac{2}{3}$

15. If $m + 1 = \frac{n-2}{3}$, what is the value of $3m - n$?

16. If $2(x - 5) = 3(2 - x)$, then $x =$

17. If $2(x - 5) = -11$, then $x = ?$

18. If $\frac{1}{2} + \frac{2}{3} + \frac{3}{4} + \frac{n}{12} = 2$, the value of n is

19. Each of w, x, y, and z is an integer.
    If $w + x = 45$, $x + y = 51$, and $y + z = 28$, what is the value of $w + z$?

20. The diagram shows a magic square in which the sum of the numbers in any row, column, or diagonal are equal. What is the value of n?

8		
9		5
4	n	

CHAPTER 9
Algebra & Geometry - 1

✓ Target Concepts and Skills

- [ ] Angles
- [ ] Areas of basic polygons
- [ ] Perimeters of basic polygons
- [ ] Volumes of basic 3-D shapes
- [ ] Setting equations by using geometric figures

Definition 9.1 – Triangle interior angles
The sum of the three interior angles in a triangle is always 180°.

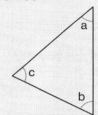

$a + b + c = 180°$

Definition 9.2 – Triangle exterior angles
The angle between any side of a polygon, and a line extended from an adjacent side.

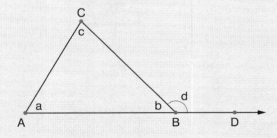

∠CBD is an exterior angle

$$\left. \begin{array}{l} a + b + c = 180 \\ b + d = 180 \end{array} \right\} \Rightarrow d = a + c$$

Definition 9.3 – Midpoint
The midpoint of the segment connecting the points (x_1, y_1) and (x_2, y_2) is

$$M = \left(\frac{x_1 + x_2}{2}, \frac{y_1 + y_2}{2} \right)$$

Definition 9.4 – Perimeter of a rectangle
The perimeter of a rectangle is the total length of all the four sides.

Perimeter of rectangle = 2L + 2W.

Definition 9.5 – Areas

Area of a triangle = $\frac{b \times h}{2}$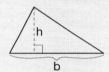

Area of a rectangle = $b \times h$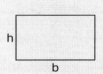

Area of an equilateral triangle
= $\frac{a^2 \sqrt{3}}{4}$

Definition 9.6 – 3D Shapes

Rectangular Prism
$S = 2(lw + lh + wh)$
l = length, w = width, h = height

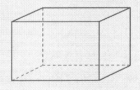

Volume = $l \times w \times h$

Cube 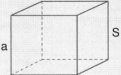 $S = a^3$

Math Fluency

CHAPTER 9

Algebra & Geometry - 1

Example 9.1

What is the perimeter of a regular octagon with side length of 5?

Since a regular octagon has 8 equal sides.

The perimeter is $5 \times 8 = 40$.

Problem 9.1

The length of a rectangle is 5 inches more than twice its width. If the perimeter of the rectangle is 250 inches, then what is the with?

Solution 9.1

Length = l   Width = w   Perimeter = 2w + 2l

Length = 2w + 5

Perimeter = 2w + 2l

250 = 2w + 2(2w + 5)	Substitute known variables
250 = 2w + 4w + 10	Distribute
250 = 6w + 10	Combine like terms
240 = 6w	Subtract 10 from each side
40 = w	Divide by 6

Problem 9.2

If a rectangle's length is 2x + 1 and its width is 2x − 1. If its area is 15 cm², what are the rectangle's dimensions and what is its perimeter?

Solution 9.2

We know that the dimensions of the rectangle in terms of x: l = 2x + 1   w = 2x − 1   A = l * w

15 = (2x + 1)(2x − 1)   x = 2

And now we have: l = 5 cm and w = 3 cm.

Therefore, the dimensions are 5 cm and 3 cm. Now, substituting these values in the formula for perimeter, we will get.

P = 2l + 2w = 16

Problem 9.3

What is the measure $\hat{B}$ in the figure right?

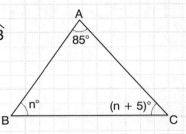

Solution 9.3

The sum of the angles of a triangle is equal to 180 degrees. To solve this, we will add all the angles together and set it equal to 180. Then we will solve for the variable.

180 = 85 + (n + 5) + n	Set the sum equal to 180.
180 = 90 + 2n	Simplify
90 = 2n	Subtract 90 from each side.
45 = n	Divide by 2

Angle B is 45 degrees.

Problem 9.4

In the diagram, the perimeter of the rectangle is 56. What is its area?

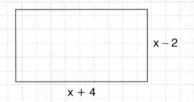

Solution 9.4

In order to find the area, we first must solve for the variable using the given perimeter.

2(x−2) + 2(x+4) = 56	Perimeter expression, 2Length + 2Height = Perimeter, set equal to 56.
2x − 4 + 2x + 8 = 56	Distribute into parentheses.
4x + 4 = 56	Combine like terms
4x = 52	Subtract 4 from each side.
x = 13	Divide by 4.
(x−2)(x+4)	Area = Base × Height
(13−2)(13+4)	Substitute 13 into expression.
(11)(17)	Simplify.
187	Multiply.

Problem Set 1 — Algebra & Geometry - 1 — **CHAPTER 9**

1. A square has a perimeter of 28 cm. The area of the square, in cm², is

2. A square has an area of 144 cm². The side length of the square is

3. The measures of two angles of a triangle are 25° and 70°. The measure of the third angle is

4. The perimeter of the figure, in cm, is

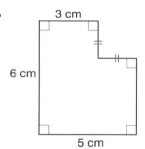

5. If x = 3, what is the perimeter of the figure shown?

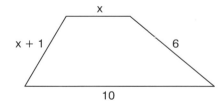

6. Write a fraction to represent the shaded area of the figure.

7. In the diagram, Q is on PR. The value of x is

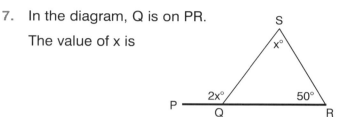

8. The lengths of the three sides of a triangle are 7, x + 4, and 2x + 1. The perimeter of the triangle is 36. What is the length of the longest side of the triangle?

9. The length of one side of square is 2.4 inches.

   How much bigger is the perimeter of square than its area?

2.4 inches

10. If the perimeter of the triangle shown is 21, what is the value of x?

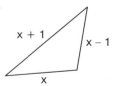

CHAPTER 9 — Algebra & Geometry - 1 — Problem Set 1

11. A rectangle has length x and width y. A triangle has base 16 and height x. If the area of the rectangle is equal to the area of the triangle, then the value of y is

12. A line segment is drawn joining the points (0, 6) and (4, 0), as shown. The area of the shaded triangle is

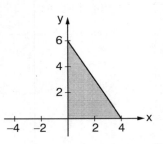

13. The volume of the rectangular prism shown is 60 cm³. What is the value of x?

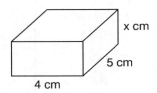

14. A rectangle has a perimeter of 32 inches and a width of 4 inches. Find the length of the rectangle.

15. In the diagram, AB and CD intersect at E. If △BCE is equilateral and △ADE is a right triangle, what is the value of x?

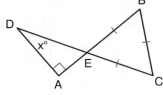

16. The volume of a rectangular block is 120 cm³. If the area of its base is 24 cm², what is its height?

17. What is the perimeter of the rectangle?

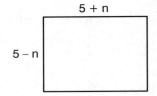

18. In the diagram, the perimeter of the triangle is equal to the perimeter of the rectangle. What is the value of x?

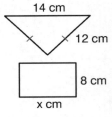

19. The equilateral triangle has sides of 2x and x + 15 as shown. The perimeter of the triangle is

20. Points P(15, 55), Q(26, 55), and R(26, 35) are three vertices of rectangle PQRS. The area of this rectangle is

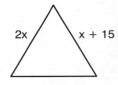

CHAPTER 10
BENCHMARK [Chapter 1-9]

1. If a is an even integer and b is an odd integer, which of the following could represent an odd integer?

   A) ab B) a + 2b C) 2a + 2b D) a + b − 1 E) a + b

2. Compute $56 - 96 \div 16 \times 2$

3. Two fractions are equally spaced between $\frac{1}{4}$ and $\frac{5}{8}$. The smaller of the two fractions is

4. $\dfrac{4 \times (0.15 + 0.45)}{1 \cdot 2} =$

5.
   ```
      a           b
   ←——•———+———•——→
     −4/5   0   7/10
   ```
   Find the distance between a and b.

6. $5r - 3(s - r) + 2s =$

7. $\dfrac{x}{3} + \dfrac{x}{2} - \dfrac{x}{6} =$

8. If $\dfrac{1 + 2x}{3} = \dfrac{4 + x}{2}$, then x =

9. Find the value of n on the square shown

   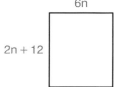

10. If the perimeter of the figure shown is 37 centimeters, what is the length of side x?

    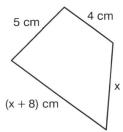

Math Fluency   63

11. What is the measure of ∠B in the figure below?

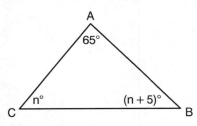

12. I am a multiple of 6, 8, and 12, and I am between 100 and 130. What number am I?

13. x is integer

    $\frac{32}{x}$, $\frac{48}{x}$, and $\frac{64}{x}$ are also integers.

    What is the greatest value of x?

14. Complete the following table by using each of the number −1, −2 and −3 only once in each row and column.

a		−1
−3		b
	−2	−3

    What is a + b?

15. $b = 10 - \frac{10}{2a + 1}$

    What is the value of b when $a = \frac{1}{2}$?

16. $-\frac{4}{5} \div \frac{a}{b} = -\frac{8}{15}$ is given.

    What is $\frac{a}{b}$?

17. If $\frac{4}{5} + \left(-\frac{3}{10}\right) = x + 1\frac{1}{2}$, then x = ?

18. To rent a car for the day, it costs $20 plus $0.25 per mile traveled. What is the total cost for renting a car for 2 days and traveling 70 miles?

19. x is 20÷ of 40 and 40 is 20÷ of Y.

    What is x + y?

20. If a, b, c are digits for which

    ```
      9 a 1
    − 4 5 b
    -------
      c 6 3
    ```

    then a + b + c =

CHAPTER 11
Equations & Inequalities

✓ Target Concepts and Skills

- [ ] Solving equations involving decimals
- [ ] Solving equations involving rational expressions
- [ ] Holistic equation solving - Cover-up method
- [ ] Absolute values
- [ ] Solving absolute value equations
- [ ] Inequalities
- [ ] Solving linear inequalities

Definition 11.1 – Simplifying an Expression

Simplifying an expression means rewriting the given expression in a compact form by implementing the order of operations.

Remark 11.1 – How to Solve Equations with One Variable (Unknown)

We solve equations with one variable by applying the following steps:
1. Combine like terms.
2. Isolate the variable.

3x, 5x, and -x are like terms. But 3x and 7 are not.

Example 11.1

$3x + 5x$ can be combined as $(3 + 5)x = 8x$ and $7x - 1 + 3x + 3$ can be combined as $7x + 3x - 1 + 3 = 10x + 2$.

Problem 11.1
Solve for x.
a) $x + 1 = 2$
b) $2x + 1 = x$
c) $\frac{x}{3} = 5$
d) $2x - 0.5 = 0.7$

Solution 11.1

a) $x + 1 = 2$,
Subtract 1 from both sides: $x = 1$.

b) $2x + 1 = x$
Subtract x from both sides: $2x + 1 - x = 0$.
Combine like terms: $x + 1 = 0$
Subtract 1 from both sides: $x = -1$.

c) $\frac{x}{3} = 5$
Multiply both sides by 3: $x = 15$.

d) $2x - 0.5 = 0.7$
Add 0.5 to both sides: $2x = 1.2$
Divide both sides by 2: $x = 0.6$

Definition 11.2

A proportion is an equation with two equivalent ratios (fractions) on each side.

Example 11.2

$\frac{1}{2} = \frac{2}{4}$ and $\frac{a}{b} = \frac{3}{4}$ are proportions.

Problem 11.2
Solve for x.

a) $\frac{x}{2} = \frac{1}{3}$

b) $\frac{x+5}{6} = \frac{2}{3}$

c) $\frac{3}{x} = \frac{1}{4}$

d) $\frac{x-1}{3x} = \frac{1}{4}$

e) $\frac{x}{1+\frac{2}{3}} = \frac{\frac{5}{2}-1}{4}$

Math Fluency

CHAPTER 11 — Equations & Inequalities

Solution 11.2

a) $\dfrac{x}{2} = \dfrac{1}{3}$

Multiply both sides by 2 : $x = \dfrac{2}{3}$.

b) $\dfrac{x+5}{6} = \dfrac{2}{3}$

Multiply both sides by 6 : $x + 5 = 6 \times \dfrac{2}{3}$,
$x + 5 = 4$

Subtract 5 from both sides: $x = -1$.

c) $\dfrac{3}{x} = \dfrac{1}{4}$

Multiply both sides by x and 4 (cross multiply):
$4 \times 3 = x \times 1$, $x = 12$.

d) $\dfrac{x-1}{3x} = \dfrac{1}{4}$

Multiply both sides by 3x and 4 (cross multiply):
$4 \times (x - 1) = 3x \times 1$, $4x - 4 = 3x$

Subtract 3x and add 4 to both sides:
$4x - 3x = 4$, $x = 4$.

e) $\dfrac{x}{1 + \frac{2}{3}} = \dfrac{\frac{5}{2} - 1}{4}$

First, we should simplify $1 + \dfrac{2}{3}$ and $\dfrac{5}{2} - 1$:

$1 + \dfrac{2}{3} = \dfrac{3}{3} + \dfrac{2}{3} = \dfrac{5}{3}$ and $\dfrac{5}{2} - 1 = \dfrac{5}{2} - \dfrac{2}{2} = \dfrac{3}{2}$.

$\dfrac{x}{\frac{5}{3}} = \dfrac{\frac{3}{2}}{4}$, $\dfrac{3x}{5} = \dfrac{3}{8}$

Multiply both sides by 5 and divide by 3: $x = \dfrac{5}{8}$.

Remark 11.2

$\dfrac{x}{\frac{5}{3}} = x \div \dfrac{5}{3} = x \times \dfrac{3}{5} = \dfrac{3x}{5}$ and

$\dfrac{\frac{3}{2}}{4} = \dfrac{3}{2} \div \dfrac{4}{1} = \dfrac{3}{2} \times \dfrac{1}{4} = \dfrac{3}{8}$.

Remark 11.3 – Cover-Up Method

This is a step-by-step fill-in-the-blank process. For example, we can solve the equation $1 + \dfrac{x}{5} = 7$ as follows:

$1 + \dfrac{x}{5} = 7$
$1 + 6 = 7$
$\dfrac{x}{5} = 6$
$\dfrac{30}{5} = 6$
$x = 30$

Example 11.3

The following equation can be solved by the cover-up method.

$1 + \dfrac{2}{1 + \frac{3}{x}} = 7$
$1 + 6 = 7$
$\dfrac{2}{1 + \frac{3}{x}} = 6$
$\dfrac{2}{\frac{1}{3}} = 6$
$1 + \dfrac{3}{x} = \dfrac{1}{3}$
$\dfrac{3}{x} = -\dfrac{2}{3}$
$9 = -2x$
$x = -4.5$

Remark 11.4 – How to Solve Equations with Two (or more) Variables (Unknowns)

Basically, there are two methods of solving equations with two or more variables.

1. Method of substitution: One variable is expressed in terms of the other one and plugged into the other equation.

2. Method of elimination: By making the coefficients of one variable opposite in both equations and adding two equations side-by-side, that variable is eliminated.

Equations & Inequalities

CHAPTER 11

Example 11.4

Let's solve the following system of equations by both methods.

$$\begin{cases} x + y = 3 \\ x - y = 1 \end{cases}$$

Method of substitution: The first equation $x + y = 3$ can be rewritten as $y = 3 - x$ and this can be plugged into the second equation $x - y = 1$:

$x - (3 - x) = 1$, $2x - 3 = 1$, $2x = 4$, $x = 2$.

$y = 3 - x = 3 - 2 = 1$.

So, the solution is $(2, 1)$ which means $x = 2$ and $y = 1$.

Method of elimination: As you can see, y variables in both equations have already opposite coefficients. Let's add these equations side-by-side:

$(x + y) + (x - y) = 3 + 1$, $2x = 4$, $x = 2$.

$y = 3 - x = 3 - 2 = 1$.

So, there is one solution, and it is $(2, 1)$.

Problem 11.3

a) $\begin{cases} \frac{1}{a} + \frac{1}{b} = 3 \\ \frac{1}{a} - \frac{1}{b} = 1 \end{cases}$

b) $\begin{cases} x + y - z = 3 \\ x - 2y + z = 2 \\ x + y + z = 1 \end{cases}$

c) $\begin{cases} a + b + c = 3 \\ a - b + c = 1 \end{cases}$ $a + c = ?$

Solution 11.3

a) $\begin{cases} \frac{1}{a} + \frac{1}{b} = 3 \\ \frac{1}{a} - \frac{1}{b} = 1 \end{cases}$

Replace $\frac{1}{a}$ by x and $\frac{1}{b}$ by y.

So, we have the system of equations in Example 11.3.

So, $\frac{1}{a} = 2$ and $\frac{1}{b} = 1$.

This means that $a = 0.5$ and $b = 1$.

b) $\begin{cases} x + y - z = 3 \\ x - 2y + z = 2 \\ x + y + z = 1 \end{cases}$

Adding all equations side-by-side, we get:

$3x + z = 6$, $z = 6 - 3x$.

Replacing z with $6 - 3x$ in the first and last equations:

$\begin{cases} x + y - (6-3x) = 3 \\ x + y + (6-3x) = 3 \end{cases}$, $\begin{cases} x + y - 6 + 3x = 3 \\ x + y + 6 - 3x = 1 \end{cases}$,

$\begin{cases} 4x + y = 9 \\ -2x + y = -5 \end{cases}$,

Multiply the first equation by (-1): $\begin{cases} -4x - y = -9 \\ -2x + y = -5 \end{cases}$,

Adding both equations side-by-side: $-6x = -14$

Divide both sides by (-6): $x = \frac{14}{6} = \frac{7}{3}$.

Replace x with $\frac{7}{3}$ in $-2x + y = -5$: $-\frac{14}{3} + y = -5$,

$y = \frac{14}{3} - 5 = -\frac{1}{3}$.

Plug x and y values in one of the original equations,

$x + y + z = 1$: $\frac{7}{3} + (-\frac{1}{3}) + z = 1$, $z = -1$.

So, there is one solution: $(\frac{7}{3}, -\frac{1}{3}, -1)$.

c) $\begin{cases} a + b + c = 3 \\ a - b + c = 1 \end{cases}$ $a + c = ?$

Adding both equations side-by-side, we get:

$2a + 2c = 4$, $2(a + c) = 4$, $a + c = 2$.

Definition 11.3

Absolute value of a real number is the distance between that real number and zero. It is denoted by two bars around the number.

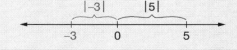

CHAPTER 11 — Equations & Inequalities

Example 11.5

a) $|5| = 5$

b) $|-3| = 3$

c) $|x| = \begin{cases} x \text{ if } x \geq 0 \\ -x \text{ if } x < 0 \end{cases}$

Problem 11.4

Solve for the integer values of x.

a) $|x| = 3$
b) $|x - 1| = 3$
c) $|2x - 1| = 3$

Solution 11.4

a) $|x| = 3$
$x = -3$ or $x = 3$. So, the solution set is $\{-3, 3\}$.

b) $|x - 1| = 3$
$x - 1 = -3$, $x = -2$ or $x - 1 = 3$, $x = 4$.
So, the solution set is $\{-2, 4\}$.

c) $|2x - 1| = 3$
$2x - 1 = -3$, $2x = -2$, $x = -1$ or
$2x - 1 = 3$, $2x = 4$, $x = 2$.
So, the solution set is $\{-1, 2\}$.

Definition 11.5

Two expressions with one of the signs <, >, ≤ or ≥ between them are called an inequality.

Example 11.6

a) $3 < 4$

b) $x < 4$ (All real numbers less than four)

c) $3 \leq x < 5$ (Three-part inequality: All real numbers greater than or equal to three and less than five)

Remark 11.5 – How to Multiply/Divide an Inequality by a Negative Number

When we multiply or divide an inequality by a negative number, we flip the inequality sign.

Example 11.7

a) $3 < 4$ changes to $-3 > -4$ when divided or multiplied by -1.

b) $-2x < 4$ changes to $x > -2$ when divided by -2.

Problem 11.5

How many integer values of x satisfy the following inequalities?

a) $4 \leq x < 10$
b) $4 \leq 2x < 10$
c) $4 \leq 2x + 3 < 10$
d) $4 \leq -2x + 3 < 10$
e) $4 \leq \dfrac{-2x + 3}{3} < 10$

Solution 11.5

a) $4 \leq x < 10$
Integer values of x are: 4,5,6,7,8,9. So, there are six integer values satisfying this inequality.

b) $4 \leq 2x < 10$
Dividing all sides of the given inequality by 2, we get $2 \leq x < 5$.
Integer values of x are: 2,3,4. So, there are three integer values.

c) $4 \leq 2x + 3 < 10$
Subtract 3 from all sides: $1 \leq 2x < 7$
Divide all sides by 2: $0.5 \leq x < 3.5$
Integer values of x are: 1, 2, 3. So, there are three integer values.

d) $4 \leq -2x + 3 < 10$
Subtract 3 from all sides: $1 \leq -2x < 7$
Divide all sides by -2: $-0.5 \geq x > -3.5$,
which means $-3.5 < x \leq -0.5$.
Integer values of x are: -3, -2, -1.
So, there are three integer values.

e) $4 \leq \dfrac{-2x + 3}{3} < 10$
Multiply all sides by 3: $12 \leq -2x + 3 < 30$
Subtract 3 from all sides: $9 \leq -2x < 27$
Divide all sides by (-2): $-13.5 < x \leq -4.5$
Integer values of x are $-13, -12, -11, -10, \ldots, -5$.
So, there are nine integer values.

Problem Set 1 — **Equations & Inequalities** — **CHAPTER 11**

1. Simplify

    $\dfrac{x + 32 + (12 - x)}{15} + 3$

2. Solve

    $\dfrac{27}{3} = \dfrac{x}{9}$

3. Solve

    $\dfrac{5}{x} + 2 = \dfrac{7}{2}$

4. Solve

    $\dfrac{(10)(6)}{5} + 3^2 = \dfrac{x}{4}$

5. Solve

    $-126 + 14 + x = 6 - 20$

6. Solve

    $0.70 + 1.65 + 10h = 2.72$

7. Solve

    $\dfrac{2}{9}x - 4 = x - 1$

8. Solve

    $2 \cdot (x + 1) - 4 = 6$

9. Solve for each variable in this system of equations:
    - $z + 2x - y = 10$
    - $6y + x - 4 = 11$
    - $3x + 1 = 10$

10. Solve

    $\dfrac{2x - 5}{7} = 11$

CHAPTER 11 — Equations & Inequalities — Problem Set 1

11. Solve

    $$\frac{2x+1}{3x-6} = \frac{1}{2}$$

12. Solve

    $$\frac{1}{3} \times (84 - 7x) = 1$$

13. $x + y = 16$
    $x + z = 1$
    $y + z = 7$
    What is x?

14. $x - y + z = 6$
    $x + y + z = 10$
    What is $x + z$?

15. $b = 4a$
    $2a + 3b = 28$
    What is a?

16. $23 + \dfrac{48}{26 - \dfrac{12}{x+3}} = 25$

17. $109 + \dfrac{50}{23 + \dfrac{30}{13 + \dfrac{x+4}{4}}} = 111$

18. $3 + \dfrac{4}{4 + \dfrac{6}{x}} = 5$

19. Solve for x:

    $$\frac{1}{x} = \frac{2}{x+1}$$

20. Solve the following equation for x:

    $$\frac{x}{2} - \frac{3}{4} = \frac{9}{8}$$

Problem Set 2 — Equations & Inequalities — CHAPTER 11

1. $\dfrac{|-8| + |4|}{|-4| - |-2|} = ?$

2. For how many x integers is the following inequality satisfied?

    $-5 < x \leq 3$?

3. What is the smallest integer value of a: satisfying

    $2 \times (a + 6) > 30$

4. What is the largest integer value of a: satisfying

    $5 \times (a + 6) < 50$

5. If $2(x - 1) \geq +3$

    then what is the smallest integer value of x?

6. If

    $\dfrac{(x + 3)}{4} = -7,$

    what is the value of x?

7. What is the sum of positive x integer values that satisfy

    $5 - 6x \geq -19$?

8. x is an integer such that

    $-4 \leq x < 2$

    What is the sum of all x values?

9. What is the smallest x integer value satisfying the following inequality?

    $\dfrac{2x + 1}{3} > 4$

10. x and y are integers that satisfy

    $-3 < x < 4$

    $-5 < y < 6$

    How many values can x + y have?

11. For how many x integer values
    $-\sqrt{5} < x < \dfrac{11}{3}$?

12. For how many x integer values
    $-2 < \dfrac{3x-1}{5} \leq 7$?

13. For how many x integer values
    $-10 < 6x + 2 \leq 32$?

14. Which of these numbers will make the inequality true?
    $\sqrt{11} < \square$
    A) 4 B) 3 C) 2 D) 1

15. What is the smallest x integer value?
    $3 < \dfrac{x}{2} + 1$

16. What is the sum of x values?
    $|x - 9| = 20$

17. What is the sum of x values?
    $|x + 14| = 5$

18. If $|x - 6| = |2x + 4|$, what is the largest value of x?

19. Find the sum of all possible integer values of x if
    $3 \leq \dfrac{3x + 3}{2} \leq 6$

20. What is the largest integer t value satisfying the following inequality?
    $9t + 5 - 12t \geq 7 + 3t + 10$

CHAPTER 12
Ratios & Proportions

✅ Target Concepts and Skills

- ☐ Defining ratios and proportions
- ☐ Solving proportion equations
- ☐ Solving real-life problems with ratios and proportions
- ☐ Applying ratios & proportions to similar figures

Definition 12.1 – Ratio

A ratio is a comparison of two (or more numbers) by division to indicate their sizes in relation to each other.

Example 12.1

The ratio of 3 to 4 can be expressed as 3:4 or $\frac{3}{4}$.

Example 12.2

For every two chickens on a farm, there are five cows. If there are 10 chickens, then how many cows are there?

We know that the ratio of 10 chickens to the unknown number of cows is 2:5, so we can set our unknown fraction equal to $\frac{2}{5}$ and set our known quantity equal to x. So we have $\frac{2}{5} = \frac{10}{x}$.
Setting 2x = 50, we divide both sides by 2 and get x = 25. Thus, there are 25 cows if there are 10 chickens.

Definition 12.2 – Proportion

An equation in which two ratios are set equal is called a proportion.

Example 12.3

$\frac{1}{3} = \frac{2}{6}$ is a proportion that includes two equivalent ratios $\frac{1}{3}$ and $\frac{2}{6}$.

Problem 12.1

Find x if

a) $\frac{x}{4} = \frac{3}{12}$

b) $\frac{3x-1}{4} = \frac{3}{12}$

c) $\frac{3x-1}{4x+2} = \frac{3}{12}$

d) $1:2:3 = 3:6:x$

Solution 12.1

a) $\frac{x}{4} = \frac{3}{12}$.

Multiply both sides by 4: $x = \frac{12}{12}$, x = 1.

b) $\frac{3x-1}{4} = \frac{3}{12}$

Multiply both sides by 4: $3x - 1 = 1$, $3x = 2$, $x = \frac{2}{3}$.

c) $\frac{3x-1}{4x+2} = \frac{\cancel{3}^{1}}{\cancel{12}_{4}}$

Multiply both sides by 4x + 2 and 4 (cross multiply): $(3x - 1) \cdot 4 = (4x + 2) \cdot 1$

$12x - 4 = 4x + 2$, $12x - 4x = 2 + 4$, $8x = 6$, $x = \frac{3}{4}$.

d) $1:2:3 = 3:6:x$

We can solve this proportion with three ratios by taking them two by two. Let's take the first and last numbers from both sides: $1:3 = 3:x$, which can be written as $\frac{1}{3} = \frac{3}{x}$.
Multiply both sides by 3 and x (cross multiply): x = 9.
Note that we could take the second and last numbers also: $2:3 = 6:x$.

Math Fluency

CHAPTER 12 — Ratios & Proportions

Definition 12.3 – Similar Figures
Figures with equivalent corresponding angles and corresponding proportional sides are similar.

Remark 12.1 – Ratios in Similar Figures
Ratios of two pairs of corresponding lengths in similar figures are equal.

Example 12.4

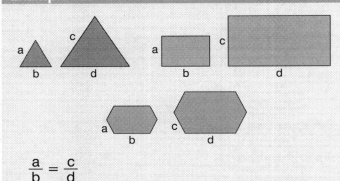

$$\frac{a}{b} = \frac{c}{d}$$

Problem 12.2
Find x if the following figures are similar.

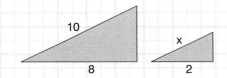

Solution 12.2
Since the figures are similar, we can set up the proportion $\frac{10}{8} = \frac{x}{2}$ and get that $x = 2.5$.

Problem 12.3
Find $\frac{x}{y}$ if $\frac{2x - y}{y} = \frac{3}{2}$.

Solution 12.3
Cross multiply: $2 \cdot (2x - y) = 3y$, $4x - 2y = 3y$, $4x = 5y$.
Divide both sides by y and then by 4: $\frac{x}{y} = \frac{5}{4}$.

Problem 12.4
Find the following ratios if $a : b : c = 1 : 2 : 3$.
a) $\frac{a+b}{b}$ b) $\frac{a+b}{a-2c}$

Solution 12.4
By the given three-part ratio, we can take $a = x$, $b = 2x$, $c = 3x$ ($x \neq 0$). Then,

a) $\frac{a+b}{b} = \frac{x+2x}{2x} = \frac{3x}{2x} = \frac{3}{2} = 1.5$.

b) $\frac{a+b}{a-2c} = \frac{x+2x}{x-6x} = \frac{3x}{-5x} = -\frac{3}{5} = -0.6$.

Problem 12.5
Perimeter of a rectangle is 48 cm. The ratio of its length to width is $5 : 3$. Find the area of this rectangle.

Solution 12.5
Let the length and width of the rectangle be ℓ and w, respectively. Then, $\frac{\ell}{w} = \frac{5}{3}$.
So, we can say that $\ell = 5x$ and $w = 3x$ ($x \neq 0$), and $48 = 2 \cdot (5x + 3x)$. Thus, $48 = 16x$, $x = 3$. This means that $\ell = 5 \cdot 3 = 15$ cm and $w = 3 \cdot 3 = 9$ cm. Therefore, rectangle's area equals $15 \cdot 9 = 135 \text{cm}^2$.

Problem 12.6
In a math class, the number of students is greater than 40 and less than 46. The ratio of the number of female students to male students is $4 : 5$. Find the number of male students.

Solution 12.6
Let the numbers of female students and male students be f and m, respectively. Then, $\frac{f}{m} = \frac{4}{5}$.
So, we can say that $f = 4x$ and $m = 5x$ ($x \neq 0$), and thereby the total number of students is 9x. This means that the total number of students is a multiple of 9 and is between 40 and 46. So, it is 45. Thus, $9x = 45$ and $x = 5$.
The number of male students is $5 \cdot 5 = 25$.

Problem Set 1 — Ratios & Proportions — CHAPTER 12

1. Find the missing value
   $\dfrac{x}{10} = \dfrac{6}{15}$

2. Find the missing value
   $\dfrac{16}{37} = \dfrac{200}{m}$

3. Find the missing value
   $\dfrac{x}{100} = \dfrac{7}{8}$

4. $\dfrac{3 \text{ pounds}}{\$7.50} = \dfrac{x}{\$10}$

5. What is x?

   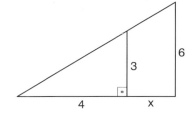

6. If $\dfrac{3}{7} \cdot A = B$, what $\dfrac{A + B}{A - B} = ?$

7. Solve for m
   $\dfrac{2m + 3}{3m - 4} = \dfrac{7}{2}$

8. Which pack is the better value?

   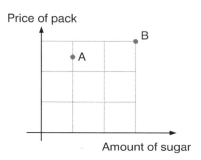

9. Where does point (9,20) lie? (Region I or II)

   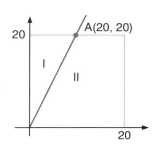

10. My printer can print 15 pages in 1/2 minutes. How many pages does it print in 3 minutes?

Math Fluency — 75

11. Find $\dfrac{a}{b}$ if $\dfrac{2a-b}{2a} = \dfrac{1}{2}$

12.
	Distance(m)	Time(sec)
Student A	90	15
Student B	80	12

Which student ran faster?

13. On a map, an 8-centimeter length represents 48 kilometers.

How many kilometers does 20-centimeter length represent?

14. The ratio of $x : y$ is $2 : 3$.
What is $\dfrac{x+y}{y-x}$?

15. The average of 4, 20, and x is equal to the average of y and 16.
What is $\dfrac{y}{x}$?

16. Given the ratios of the sides $x : y : z = 1 : 2 : 5/2$ and the perimeter of the triangle is 22 cm. What is z?

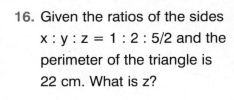

17. There are between 250 and 350 students in a school. The ratio of boys to girls is $4 : 7$.
How many students in the school?

18. If $\dfrac{a}{5} = \dfrac{b}{3} = \dfrac{c}{2}$ and $a + b + 2c = 36$
What is $a = $?

19. If $a : b = 3/4$ and $b : c = 3/5$ then what is $a : c$?

20. If $b = 2c$ and $a = 3b$,
What is the value of $\dfrac{a+b-c}{b}$?

Problem Set 2 — **Ratios & Proportions** — **CHAPTER 12**

1. The number that goes into the □ to make $\frac{3}{7} = \frac{\square}{63}$ true is

2. If $\frac{x}{4} = \frac{18}{12}$ what is the value of x?

3. $\frac{x}{4} = \frac{18}{12}$
   a = _____

4. $\frac{z+1}{10} + 6 = 3$
   z = _____

5. If $\frac{3}{5} = \frac{M}{20} = \frac{15}{N}$, what is M + N?

6. If $\frac{x+3}{4} = \frac{x-8}{5}$, what is the value of 2x?

7. $\frac{1}{\square}$ of 24 = $\frac{1}{6}$ of 12
   What number goes in the box?

8. If $\frac{1}{n+3} = \frac{1}{7}$ then $\frac{1}{n^2 + 9}$ is equal to?

9. $5 : x + 2 = 4 : x$

10. Solve the proportion $25 : q = 5 : 2$ for q.

CHAPTER 12 — Ratios & Proportions — Problem Set 2

11. If
$$\frac{x+3}{18} = \frac{x-a}{17}$$
and $a = 5$,

what is the value of x?

12. Solve for x: $\dfrac{12}{x-2} = \dfrac{32}{x+8}$

13. If
$$\frac{a+b}{a-b} = 4,$$
what is the value of $\dfrac{a}{b}$?

14. $\dfrac{x+3y}{x-y} = 3$

what is the value of $\dfrac{x}{y}$?

15. If
$$\frac{4a-b}{3a+2b} = \frac{2}{3}$$
what is $\dfrac{a}{b}$?

16. If
$$3 \cdot x = 4 \cdot y$$
What is $\dfrac{x+2y}{3x-y}$?

17. An oil tank with a capacity of 200 gallons contains 50 gallons of oil.

Find the ratio of the number of gallons of oil in the tank to the capacity of the tank.

18. $\dfrac{x}{6} = \dfrac{y}{8}$ and $y - x = 15$

What is the value of x?

19. The perimeter of a triangle is 60 feet. If the sides are in the ratio 3 : 4 : 5, find the length of each side of the triangle.

20. There are between 25 and 35 students in a class. The ratio of boys to girls is 4 : 7. How many students are in the class?

CHAPTER 13
Operations & Functions

Target Concepts and Skills

- [ ] Defining functions & binary operations.
- [ ] Representing linear functions in various forms.
- [ ] Solving equations involving functions & binary operations.
- [ ] Applying linear equations to real-life situations.

Definition 13.1 – Function

A function is a relationship between two sets (input and output sets), which pairs **each** member of one set (input set=domain) with **exactly one** member of the other set (output set=range). In general, functions are named by lowercase letters like f, g, or h.

Example 13.1

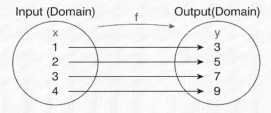

The relationship given above by the diagram defines the function f from the input set {1, 2, 3, 4} to the output set {3, 5, 7, 9}. Input values are represented by the variable x (independent variable), and output values are represented by the variable y (dependent variable).

This function can be represented in the following ways as well:

Algebraically (by the formula): $f(x) = 2x + 1$ since
$f(1) = 2 \cdot 1 + 1 = 3$,
$f(2) = 2 \cdot 2 + 1 = 5$,
$f(3) = 2 \cdot 3 + 1 = 7$,
$f(4) = 2 \cdot 4 + 1 = 9$.

By a table of x & y values:

x	y = f(x)
1	3
2	5
3	7
4	9

Verbally: Double x and add one.

Depending on the situation, one way of representing a function might be more convenient than the other ways.

Graphically:

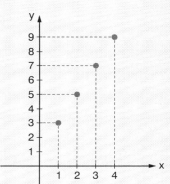

Example 13.2

All words in the English language and an English dictionary illustrate a function since each word is paired with exactly one letter in the dictionary.

Problem 13.1

Evaluate the following expressions if $f(x) = 3x - 1$
a) $f(5)$ c) $2 \cdot f(4) + f(5)$
b) $f(4) + f(5)$ d) $f(2a)$

CHAPTER 13 — Operations & Functions

Solution 13.1
a) $f(5) = 3 \cdot 5 - 1 = 15 - 1 = 14$.
b) $f(4) = 3 \cdot 4 - 1 = 12 - 1 = 11$. So,
   $f(4) + f(5) = 11 + 14 = 25$.
c) $2 \cdot f(4) + f(5) = 2 \cdot 11 + 14 = 22 + 14 = 36$.
d) $f(2a) = 3 \cdot (2a) - 1 = 6a - 1$.

Problem 13.2
For what value(s) of x, $f(x) = 14$ if $f(x) = 3x - 1$.

Solution 13.2
$f(x) = 14$ means we need to replace $f(x)$ with 14 in the equation of the given function $f(x) = 3x - 1$. Thus, we have the equation:
$14 = 3x - 1$ from which we get $15 = 3x$, $5 = x$.

Definition 13.2 – Linear Equation
A function of the form $f(x) = mx + b$ or $y = mx + b$ where m & b are constants, x is a variable and $m \neq 0$, is called a linear function. The graph of a linear function is a straight line.

Problem 13.3
Determine the linear function $f(x)$ if $f(1) = 3$ and $f(2) = 5$.

Solution 13.3
Since f is a linear function, we can assume that $f(x) = mx + b$.
Then, $f(1) = m \cdot 1 + b$ and $f(2) = m \cdot 2 + b$.
Thus, we have a system of equations:
$\begin{cases} m + b = 3 \\ 2m + b = 5 \end{cases}$ (Remember that $f(1) = 3$ and $f(2) = 5$)
The first equation can be expressed as: $b = 3 - m$
By substitution method: $2m + 3 - m = 5$,
$m + 3 = 5$, $m = 2$.
Plugging m value into the first equation:
$2 + b = 3$, $b = 1$.
So, we have $f(x) = 2x + 1$.

Problem 13.4
Find $f(g(x))$ if $f(x) = 3x + 1$ and $g(x) = x - 1$

Solution 13.4
$f(g(x)) = f(x - 1) = 3 \cdot (x - 1) + 1 = 3x - 3 + 1 = 3x - 2$. So, $f(g(x)) = 3x - 2$.

Alternatively, we could begin in a slightly different way:
$f(g(x)) = 3 \cdot (g(x)) + 1 = 3 \cdot (x - 1) + 1 = 3x - 3 + 1 = 3x - 2$.
Thus, $f(g(x)) = 3x - 2$.

Problem 13.5
The point (2,n) is on the line represented by the function $y = 2x - 1$. Find n.

Solution 13.5
The first coordinate of a point is the input (x) value, and the second coordinate is the output (y) value. So, we can replace x with 2 and y with n in the given function's equation:
$n = 2 \cdot 2 - 1$ $n = 4 - 1$ $n = 3$.

Problem 13.6
Rental cost y of a construction machine for x days can be modeled by the linear equation
$y = 200x + 300$ dollars.
Find the number of rental days if the total rental cost is $1900.

Solution 13.6
The total rental cost is $1900. So, y can be replaced by 1900 in the given function:
$1900 = 200x + 300$. Then, to find the number of rental days, we solve the equation for x.
$1900 = 200x + 300$, $1600 = 200x$, $x = 8$.

Operations & Functions

CHAPTER 13

Remark 13.1 – How to Determine the Domain of a Function?

When not specified, the domain of a function includes all defined values of real numbers.

Example 13.3

Let's determine the domains of the following functions:

a)
x	y = f(x)
5	3
7	5
9	7
20	9

Domain = {5,7,9,20}

b) $y = x - 1$

Domain= All real numbers since x can be replaced by any real number.

c)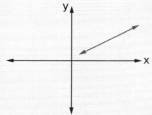

Domain = All real numbers

d)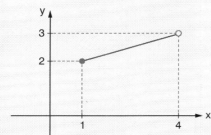

Domain= [1,4) which means "all real numbers from 1 (inclusive) to 4 (exclusive)".

Definition 13.2 – Binary Operation

A binary operation is a function with two input values corresponding to one output value.

Example 13.4

Let's define an operation # such that
$a \# b = a + b - 1$ where a and b real numbers.
According to the given definition,
$1 \# 2 = 1 + 2 - 1$, $1 \# 2 = 2$
$3 \# 7 = 3 + 7 - 1$, $3 \# 7 = 9$.

Problem 13.7

Evaluate the following expressions if
$a * b = a - b + 5$.

a) $3 * 4$
b) $3 * (4 * 5)$
c) 3^{4*5}
d) $3^{4*5} + (3 * 4)$

Solution 13.7

a) $3 * 4 = 3 - 4 + 5 = 4$.

b) $3 * (4 * 5) = 3 * (4 - 5 + 5) = 3 * 4 = 3 - 4 + 5 = 4$.

c) $3^{4*5} = 3^{4-5+5} = 3^4 = 81$.

d) By part (a), we have $3 * 4 = 4$, and by part (c), $3^{4*5} = 81$. Thus,
$3^{4*5} + (3 * 4) = 81 + 4 = 85$.

Problem 13.8

Find x if $a \Delta b = a \cdot b + \dfrac{a}{b}$.

a) $x \Delta 2 = 15$
b) $2 \Delta x = 2x + 4$

Solution 13.8

a) $x \Delta 2 = x \cdot 2 + \dfrac{x}{2} = \dfrac{5x}{2}$. So, $\dfrac{5x}{2} = 15$, $5x = 30$, $x = 6$.

b) $2 \Delta x = 2 \cdot x + \dfrac{2}{x}$. So, $2x + \dfrac{2}{x} = 2x + 4$, $\dfrac{2}{x} = 4$, $2 = 4x$, $\dfrac{2}{4} = x$, $x = \dfrac{1}{2}$.

CHAPTER 13 — GAME 24 — Puzzle

Make the number 24 from the four numbers shown. You can add, subtract, multiply, and divide. Use all four numbers on the card, but use each number only once. You do not have to use all four operations.

1. a)

   b)

   c)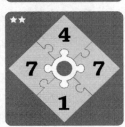

2. a)

   b)

   c)

3. a)

   b)

   c)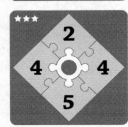

4. a)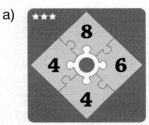

   b)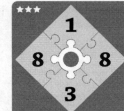

   c)

Problem Set 1 — **Operations & Functions** — **CHAPTER 13**

1. If $a \triangle b = a + b - ab$, find $4 \triangle 9$.

2. If $a * b = a \times b - 2a - 2b$,
   find $(6 * 7)$

3. The operation is defined so that
   $a \triangle b = a \times b + a + b$.
   For example,
   $2 \triangle 5 = 2 \times 5 + 2 + 5 = 17$.
   If $a \triangle 3 = 39$, the value of a is

4. If $a * b$ is equivalent to $\frac{a}{b} + a \times b$,
   what is the value of $a * b$ when $a = 4$ and $b = -2$?

5. Suppose $a \square b$ means $4a - 3b$
   What is the value of x if $(4 \square x) = 1$

6. If $a \bigcirc b = \dfrac{a \times b}{a + b}$ and $\dfrac{1}{2} \bigcirc a = \dfrac{1}{4}$,
   What is the value of a?

7. If $<4> = 1 + 2$, $<6> = 1 + 2 + 3$, and $<12> = 1 + 2 + 3 + 4 + 6$, then
   what is $<28> = ?$

8. For positive number a and b the operation $?(a, b)$ is defined as $?(a, b) = a - \dfrac{1}{b}$.
   What is $?(4, ?(4, 4))$?

9. If $f(x) = 4x + a$,
   What is the value of a satisfying $f(2) = 6$?

10. If $f(x) = 2x + n$ and $f(8) = 20$,
    find the value of $f(4) = ?$

CHAPTER 13 — Operations & Functions — Problem Set 1

11. If point P(a, 2) is on the line $3x + y - 12 = 0$, what is a?

12.

N	1	2	3	4	5	...	15
F(n)	5	9	13	17	21	...	x

What is x?

13. What is the 51st number in the sequence

7, 17, 27, 37, ...

14. The cost of hiring a tennis court for h hour is $5h + 8$.

What is the cost of hiring for 6 hours?

15. Given a line $Y = mx + 6$ that passes through the point (24, 6), what is m?

16. Define the operation a@b to be

$3 + ab + a + 2b$.

If $x@2 = 16$

What is x?

17. Let $a@b = \dfrac{a}{2} + b$, what is $2@4 - 6@2$?

18. If $f(x) = \dfrac{3x + 1}{x - 2}$, what is $f(0) + f(3) = ?$

19.

Planting Years	Height
3	10
4	13
5	16

What is the height of the tree 50 years after it was planted?

20. Define $x * y = x^2 - y$ what is a if $a * (a * a) = 4$

Problem Set 2 — Operations & Functions — CHAPTER 13

1.
input		output
x	→	4x + 7
3	→	y

   What is y?

2. $f(x) = 8x - 5$

   What is $f(2)$?

3. If $A * B = \dfrac{A + B}{2}$, then $(3 * 5) = ?$

4. If $a \otimes b = \dfrac{a + b}{a - b}$, then $(6 \otimes 4) = ?$

5. Use the table to determine the rule.

Input △	Output □
2	8
7	13
12	18
40	46

   What is the rule for the function?

   A) △ × 4 = □
   B) (△ × 3) − 1 = □
   C) △ + 5 = □
   D) △ + 6 = □

6. If $f(x) = 2x$, what is the value of $f(-4)$?

7. If p and q is equivalent to $\dfrac{p}{q} + pq$, what is the value of q and p when $p = 4$ and $q = -2$?

8. Suppose that $x*$ means $\dfrac{1}{x}$, the reciprocal of x. For example, $5* = \dfrac{1}{x}$.

   What is $2* + 4*$?

9. f is a function and $f(x) = 4x - 6$.

   What is the value of $f(1) + f(3)$?

10. $f(a) = 2a + 4$

    Find $f(3)$

CHAPTER 13 — Operations & Functions — Problem Set 2

11. $g(t) = 2t - 3$

Find $g(5)$.

12. $g(x) = 2x - 5$

$h(x) = 4x + 5$

Find $g(3) - h(3)$

13. For real numbers x and y, define

$x \spadesuit y = (x + y)(x - y)$.

What is $3 \spadesuit (4 \spadesuit 5)$?

14. Write a rule for the relationship between x and y.

x	y
1	4
2	9
3	14
4	19
5	24

15. The cost of hiring a tennis court for h hours is given by the formula $C(h) = 5h + 8$ dollars.

Find the cost of hiring the tennis court for 4 hours.

16. If $f(x) = 2x + a$, what is the value of a satisfying $f(2) = 2$?

17. $f(x) = 3x + 12$ is a function and a is a constant.

$f(a) + f(2a) = 42$.

Find a.

18. Which equation represents the relationship between the values of x and y in the table?

x	y
1	1.5
2	3
3	4.5
4	6

A) $y = x + 0.5$

B) $y = 1.5x$

C) $y = 0.5x + 1$

D) $y = 2x - 0.5$

19. The binary operation $\otimes$ satisfies

$x \otimes y = xy + x - y$ for any pair of real numbers x and y.

Find a value of a such that $3 \otimes a = a \otimes 5$.

20. $f(x) = 2x + 4$ is a function and $f(b) + f(3b) = 40$.

Find b.

CHAPTER 14
Exponents & Radicals

✓ Target Concepts and Skills

- ☐ Defining exponential numbers.
- ☐ Defining the square root of a number.
- ☐ Using the rules of exponents and square roots for simplifying expressions.
- ☐ Using the rules of exponents and square roots for solving equations.

Definition 14.1 – Exponential Number

a^b is read as "a to the power of b" and is equal to a being multiplied by itself b times. For example, $2^5 = 2 \cdot 2 \cdot 2 \cdot 2 \cdot 2 = 32$. Here, 2 is called the base and 5 is called the exponent.

Remark 14.1 – Rules of Exponents

1. $a^m \cdot a^n = a^{m+n}$
2. $\dfrac{a^m}{a^n} = a^{m-n}$
3. $(a^m)^n = a^{m \cdot n}$
4. $\dfrac{a^m}{b^m} = \left(\dfrac{a}{b}\right)^m$
5. $a^0 = 1$
6. $a^{-m} = \dfrac{1}{a^m}$

where a & b are nonzero real numbers, n & m integers.

Example 14.1

Using the rules of exponents, we can rewrite the following as an exponential number.

a) $4 \cdot 4 \cdot 4 = 4^3$

b) $5 + 5 + 5 + 5 + 5 = 5 \cdot 5 = 5^2$

c) $\dfrac{21^3}{7^2 + 7^2 + 7^2 + 7^2 + 7^2 + 7^2 + 7^2} = \dfrac{21^3}{7 \cdot 7^2} = \dfrac{21^3}{7^3} = \left(\dfrac{21}{7}\right)^3 = 3^3$.

d) $\dfrac{2^7 + 2^7}{4^5 + 4^5} = \dfrac{2 \cdot 2^7}{2 \cdot 4^5} = \dfrac{2^7}{4^5} = \dfrac{2^7}{(2^2)^5} = \dfrac{2^7}{2^{10}} = 2^{7-10} = 2^{-3}$.

Problem 14.1

Solve the following equations for x.

a) $3^x = 9$
b) $3^{x-2} = 27$
c) $3^x + 3^{x-1} = 12$

Solution 14.1

a) $3^x = 9$, $3^x = 3^2$, $x = 2$.

b) $3^{x-2} = 27$, $3^{x-2} = 3^3$, $x - 2 = 3$, $x = 5$.

c) Notice that $3^{x-1} = \dfrac{3^x}{3}$. So, $3^x + 3^{x-1} = 12$ can be written as $3^x + \dfrac{3^x}{3} = 12$.

Thus, $3^x \cdot \left(1 + \dfrac{1}{3}\right) = 12$, $3^x \cdot \dfrac{4}{3} = 12$, $3^x = 9$, $3^x = 3^2$, $x = 2$.

Problem 14.2

Solve the following equations for x.

a) $2^x = 1$
b) $2^x = 3^x$
c) $x^2 = x^3$

Solution 14.2

a) $2^x = 1$, $2^x = 2^0$, $x = 0$.

b) Since bases are not equal and cannot be expressed in terms of each other, this equation is true only when $x = 0$.

c) Since exponents are not equal and bases are equal, this equation is true only for some special cases that are $x = 0$ & $x = 1$.

Math Fluency

CHAPTER 14

Exponents & Radicals

Problem 14.3
Find the following if $7^x = 2$.
a) $7^x - 1$
b) 7^{x-1}
c) $5 \cdot 7^{x-1} + 7^x$
d) 49^x

Solution 14.3
Notice that we are not asked to find x.
a) $7^x - 1 = 2 - 1 = 1$.
b) $7^{x-1} = \dfrac{7^x}{7} = \dfrac{2}{7}$.
c) $5 \cdot 7^{x-1} + 7^x = 5 \cdot \dfrac{2}{7} + 2 = \dfrac{10}{7} + \dfrac{14}{7} = \dfrac{24}{7}$.
d) $49^x = (7^2)^x = 7^{2 \cdot x} = 7^{x \cdot 2} = (7^x)^2 = 2^2 = 4$.

Definition 14.2 – Square Root of a Number
The square root of the non-negative real number **b** is the number whose square is equal to **b**.

Remark 14.2 – The Principal Square Root
According to the definition above, any positive real number b has two square roots, which are $\sqrt{b}$ & $-\sqrt{b}$.

The positive square root $\sqrt{b}$ is called the principal square root of the number b.

Example 14.2
The square roots of 9 are –3 and 3.
However, $\sqrt{9} = 3$.

Remark 14.3
$\sqrt{x^2} = |x| = \begin{cases} x & \text{if } x \geq 0 \\ -x & \text{if } x < 0 \end{cases}$

Example 14.3
a) $\sqrt{(-7)^2} = |-7| = 7$
b) $\sqrt{(a-b)^2} = |a-b| = b - a$ if $b > a$.
c) $\sqrt{(3-\pi)^2} = |3-\pi| = \pi - 3$ since $\pi \approx 3.14$

Remark 14.4 – Rules of Square Roots
For non-negative real numbers a & b and $b \neq 0$, we have

1. $\sqrt{a} \cdot \sqrt{b} = \sqrt{a \cdot b}$
2. $\dfrac{\sqrt{a}}{\sqrt{b}} = \sqrt{\dfrac{a}{b}}$
3. $b\sqrt{a} + c\sqrt{a} = (b+c)\sqrt{a}$
4. $b\sqrt{a} - c\sqrt{a} = (b-c)\sqrt{a}$
5. $\sqrt{a} = a^{\frac{1}{2}}$

Problem 14.4
Simplify the following expressions.
a) $\sqrt{16}$
b) $\sqrt{32}$
c) $\sqrt{0.09}$
d) $\dfrac{\sqrt{27}}{\sqrt{3}}$
e) $2\sqrt{7} + 3\sqrt{7}$
f) $\sqrt{32} - 3\sqrt{2}$
g) $\sqrt{28} + \sqrt{45}$
h) $\dfrac{\sqrt{(3-\pi)^2}}{\pi - 3}$

Solution 14.4
a) $\sqrt{16} = \sqrt{4^2} = 4$.
b) $\sqrt{32} = \sqrt{16 \cdot 2} = \sqrt{16} \cdot \sqrt{2} = 4 \cdot \sqrt{2} = 4\sqrt{2}$.
c) $\sqrt{0.09} = \sqrt{\dfrac{9}{100}} = \dfrac{\sqrt{9}}{\sqrt{100}} = \dfrac{\sqrt{3^2}}{\sqrt{10^2}} = \dfrac{3}{10} = 0.3$
d) $\dfrac{\sqrt{27}}{\sqrt{3}} = \sqrt{\dfrac{27}{3}} = \sqrt{9} = \sqrt{3^2} = 3$.
e) $2\sqrt{7} + 3\sqrt{7} = (2+3)\sqrt{7} = 5\sqrt{7}$.
f) $\sqrt{32} - 3\sqrt{2} = 4\sqrt{2} - 3\sqrt{2} = (4-3)\sqrt{2} = \sqrt{2}$.
g) $\sqrt{28} + \sqrt{45} = \sqrt{4 \cdot 7} + \sqrt{9 \cdot 5} = 2\sqrt{7} + 3\sqrt{5}$.
h) Notice that $\pi \approx 3.14$ and $|3 - \pi| = \pi - 3$ since $\pi > 3$.

So, $\dfrac{\sqrt{(3-\pi)^2}}{\pi - 3} = \dfrac{|3-\pi|}{\pi - 3} = \dfrac{\pi - 3}{\pi - 3} = 1$.

Remark 14.5
1. Notice that $\sqrt{a} + \sqrt{b} \neq \sqrt{a + b}$.
   For example, $\sqrt{4} + \sqrt{9} \neq \sqrt{4 + 9}$.
2. $\sqrt{16} = \pm 4$ is a false statement. The true statement is $\sqrt{16} = 4$.

Exponents & Radicals

CHAPTER 14

Problem 14.5

Find the nearest integer to the given number below.

a) $2\sqrt{10}$

b) $\sqrt{72} - \sqrt{32}$

c) $\dfrac{\sqrt{90}}{\sqrt{5}} + \sqrt{8}$

Solution 14.5

a) $2\sqrt{10} = \sqrt{4} \cdot \sqrt{10} = \sqrt{4 \cdot 10} = \sqrt{40}$.

There are two perfect square integers around 40: $36 < 40 < 49$ and 36 is closer to 40. This means that $\sqrt{36} = 6$ is closer to $\sqrt{40} = 2\sqrt{10}$.

b) $\sqrt{72} - \sqrt{32} = \sqrt{36 \cdot 2} - \sqrt{16 \cdot 2}$
$= \sqrt{36} \cdot \sqrt{2} - \sqrt{16} \cdot \sqrt{2} = 6\sqrt{2} - 4\sqrt{2} = 2\sqrt{2}$
$= \sqrt{4 \cdot 2} = \sqrt{8}$.

Notice that nearest perfect square integers around 8 are 4 and 9 such that $4 < 8 < 9$ and 9 is closer to 8. This means that $\sqrt{9} = 3$ is closer to $\sqrt{8} = \sqrt{72} - \sqrt{32}$.

c) $\dfrac{\sqrt{90}}{\sqrt{5}} + \sqrt{8} = \sqrt{\dfrac{90}{5}} + \sqrt{4 \cdot 2} = \sqrt{18} + \sqrt{4} \cdot \sqrt{2}$
$= \sqrt{9 \cdot 2} + \sqrt{4} \cdot \sqrt{2} = \sqrt{9} \cdot \sqrt{2} + 2 \cdot \sqrt{2}$
$= 3\sqrt{2} + 2\sqrt{2} = 5\sqrt{2} = \sqrt{25 \cdot 2} = \sqrt{50}$.

The nearest perfect square integers around 50 are 49 and 64, such that $49 < 50 < 64$ and 49 is closer to 50.
Thus, $\sqrt{49} = 7$ is closer to $\sqrt{50} = \dfrac{\sqrt{90}}{\sqrt{5}} + \sqrt{8}$.

Problem 14.6

Solve the following equations for x.

a) $x^2 = 16$

b) $\sqrt{x} = 4$

c) $\sqrt{x} = -4$

d) $\sqrt{3x - 2} = 4$

e) $\sqrt{3 - \sqrt{x}} = 4$,

Solution 14.6

a) $x^2 = 16$, $x = \pm\sqrt{16}$, $x = \pm 4$

b) $\sqrt{x} = 4$,

Square both sides to remove the square root sign: $(\sqrt{x})^2 = 4^2$, $x = 16$. Plug this value into the original equation to check whether the equation holds true: $\sqrt{16} = 4$ (True).

So, the solution is 16.

c) No real number solution since $\sqrt{x}$ must always be equal to a non-negative value.

d) $\sqrt{3x - 2} = 4$,

Square both sides to remove the square root sign:

$(\sqrt{3x - 2})^2 = 4^2$, $3x - 2 = 16$, $3x = 18$, $x = 6$.

Plug this value into the original equation to check whether the equation holds true:

$\sqrt{3 \cdot 6 - 2} = 4$ (True). So, the solution is 6.

e) $\sqrt{3 - \sqrt{x}} = 4$,

Square both sides to remove the bigger square root sign:

$(\sqrt{3 - \sqrt{x}})^2 = 4^2$,

$3 - \sqrt{x} = 16$, $-\sqrt{x} = 13$, $\sqrt{x} = -13$

Square both sides to remove the smaller square root sign:

$(\sqrt{x})^2 = (-13)^2$, $x = 169$.

Plug this value into the original equation to check whether the equation holds true:

$\sqrt{3 - \sqrt{169}} = 4$, $\sqrt{3 - 13} = 4$, $\sqrt{-10} = 4$ (False).

So, since there is no other number to plug in, there is no solution.

CHAPTER 14 — Count Down Number Game — Puzzle

SCORING: For each of the target integers, you will receive 10 points for reaching the exact target, or 9 points for finding an integer that is 1 away from the target, or 8 points for finding an integer that is 2 away from the target, etc. or 1 point for finding an integer that is 9 away from the target.

Using each of the given numbers exactly once (you don't have to use all numbers) and only addition, subtraction, multiplication, division, and parenthesis, your goal is to get to the target number or an integer as close to the target number as you can

Example: If the given numbers are 1, 2, 3, 4, 10, 50 and target number is 605, then

$608 = (10 + 2) \times 50 + (1 + 3 + 4)$ would receive 7 points.

Given Numbers: 2, 3, 4, 5, 10, 75	
Target Number	**Solution**
201	
221	
241	
261	
281	
301	
311	
321	
331	
341	

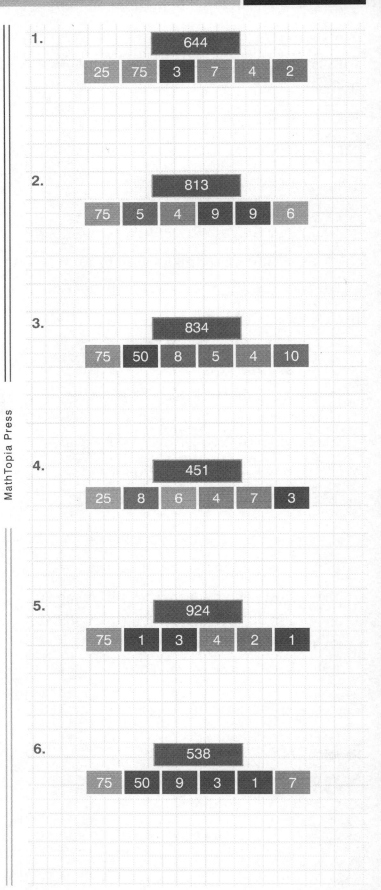

1. 644 — 25, 75, 3, 7, 4, 2
2. 813 — 75, 5, 4, 9, 9, 6
3. 834 — 75, 50, 8, 5, 4, 10
4. 451 — 25, 8, 6, 4, 7, 3
5. 924 — 75, 1, 3, 4, 2, 1
6. 538 — 75, 50, 9, 3, 1, 7

Problem Set 1 — Exponents & Radicals — CHAPTER 14

1. $9 \cdot 9 \cdot 9(9 + 9 + 9) = ?$

2. The expression $2^5 - 2^4$ has a value equal to

3. a) $x \times x \times x \times x \times x \times x \times x \times x \times x \times x$
   b) $4 \times 4 + n \times n$

4. $5^2 + 2^3 + 7 = ?$

5. If
   $A \times A \times A = 12^3$
   $7 \times 7 = 7^B$
   What is $A + B$?

6. If
   $(-1)^6 + (-2)^2 = A$
   $(-3)^1 + (-1)^7 = B$
   What is $A + B$?

7. If
   $4^{x+1} = 64$
   What is the value of x?

8. $5^{x+4} = 1$

9. $\dfrac{2^{11} + 2^{11}}{4^4 + 4^4} = ?$

10. $7^{x-2} = 1$
    What is x?

CHAPTER 14 — Exponents & Radicals — Problem Set 1

11. If $2^x + 3^y = 43$, where x and y are integers, then the value of x + y is

12. If
    $3^x = 2$
    What is 9^x?

13. If
    $2^{x-1} = 5$,
    What is 4^x?

14. If
    $7^{3x+y-3} = 13^{x-y-5}$
    What is x + y?

15. $\dfrac{5 \cdot 5 \cdot 5 \cdot 5 \cdot 5}{5^2 + 5^2 + 5^2 + 5^2 + 5^2} = ?$

16. If
    $3^x + 3^{x-2} = 30$
    What is x?

17. $\dfrac{1111^5 + 1111^5}{1111^4 + 1111^4} = ?$

18. Compute
    $2^{10} \cdot [2^{-9} - 2^{-8} + 2^{-7}]$

19. If
    $2^x \cdot 2^{2x} \cdot 2^{3x} = 4 \cdot 8 \cdot 128$
    What is x?

20. What is $\dfrac{1}{4}$ of 4^4?

Problem Set 2 — Exponents & Radicals — CHAPTER 14

1. The value of $\sqrt{81}$ is equal to

2. If $\sqrt{b} = 5$ then what is b?

3. $\sqrt{3^2 + 4^2} = ?$

4. $\sqrt{0.16} + \sqrt{0.36} = ?$

5. $\sqrt{8 + 2 \cdot \sqrt{7 + \sqrt{81}}} = ?$

6. $\sqrt{25} + \sqrt{49} - \sqrt{16} = ?$

7. If $x + \sqrt{25} = \sqrt{36}$, then x equals

8. Solve the equation $\sqrt{9 + 4y} = 11$.

9. $\sqrt{13 + \sqrt{7 + \sqrt{4}}}$ is equal to

10. Find n if $\sqrt{n} = \sqrt{81} - \sqrt{16}$.

CHAPTER 14 — Exponents & Radicals — Problem Set 2

11. Which perfect cubes less than 100 have square roots that are integers?

12. $\sqrt{x-1} = 4$
    What is the value of x?

13. $\sqrt{0.09} + \sqrt{0.16}$

14. Find the integer nearest to $\sqrt{98} - \sqrt{50}$.

15. What values of n satisfy the inequality $\frac{1}{n} \geq 6$?

16. What integer is closest to $-\sqrt{23}$?

17. What is the value of the expression $\sqrt{x^3 - 2^y}$ when $x = 5$ and $y = 2$?

18. $\dfrac{\sqrt{18} \cdot \sqrt{12}}{\sqrt{24}}$

19. $\dfrac{\sqrt{0.016} + \sqrt{0.009}}{\sqrt{0.1}}$

20. What is the greatest integer that is less than $\sqrt{80} + \sqrt{120}$?

Problem Set 3 — **Exponents & Radicals** — **CHAPTER 14**

1. $5^0 3^2 + 4^3 - 5^1 = ?$

2. $\sqrt{5^2 + 12^2} = ?$

3. Find the value of x which satisfies
   $10^x \times 10^{2x} = 10^{12}$

4. $\sqrt{20 + \sqrt{n}} = 5$,
   What is the value of n?

5. Find one quarter of the number 4^{20}.

6. Divide: $\dfrac{a^2}{x} \div \dfrac{x}{a^2}$.

7. $\dfrac{(x^9)(x^6)}{x^3} = ?$

8. $\sqrt{0.49} + \sqrt{0.09} + \sqrt{12^2 + 5^2}$

9. If $\sqrt{121x} = 26$, what is the value of x?

10. If $\sqrt{a + 4} = 5$, what is the value of a?

CHAPTER 14 — Exponents & Radicals — Problem Set 3

11. $3^{x+2} + 3^{x-1} = 84$

    What is x?

12. x and y are integers.

    $3^{x+4} = 7^{x+y+8}$

    What is y?

13. $3^{x+4} = 3^{2x-1}$

    What is x?

14. What is half of 10^{10}?

15. Solve the following equation for x.

    $\sqrt{5x - 6} = x$

16. $\sqrt{40} - (\sqrt{5} + \sqrt{2})^2 = ?$

17. $\dfrac{\sqrt{2} \cdot \sqrt{2} \cdot \sqrt{2}}{\sqrt{2} + \sqrt{2}} = ?$

18. $\dfrac{\sqrt{60} \cdot \sqrt{12}}{\sqrt{15}} = ?$

19. Solve

    $\sqrt{3x + 1} - 3 = 7$ for x.

20. Evaluate $\sqrt{\dfrac{11}{4}} + \sqrt{1 + \dfrac{9}{16}}$

CHAPTER 15
Geometry Basics

Target Concepts and Skills

- [ ] Basic properties of a rectangle and a square
- [ ] Angle properties of a triangle
- [ ] Side properties of a triangle
- [ ] Special right triangles
- [ ] The Pythagorean Theorem
- [ ] Triangle similarities

Definition 15.1 – Rectangle

A two-dimensional quadrilateral with four right angles (90°) is called a rectangle.

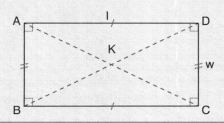

Remark 15.1 – Basic Properties of a Rectangle

1. Perimeter of a rectangle is $P = 2 \cdot (l + w)$
2. Area of a rectangle is $A = l \cdot w$
3. Diagonals of the rectangle ABCD are equal in length: AC = BD. They also bisect each other: KA = KB = KC = KD

Definition 15.2 – Square

A rectangle with four equal sides is called a square.

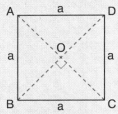

Remark 15.2 – Basic Properties of a Square

1. Perimeter of a square is $P = 4 \cdot a$
2. Area of a square is $A = a \cdot a = a^2$
3. Diagonals of the square ABCD, given in Definition 15.2, are equal in length: AC = BD. They bisect each other and are perpendicular to each other: OA = OB = OC = OD.

Example 15.1

Let's find the area and the perimeter of the square with a diagonal length equal to $3\sqrt{2}$.

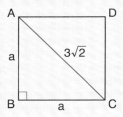

Let one side of the square have side length a, then by Pythagorean theorem we have:
$a^2 + a^2 = (3\sqrt{2})^2$, $2a^2 = 18$, $a^2 = 9$, $a = 3$. So, $P(ABCD) = 4 \cdot 3 = 12$ and $A(ABCD) = 3^2 = 9$.

Definition 15.3 – Triangle

A triangle is a two-dimensional polygon with three straight sides and three angles.

CHAPTER 15

Geometry Basics

Remark 15.3

1. The sum of the interior angles of a triangle are equal to 180°.

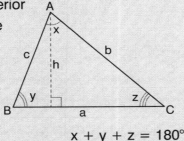

$$x + y + z = 180°$$

2. For the triangle ABC given above, let the side lengths opposite to the vertices A, B, and C be a, b, and c, respectively. Then, the perimeter of the triangle ABC is $P = a + b + c$.

3. The area of the triangle ABC given above is $A = \dfrac{a \cdot h_a}{2}$, where h_a is the height drawn from vertex A to the opposite side.

   Notice that the same area can be calculated in three ways since there are three sides.
   That is, $A = \dfrac{b \cdot h_b}{2} = \dfrac{c \cdot h_c}{2}$

Example 15.2

For the given triangle below, let's find:

a) The measure of the missing angle
   $= 180° - (75° + 50°) = 55°$.

b) The perimeter $= 5.6 + 6 + 7.08 = 18.68$.

c) The area $= \dfrac{6 \cdot 5.42}{2} = 16.26$.

d) The length of another height,
   h_b: $A(\triangle ABC) = \dfrac{b \cdot h_b}{2}$, $16.26 = \dfrac{7.08 \cdot h_b}{2}$,
   $\dfrac{16.26 \cdot 2}{7.08} = h_b$, $h_b = 4.59$
   (rounded to two decimal digits).

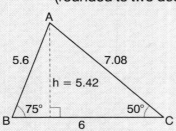

Definition 15.4 – Types of Triangles

1. A triangle is called an equilateral triangle if all three sides have the same length. An equilateral triangle is also equiangular, i.e., all three internal angles are each equal to 60°.

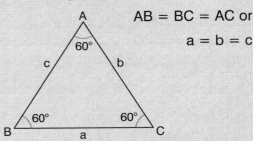

$AB = BC = AC$ or
$a = b = c$

2. A triangle is called an isosceles triangle if at least two sides have the same length. In an isosceles triangle, the angles opposite to the equivalent sides are also equivalent.

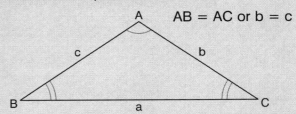

$AB = AC$ or $b = c$

3. In the following isosceles triangle, the height drawn from the vertex of angle A to the base BC, divides the base into two equal parts.

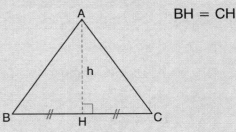

$BH = CH$

4. A triangle is called a right triangle if one of its angles is equal to 90°. The longest side (which is opposite to 90°) of a right triangle is called the hypotenuse, and the other two sides are called the legs.

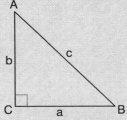

Geometry Basics

CHAPTER 15

Remark 15.4 – The Pythagorean Theorem

In a **right** triangle, the sum of squares of lengths of shorter sides (legs) is equal to the square of the length of the hypotenuse. So, in the figure given above: $a^2 + b^2 = c^2$.

There are more than three hundred proofs of this theorem.

Remark 15.5 – A Special Right Triangle with Angles 30° - 60° - 90°

In the following triangle, the length of the side opposite to 30° is one-half of the length of the hypotenuse. This is because this special triangle is one-half of an equilateral triangle. Also, by the Pythagorean theorem, we see that the other leg is $\frac{\sqrt{3}}{2}$ times the length of hypotenuse.

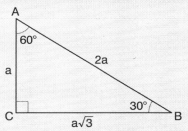

Problem 15.1

Find the following for the given right triangle.

a) The measure of the angle B.
b) The length of the side BC.
c) The area of the triangle ABC.
d) The length of the height drawn from the vertex C.

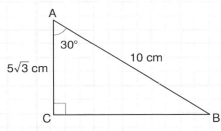

Example 15.3

If a right triangle with an acute angle of 30° has the hypotenuse equal to 10 cm, then its legs are equal to 5 cm and $5\sqrt{3}$ cm.

Remark 15.6 – Similar Triangles

Two triangles are called similar if their angle measures are equal and the side lengths opposite to these angles are proportional.

Example 15.4

In the following figure, the triangles are similar since their angle measures are equal and their corresponding sides are proportional, i.e.,

$$\frac{AB}{DE} = \frac{BC}{EF} = \frac{AC}{DF} = \frac{1}{2}.$$

In this case, we write $\triangle ABC \sim \triangle DEF$. Notice that the letters in the same order correspond to the same angles in each triangle.

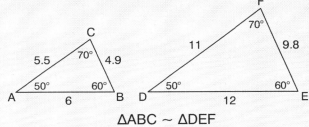

$\triangle ABC \sim \triangle DEF$

Solution 15.1

a) The measure of the angle B is equal to $180° - (30° + 90°) = 60°$.

b) By the Pythagorean theorem, $AC^2 + BC^2 = AB^2$
$BC^2 + (5\sqrt{3})^2 = 10^2$, $BC^2 = 25$, $BC = 5$ cm.

c) The area of the triangle ABC is
$$A(\triangle ABC) = \frac{AC \cdot BC}{2} = \frac{5\sqrt{3} \cdot 5}{2} = \frac{25\sqrt{3}}{2} \text{ cm}^2$$

d) Let the length of the height drawn from the vertex C be h_c, then
$$A(\triangle ABC) = \frac{AB \cdot h_c}{2}, \frac{25\sqrt{3}}{2} = \frac{10 \cdot h_c}{2},$$
$$\frac{25\sqrt{3}}{10} = h_c, h_c = \frac{5\sqrt{3}}{2} \text{ cm}.$$

CHAPTER 15

Geometry Basics

Problem 15.2

In the figure with two 90° angles given below, find
a) The length EB.
b) The length AD.
c) The length BC.

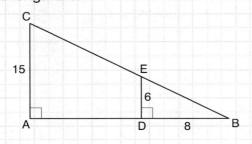

Solution 15.2

a) BDE is a right triangle. By the Pythagorean theorem, we have: $DB^2 + DE^2 = BE^2$, $6^2 + 8^2 = BE^2$, $100 = BE^2$, $BE = 10$.

b) Notice that the triangles DBE and ABC are similar. So, $\dfrac{DB}{AB} = \dfrac{BE}{BC} = \dfrac{DE}{AC} = \dfrac{6}{15}$.

Let $AD = x$, then $\dfrac{6}{15} = \dfrac{8}{8+x}$.

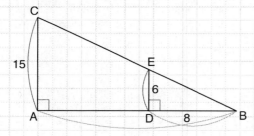

Cross multiply:

$(8 + x) \cdot 6 = 15 \cdot 8$, $48 + 6x = 120$,

$6x = 72$, $x = 12$.

c) ABC is a right triangle.

Then, by the Pythagorean theorem, we have: $AB^2 + AC^2 = BC^2$, and $AB = 8 + 12 = 20$. So, $20^2 + 15^2 = BC^2$, $625 = BC^2$, $BC = 25$.

Square Number Puzzles

1.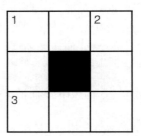

   Complete this crossnumber using eight different non-zero digits.

   Across
   1. A square
   3. A cube

   Down
   1. A prime
   2. A prime

2. Complete this crossnumber.

1	2
3	

   Across
   1. A prime number
   3. The square of a square

   Down
   1. The square of a square
   2. A prime

3. | 13 | | |
   |----|----|----|
   | 5 | | 15 |
   | x | | |

   In a magic square, each row, each column, and both main diagonals have the same total.

   What number should replace x in this partially completed magic square?

   Junior Mathematical Challenge, 2000

Problem Set 1 — Geometry Basics — CHAPTER 15

1. What is perimeter of the rectangle?

2. In the diagram, the value of x is

   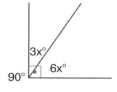

3. For the triangle shown, what is the value of x?

   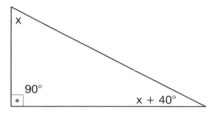

4. Find the measure of the angle labeled x in the diagram.

   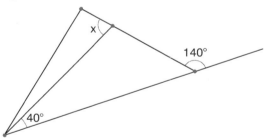

5. What is the area of the whole figure?

   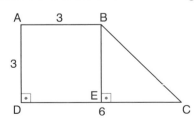

6. If PQ is a straight line segment, then the value of x is

   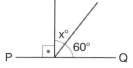

7. In the diagram, AC = 4, BC = 3, and BD = 10. The area of the shaded triangle is

   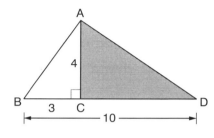

8. What is the missing dimension for x?

   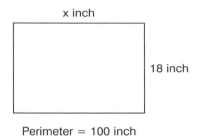

   Perimeter = 100 inch

9. The area of a square is 25 square meters. What is the perimeter of the square?

10. In the squares in the figure, express the area of unshaded region?

    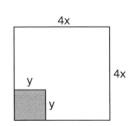

CHAPTER 15 — Geometry Basics — Problem Set 1

11. The equilateral triangle AFB and the rectangle ABCD have the same perimeter.

    If AB = 8 cm, what is the area of rectangle ABCD?

    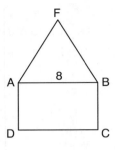

12. Square A has an area of 100 cm². The area of square B is four times the area of square A. The perimeter of square B is

13. In the 9 by 7 rectangle shown, what is the area of the shaded region?

    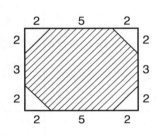

14. In the figure shown, x =

    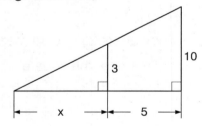

15. The perimeter of a rectangle is 36. If the length is 12, what is the area?

16. How many centimetres are equal to 36 meters?

17. In the figure shown, x =

    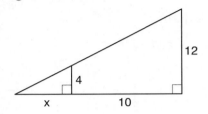

18. A right triangle has two legs of length 8 m and 10 m respectively.

    Find the length of the hypotenuse.

19. How many rectangles (including squares) are in the following figure?

20. In the figure, the area of three rectangles are given.

    What is the shaded area?

    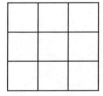

Problem Set 2 — Geometry Basics — CHAPTER 15

1. In triangle ABC, the interior angles are equal to 2x, 3x, & 4x. Determine each angle.

   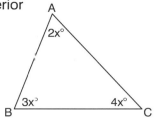

2. In the following figure, B is a point on AC. Find the measure of angle BDC.

   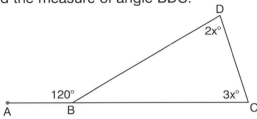

3. In the following isosceles triangle, one of the base angles is equal to 30°. Find the vertex angle.

   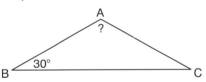

4. If a right triangle with an acute angle of 30 degrees has the hypotenuse equal to 8 cm, then what is the perimeter of the triangle?

5. Find the maximum integer value of the perimeter of an equilateral triangle with a side length between 1 cm and 1.4 cm.

6. In the following figure, ABD is an equilateral triangle with a side length of 12 cm. Find the perimeter of the rectangle ABCE.

   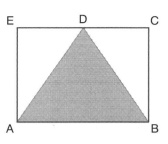

7. Find the perimeter of an equilateral triangle with a height of $3\sqrt{3}$ cm.

8. In the following figure, ABC is an isosceles right triangle with AB = $\sqrt{2}$ inches. Find the perimeter of the rectangle ACDE.

   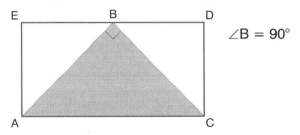

   $\angle B = 90°$

9. In the following isosceles triangle, find the distance between the vertex C and the line AB if the base AC is equal to 40 cm and one of the base angles is equal to 30°.

   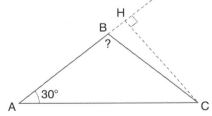

10. Find the area of an isosceles triangle with a height of 4 cm if this height is drawn to the base and the base length is 6 cm.

11. Find the perimeter of an isosceles triangle with a height of 5 if this height is drawn to the base and the base length is 24 cm.

12. Find the area of an equilateral triangle with a height of $3\sqrt{3}$ cm.

13. Find the area of an equilateral triangle with a side of 12 cm.

14. ABC and DEF are equilateral triangles with AB = 3 and DE = 4.
Find the ratio of the area of the triangle ABC to the area of the triangle DEF.

15. A rectangle with a perimeter of 30 centimeters is twice as long as it is wide. What is the area of the rectangle in square centimeters?

16. ABCD is a square with the diagonal AC = $4\sqrt{2}$ inches. Find the area of the square ABCD.

17. In the following figure, ABC and CDB are right triangles with AD = 2 inches, BD = 4 inches. Find CD.

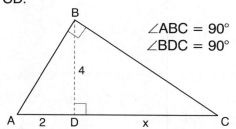

∠ABC = 90°
∠BDC = 90°

18. In the following figure, ABC is a right triangle. Find the area of the square ACIH if the areas of the squares ABFG and BCDE are 64 cm² and 225 cm², respectively.

19. In the following figure, ABC is a right triangle. Find the area of the equilateral triangle BCD if the areas of the equilateral triangles FAC and ABE are 625 cm² and 49 cm², respectively.

20. In the following picture, find the height of the building if the two-meter tall man is standing on the shadow of the building 3 meters away from its tip and the building's shadow is 18 meters long.

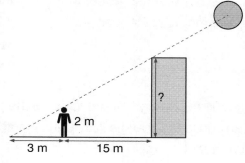

CHAPTER 16
Coordinate Geometry

Target Concepts and Skills

- [ ] Defining the coordinate plane.
- [ ] Applying the Distance & Midpoint Formulas in the coordinate plane.
- [ ] Applying the rules of reflection in the coordinate plane.
- [ ] Area & Perimeter in the coordinate plane

Remark 16.1 – Coordinate Plane (Cartesian Coordinate System)

A coordinate plane is a two-dimensional surface formed by two number lines.

Two real numbers (coordinates) are used to uniquely determine the position of a point in a coordinate plane. Each of these two coordinates for a given point is located on an axis. The first coordinate is on the horizontal number line (the x-axis), and the second is on the vertical number line (the y-axis). So, a pair of the coordinates of a point is called an ordered pair. These two axes are assumed to be perpendicular to each other and infinitely long in both positive and negative directions.

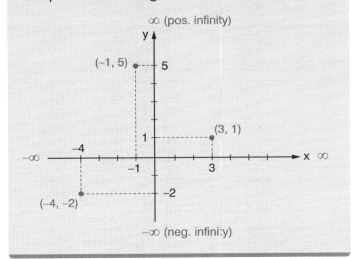

Example 16.1

Let's find the distance between the following points.

a) (5,0) & (8,0)

b) (5,0) & (8,4)

Notice that the points in part (a) are on the regular real number line. So, the distance between them, which is horizontal, is equal to $8 - 5 = 3$.

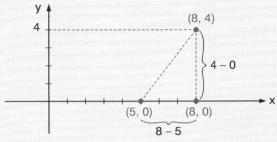

Can we say that the distance in part (b) is equal to the sum of the horizontal distance $(8 - 5)$ and the vertical distance $(4 - 0)$? Answer: No.

However, it is a combination of these two distances. These horizontal and vertical distances are sides of a right triangle whose hypotenuse is the distance we are looking for. Thus, we can write the following equation, which is called the distance formula for the points (5,0) & (8,4):

$$d^2 = (8 - 5)^2 + (4 - 0)^2$$

Remark 16.1 – The Distance Formula

The distance between the points (x_1, y_1) & (x_2, y_2) is $d = \sqrt{(x_2 - x_1)^2 + (y_2 - y_1)^2}$

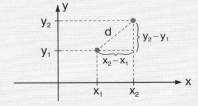

Math Fluency

CHAPTER 16 — Coordinate Geometry

Problem 16.1
Find the distance between the following points.
a) (5, 1) & (8, 5)
b) (5, −1) & (−8, 5)

Solution 16.1
a) By the distance formula:
$d = \sqrt{(8-5)^2 + (5-1)^2} = \sqrt{3^2 + 4^2} \sqrt{9 + 16}$
$= \sqrt{25} = 5.$

b) Similarly, $d = \sqrt{(-8-5)^2 + (5-(-1))^2}$
$= \sqrt{(-13)^2 + (5+1)^2} = \sqrt{(-13)^2 + 6^2}$
$= \sqrt{169 + 36} = \sqrt{205}.$

Problem 16.2
Find x if the distance between points A(x, −5) and B(−3, −14) is 9 units.

Solution 16.2
By the distance formula,
$9^2 = (x + 3)^2 + (-5 + 14)^2$, $9^2 = (x + 3)^2 + 9^2$,
$0 = (x + 3)^2$, $x = -3.$

Remark 16.1 – The Midpoint Formula
In the coordinate plane, the midpoint between the points (x_1, y_1) & (x_2, y_2) is $\left(\dfrac{x_1 + x_2}{2}, \dfrac{y_1 + y_2}{2}\right)$.

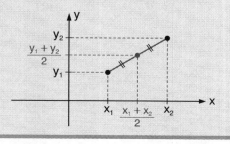

Example 16.2
The midpoint between points (2, 5) & (−6, 3) is
$\left(\dfrac{2 + (-6)}{2}, \dfrac{5 + 3}{2}\right) = (-2, 4).$

Problem 16.3
Find the coordinates of the point (x, y) if (3, 4) is the midpoint between (x, y) and (7, 2).

Solution 16.3
By the midpoint formula, we have:
$\dfrac{x + 7}{2} = 3, \quad \dfrac{y + 2}{2} = 4$
Then, $x + 7 = 6$, $x = -1$ and $y + 2 = 8$, $y = 6.$

Problem 16.4
The midpoint of the line segment joining the points A(1, 2) and B(a, 6) is P(x, y), and the point P is located on the line represented by the equation $y = -x + 3$. Find a.

Solution 16.4
Since the point P is located on the line represented by $y = -x + 3$, we can rewrite the point P with the coordinates $(x, -x + 3)$ and by the midpoint formula,
$\dfrac{a + 1}{2} = x, \quad \dfrac{6 + 2}{2} = -x + 3$
Thus, $a = 2x - 1$ and $x = -1.$
So, $a = 2 \cdot (-1) - 1 = -3.$

Problem 16.5
Find the area of the triangle with vertices at
a) A(4, 8), B(2, 3), and C(6, 3).
b) D(7, 8), B(2, 3), and C(6, 3).
c) E(7, 9), B(2, 3), and C(6, 3).

Solution 16.5

Notice that the line segment BC is horizontal, and the heights drawn from the vertices A and D have the same length. That is $h_A = h_D = 5$. Also, $h_E = 6$.

a) $A(ABC) = \dfrac{BC \cdot h_A}{2} = \dfrac{4 \cdot 5}{2} = 10.$

b) $A(DBC) = \dfrac{BC \cdot h_D}{2} = \dfrac{4 \cdot 5}{2} = 10.$

c) $A(EBC) = \dfrac{BC \cdot h_E}{2} = \dfrac{4 \cdot 6}{2} = 12.$

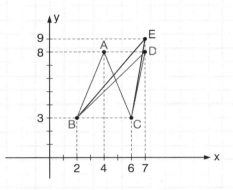

Problem 16.6

What is the perimeter of quadrilateral WXYZ in the graph below?

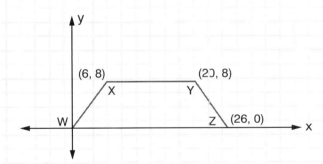

Solution 16.6

From the distance formula
$WX = YZ = \sqrt{(6-0) + (8-0)^2} = \sqrt{100} = 10$
Total = WX + XY + YZ + WZ
= 10 + 14 + 10 + 26 = 60

Problem 16.7

Find the coordinates of the image(reflection) of point B(1, 2) if point B(1, 2) is reflected across
a) The x-axis
b) The y-axis
c) The origin (0, 0).
d) Point C(3, 1).

Solution 16.7

a) The x-axis: As seen in the following figure, the image point B_x has the coordinates (1, –2). So, when a point is reflected across the x-axis, the y-coordinate's sign changes to the opposite sign.

b) The y-axis: Similarly, the image point B_y has the coordinates (–1, 2). So, when a point is reflected across the y-axis, the x-coordinate's sign changes to the opposite sign.

c) The origin (0,0): The image point B_O has the coordinates (–1, –2). This means that the point is reflected across both the x and y axes.

d) Point C(3, 1): This means that the point C(3, 1) is the midpoint between the points B(1, 2) and the image B_C. Let the coordinates of the point B_C be (x,y). Then, by the midpoint formula,

$$\dfrac{x+1}{2} = 3, \quad \dfrac{y+2}{2} = 1$$

Thus, $x + 1 = 6$, $x = 5$ and $y + 2 = 2$, $y = 0$.
So, B_C has the coordinates (5, 0).

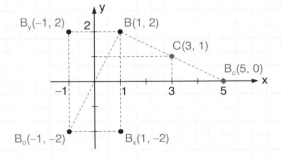

CHAPTER 16 — KENKEN NUMBER & OPERATIONS PUZZLE

KEN KEN.

RULES FOR KENKEN

Fill the grid with digits so as not to repeat a digit in any row or column, and so the digits within each heavily outlined box or boxes (called a cage) will produce the target number shown in that cage by using the operation (addition, subtraction, multiplication, or division) shown by the symbol after the numeral.

For single box cages, simply enter the number that is shown in the corner. So, for example, the notation 6+ means that the numerals in the cage should add up to 6, and the notation 48× means that by multiplying the numbers in the cage you will get 48. A 4×4 grid will use the digits 1-4. A 5×5 grid will use 1-5. A 6×6 grid will use 1-6, and so on.

Example:

3	10+	
1–		

Solution:

3	10+ 1	2
1– 2	3	1
1	2	3

1.

2–		2
1–	2–	
	5+	

2.

3	2×	
2÷		3×
6×		

3.

3÷	6×	
	3÷	2–
2		

4.

12×		2÷	
2÷		12×	3–
2÷	3		
	3+		3

5.

4	12×	2–	
2÷			3–
	11+		
4+			2

Problem Set 1 — Coordinate Geometry — CHAPTER 16

1. Which of these ordered pairs lies on both the x- and y- axes?

   A) (1, 1)   B) (1, 0)   C) (0, 1)   D) (0, 0)

2. What is the distance between (−4, 0) and 1, 0)?

3. What is the distance between (1, 5) and (1, −4)?

4. What is the midpoint of (4, 3) and (6, −1)?

5. What is the area of △ OAB?

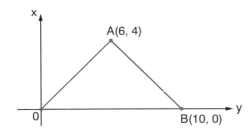

Answer questions 6–8

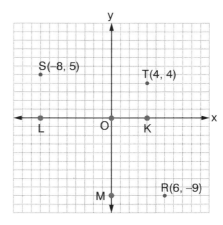

6. What is the area of △ OKT?

7. What is the area of △ OLS?

8. What is the area of △ OMR?

9. Given A(−1, 3) and B(5, −1), find the midpoint of AB.

10. Given P(0, −2) and Q(−5, 1), find the midpoint of PQ

CHAPTER 16 — Coordinate Geometry — Problem Set 1

11. If the point (3, 4) is reflected in the x-axis, what are the coordinates of its image?

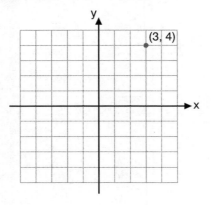

Answer questions 12–14

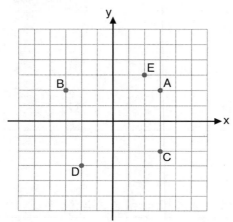

12. In the diagram, the point with coordinates (–2, –3) is located at

13. The point with coordinates (2, 3) is located at

14. What is the distance between points A and C?

15. In the diagram, the coordinates of point P could be

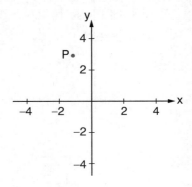

16. What are the coordinates of vertex H of rectangle EFGH shown in the figure below?

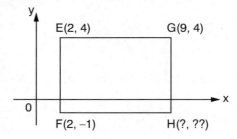

17. Points C(2, 5) and D(8, 11) lie in the standard (x, y) coordinate plane. What is the midpoint of $\overline{CD}$?

18. In the standard (x, y) coordinate plane, what is the midpoint of the line segment that has endpoints (3, 8) and (1, –4)?

19. What is the area of the trapezoid?

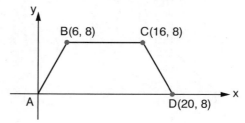

20. What is the distance between the points (4, 0) and (0, 3)?

Problem Set 2 — Coordinate Geometry — CHAPTER 16

Find the distance from:

1. A(1, 6) to B(3, 3)

2. M(2, 4) to N(−1, −3)

3. R(3, −2) to S(5, −2)

Problem 4 – 6

On the map below, each grid unit represents 1 km.

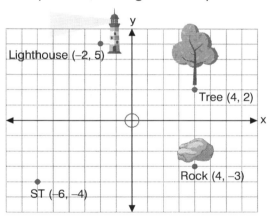

Find the distance between:

4. the lighthouse and the tree

5. the ST and the lighthouse

6. the rock and the tree

7. The points A(2, −1), B(5, 1), and C(0, 2) form a triangle ABC.

   Use the distance formula to classify the triangle as equilateral, isosceles, or scalene.

Problem 8 – 9

Use the distance formula to check that

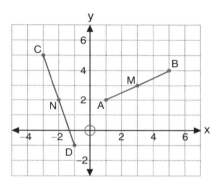

8. M is the midpoint of AB

9. N is the midpoint of CD.

10. M is the midpoint of AB. If A is (−1, 4) and M is (3, 4), find the coordinates of B.

11. PQ is the diameter of a circle, center C. If P is (4, −7) and Q is (−2, −3), find the coordinates of C.

12. Use midpoints to find the fourth vertex of the given parallelogram:

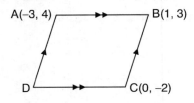

13. Find the equation of the line passing through: (2, 2) and (2, −2)

14. Find the equation of the line passing through: (2, −2) and (−2, −2).

15. Find the area, in square units, of rectangle ABCD plotted below.

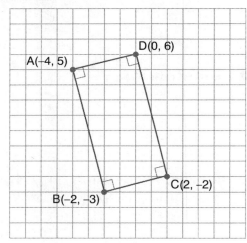

16. In the standard (x, y) coordinate plane below, the points (0, 2), (8, 2), (3, 6), and (11, 6) are the vertices of a parallelogram. What is the area, in square units, of the parallelogram?

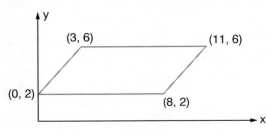

17. The point in the xy-plane with coordinates (2000; 2023) is reflected across the line y = 2000. What are the coordinates of the reflected point?

18. (CEMC-2000-Gauss8-13)

The coordinates of the vertices of rectangle PQRS are given in the diagram. The area of rectangle PQRS is 120. The value of p is

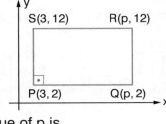

Problem 19 – 20

Use the diagram below to answer the question that follows.

Quadrilateral ABCD is constructed on a coordinate plane, as shown in the diagram. $\overline{EF}$ bisects $\overline{DC}$ and $\overline{AB}$ and triangle AGF is isosceles.

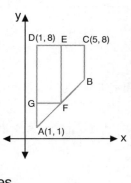

19. What is the area DEFG?

20. What is the are of triangle AGF?

CHAPTER 17
Geometry 3-D

✓ Target Concepts and Skills

- [ ] Defining prisms.
- [ ] Finding the surface area and volume of prisms.
- [ ] Finding the circumference, area, arc length, and sector area of a circle.
- [ ] Finding the surface area and volume of a cylinder.

Definition 17.1 – Prism

A prism is a solid (3-D) geometric figure whose two end faces (bases) are similar, equal, and parallel and whose lateral faces are parallelograms.

If the lateral sides of a prism are perpendicular to the base, then it is a right prism. Otherwise, it is an oblique prism.

Example 17.1

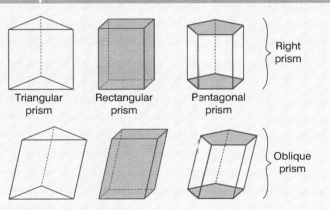

Triangular prism, Rectangular prism, Pentagonal prism — Right prism

Oblique prism

Remark 17.1 – Right & Oblique Prisms

If a prism is not specified as oblique, then it is assumed to be a right prism.

Remark 17.2 – Surface Area and Volume of a Prism

For any prism:

Surface Area = Sum of areas of all lateral and end faces (bases)

Volume = Area of base × Height

Problem 17.1

Find the surface area and the volume of the triangular prism whose height is 12 cm and whose bases are right triangles with legs of 6 cm & 8 cm.

Solution 17.1

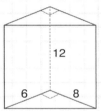

Area of bases = $2 \times \left(\dfrac{6 \times 8}{2}\right) = 48$ cm², because the hypotenuse of the base equals 10 cm.

Lateral area = $(6 \times 12) + (8 \times 12) + (10 \times 12)$
$= 288$ cm²

Thus, surface area = $48 + 288 = 336$ cm².

Volume = $\dfrac{6 \times 8}{2} \times 12 = 288$ cm³.

Definition 17.2 – Cube

A cube is a right rectangular prism with all three dimensions (length-width-height) having equal lengths.

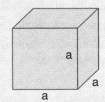

Volume = a^3

Surface area = $6 \cdot a^2$

Math Fluency

CHAPTER 17 — Geometry 3-D

Example 17.2

Let's find (a) The volume of a cube with one edge of 3 cm. (b) The edge length of a cube with a surface area of 216 cm².

(a) Volume = $3 \times 3 \times 3 = 27$ cm³

(b) $6a^2 = 216$, $a^2 = 36$, $a = 6$ cm.

Problem 17.2

Find the ratio of the surface areas and volumes of two rectangular prisms with edges of 6-8-10 cm & 3-4-5 cm.

Solution 17.2

We are given the following prisms.

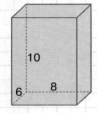

Surface area₁
$= 2 \times (6 \times 8) + 2 \times (6 \times 10) + 2 \times (8 \times 10)$
$= 2 \times (48 + 60 + 80) = 376$ cm²

Surface area₂
$= 2 \times (3 \times 4) + 2 \times (3 \times 5) + 2 \times (4 \times 5)$
$= 2 \times (12 + 15 + 20) = 94$ cm²

Thus, $\dfrac{\text{Surface area}_1}{\text{Surface area}_2} = \dfrac{376}{94} = 4$.

Volume₁ = $6 \times 8 \times 10 = 480$ cm³,
Volume₂ = $3 \times 4 \times 5 = 60$ cm³.

So, $\dfrac{\text{Volume}_1}{\text{Volume}_2} = \dfrac{480}{60} = 8$.

Remark 17.3 – Ratios of Surface Areas & Volumes of Two Similar Prisms

If two prisms are similar (their edge lengths are in proportion) with the similarity ratio k, then the ratio of their surface areas and volumes are equal to k^2 and k^3 respectively.

In the previous problem, the similarity ratio is $k = 2$.

Problem 17.3

Find the volume of the following triangular prism with right triangle bases if EC = 10, EF = 6, DF = 12.

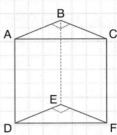

Solution 17.3

We need to find the lengths of the edges ED and CF. Notice that ECF is a right triangle, with EC being the hypotenuse. So, by the Pythagorean theorem,

$EF^2 + FC^2 = EC^2$, $6^2 + FC^2 = 10^2$,

$FC^2 = 100 - 36 = 64$, $FC = 8$.

Similarly, EDF is a right triangle with DF being hypotenuse and $ED^2 + EF^2 = DF^2$,

$ED^2 + 6^2 = 12^2$, $ED^2 = 108$, $ED = 6\sqrt{3}$.

Volume = Area of base × Height

$= \dfrac{ED \times EF}{2} \times FC = \dfrac{6\sqrt{3} \times 6}{2} \times 8 = 144\sqrt{3}$.

Remark 17.4 – Circumference and Arc of a Circle

Circumference is the perimeter of a circle and is $C = 2\pi r$, where r is the radius.

Arc of a circle is a fraction of that circle.

So, arc length is $l = 2\pi r \cdot \dfrac{\theta}{360°}$, where θ is the central angle corresponding to the arc.

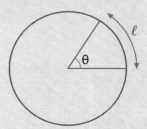

Geometry 3-D
CHAPTER 17

Remark 17.5 – Area of a Circle and a Sector

When we say area of a circle, we mean the area enclosed by a circle. The area of a circle is $A = \pi r^2$ and area of a sector, which is a fraction of the area of a circle is
$S = \pi r^2 \cdot \dfrac{\theta}{360°}$.

Notice that when we say "a fraction of a circle", we really mean a fraction, which is $\dfrac{\theta}{360°}$.

Here, θ is the central angle, which corresponds to the arc and 360° is the full central angle, which corresponds to the full circle.

Remark 17.6 – Surface Area and Volume of a Cylinder

Surface Area = Lateral Area + Area of bases
$= 2\pi rh + 2\pi r^2$ (For a right cylinder)

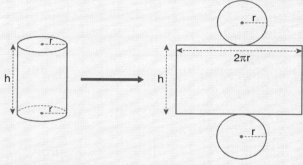

Volume = Area of base × Height = $\pi r^2 \times h$

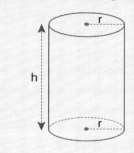

Example 17.3

Let's find the circumference, area, arc length, and sector area of a circle with a radius of 8 cm and a central angle of 60°.

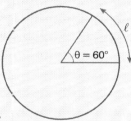

$C = 2\pi r = 2\pi \cdot 8 = 16\pi$ cm.
$A = \pi r^2 = \pi \cdot 8^2 = 64\pi$ cm².
$l = 2\pi r \cdot \dfrac{\theta}{360°} = 2\pi \cdot 8 \cdot \dfrac{60°}{360°} = 16\pi \cdot \dfrac{1}{6} = \dfrac{16\pi}{6}$
$= \dfrac{8\pi}{3}$ cm
$S = \pi r^2 \cdot \dfrac{\theta}{360°} = \pi \cdot 8^2 \cdot \dfrac{60°}{360°} = 64\pi \cdot \dfrac{1}{6} = \dfrac{32\pi}{3}$ cm².

Example 17.4

Let's find the surface area and the volume of a cylinder with a height of 7 cm and a base's area of 9π cm².

Surface Area = $2\pi rh + 2\pi r^2$. The radius is not given directly. It is hidden in the base area.
$9\pi = \pi r^2$, $\dfrac{9\pi}{\pi} = \dfrac{\pi r^2}{\pi}$, $9 = r^2$, $r = 3$ cm.
Surface Area $= 2\pi rh + 2\pi r^2$
$= 2\pi \cdot 3 \cdot 7 + 2\pi \cdot 3^2 = 60\pi$ cm²
Volume $= \pi r^2 h = \pi \cdot 3^2 \cdot 7 = 63\pi$ cm³.

Definition 17.3 – Cylinder

A prism with a circular base is called a cylinder.

CHAPTER 17 — Open Middle Geometry Puzzles — Puzzle

1. INTERIOR AND EXTERIOR ANGLES OF TRIANGLES

Directions: In triangle ABC, angle ABC is obtuse. Using the digits 1 to 9 at most one time each, place a digit in each box to make angle ACB the smallest possible acute angle.

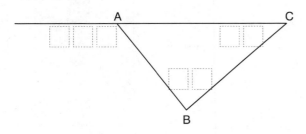

Hint:

What does the first number in the three-digit number have to be?

What does the first number in the obtuse angle have to be?

What numbers do not work as the first digit of the acute angle? Why?

2. MAXIMUM VOLUME OF A CYLINDER

Directions: Using the digits 0 to 9 at most one time each, place a digit in each box to give this cylinder the maximum volume possible.

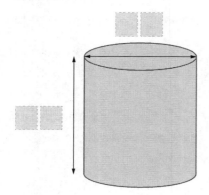

Hint:

Which dimension has a bigger impact on the volume? (Diameter or Height)

3. TRIANGLE SUM THEOREM

Directions: Using the digits 1-9 at most one time each, fill in the blanks so that when you solve for x, it is a whole number?

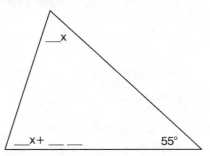

Hint:

How many degrees must the two unknown angles sum to? Can you write an equation to represent the sum of the two unknown angles?

4. PYTHAGOREAN THEOREM

Directions: What could the lengths of the legs be such that the lengths are integers and x is an irrational number between 5 and 7?

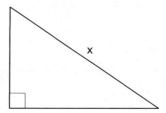

Hint:

What is a wrong answer? How can you use this wrong answer to move towards an answer?

5. WHICH CIRCLE IS BIGGER? (MIDDLE SCHOOL)

Directions: Which circle is bigger: one with an area of 30 square units or one with a circumference of 30 units? How do you know?

Hint:

What information do we need to compare these two circles?

Answer questions 1–4

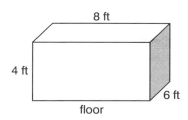
floor

1. What is the area of the floor?

2. What is the perimeter of the floor?

3. What is the total surface area of the figure?

4. What is the volume of the figure?

5. What is the volume of the triangular prism?

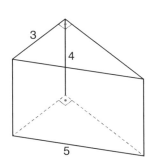

6. What is the total surface area?

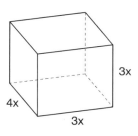

7. What is the volume of the cylinder?

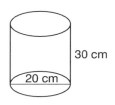

8. Cube A has edges of length 4 cm and Cube B has edges of length 6 cm. What would be the result if the volume of Cube A is divided by the volume of Cube B?

9. How many square units is the total surface area of the rectangular prism shown?

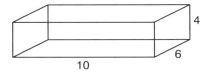

10. What is the diameter of a circle whose area is 64π?

11. BC is a diameter of the circle with center O and radius 5, as shown. If A lies on the circle and AO is perpendicular to BC, the area of triangle ABC is

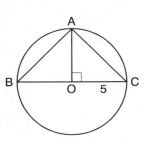

12. A cube has a volume of 125 cm³. What is the area of one face of the cube?

13. In the diagram, a sector of a circle has central angle 120°. The area of the whole circle is 9π. What is the area of this sector?

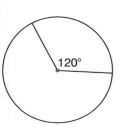

14. The circumference of a circle is 20 cm. What is the length, in centimeters, of the radius of the circle?

15. The diameter of a circle is 6 feet. What is the area, in square feet, of the circle?

16. If the circumference of a circle is 36π cm, then its area is xπ cm². What is x?

17. What is the volume of a cube that has a face with an area 16?

18. If the total surface area of a cube is 96 cm². What is the volume of the cube, in cm³?

19. A triangular prism with a volume of 240 cm³ has two edges of the triangular faces measuring 6 cm and 8 cm, as shown. The height of the prism, in cm, is

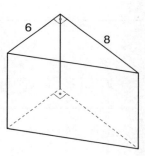

20. A rectangular pool is 6 m wide 18 m long and 4 m deep. If the pool is one-third full of water, what is the volume of the water in the pool?

CHAPTER 18

Linear Equations

Target Concepts and Skills

- [ ] Defining linear equations with one or two variables.
- [ ] Solving linear equations.
- [ ] Defining linear functions.
- [ ] Graphing linear functions.

Definition 18.1

1) An equation of the form $ax + b = 0$, where a and b are real numbers, $a \neq 0$, and x is the variable, is called a linear equation with one variable.
2) A value of x for which the equation $ax + b = 0$ holds is called a solution to this equation.

Example 18.1

$2x + 1 = 0, -3x + 2 = 0, 5x = 2$ are linear equations in one variable. The number $-\frac{1}{2}, \frac{2}{3}$, and $\frac{2}{5}$ are the solutions to these equations, respectively.

Problem 18.1

Solve for x.
a) $4x - 12 = 0$
b) $-2x = 7$
c) $4(x - 2) - 2(3x - 1) = 5$
d) $2(x - 2) - (x + 1) = x + 11$
e) $2(x - 2) - (x + 1) = x - 5$

Solution 18.1

a) $4x - 12 = 0, 4x = 12, x = 3$.
b) $-2x = 7, x = -3.5$
c) $4(x - 2) - 2(3x - 1) = 5, 4x - 8 - 6x + 2 = 5,$
   $-2x - 6 = 5, -2x = 11, x = -5.5$.
d) $2(x - 2) - (x + 1) = x + 11,$
   $2x - 4 - x - 1 = x + 11, x - 5 = x + 11,$
   $-5 = 11$ (false statement). No solution.
e) $2(x - 2) - (x + 1) = x - 5, 2x - 4 - x - 1 = x - 5,$
   $x - 5 = x - 5, -5 = -5$ (True statement). Infinitely many solutions. This means that any x value satisfies this equation.

Definition 18.2

1) An equation of the form $ax + by + c = 0$, where a, b and c are real numbers, $a \neq 0$, $b \neq 0$ and x and y are the variables, is called a linear equation in two variables.
2) A pair of (x, y) values for which the equation $ax + by + c = 0$ holds is called a solution to this equation.

Example 18.2

$2x + y - 3 = 0$ is a linear equation in two variables. The pairs (0, 3), (−3, 9) are some solutions to this equation. Notice that we can find infinitely many pairs (solutions) satisfying this equation.

Definition 18.3

1) If the linear equation $ax + by + c = 0$ is written in the form $y = -\frac{a}{b}x - \frac{c}{b}$ or $y = mx + n$, then we call it a linear function.
2) Pairs of (x, y) values that satisfy the equation $y = mx + n$ are the points on the coordinate plane which form a straight line. So, the graph of a linear function is a straight line with slope (steepness) **m** and y-intercept **n**.

Math Fluency

CHAPTER 18 — Linear Equations

Example 18.3

The equation $2x + y - 3 = 0$ can also be written as $y = -2x + 3$, which is a linear function. To graph this linear function, finding the coordinates of **two** points is sufficient. That is, two pairs of (x,y) values for which $y = -2x + 3$ holds.

For $x = 0$, $y = -2 \cdot 0 + 3$, $y = 3$. So, the first pair is (0, 3).

For $x = 1$, $y = -2 \cdot 1 + 3$, $y = 1$. The second pair is (1, 1).

We can make a table of x and y values: We get the following graph by plotting these two points on the coordinate plane and joining them with a straight line.

x	y
0	3
1	1

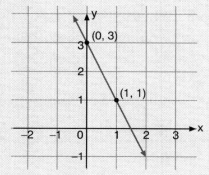

Notice that we could choose **any** two points to graph this function.

For the graphed straight line, the slope $m = -2$, which can also be obtained through the right triangle formed by the x & y axes and the line:

$m = \dfrac{y_2 - y_1}{x_2 - x_1} = \dfrac{\text{Rise}}{\text{Run}} = -2$, where (x_1, y_1) and (x_2, y_2) are any two points on the line.

Notice:

1) The coordinates of any point on the plotted line above satisfy the equation $y = -2x + 3$.
2) If a line is horizontal, then the slope is zero.
3) If a line is vertical, then the slope is undefined.
4) If a line is slanted to the right, then its slope is positive. If it is slanted to the left, the slope is negative.

Problem 18.2

Determine whether the following points lie on the line represented by $y = 5x + 1$.

a) (1, 7)
b) (−2, −9)

Solution 18.2

We need to plug the coordinates of these points into the given equation.

a) $7 = 5 \cdot 1 + 1$, $7 = 6$ (False). This point does not lie on the given line.
b) $-9 = 5 \cdot (-2) + 1$, $-9 = -9$ (True). This point lies on the given line.

Problem 18.3

Put the values of the slopes of the lines in increasing order.

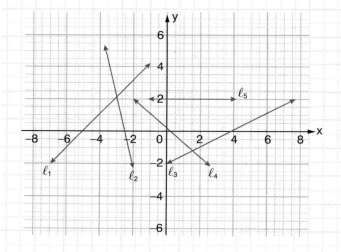

Solution 18.3

The lines l_2 and l_4 are slanted to the left. This means their slopes are negative and $m_2 < m_4$.

The lines l_1 and l_3 are slanted to the right. So, their slopes are positive and $m_3 < m_1$. Finally, the line l_5 is parallel to the x-axis, which means that its slope is zero.

Therefore, $m_2 < m_4 < m_5 < m_3 < m_1$.

Linear Equations

CHAPTER 18

Problem 18.4

Find the following for the given points (2, 3) and (5, −1).

a) The slope of the line passing through these points.
b) The equation of the line passing through these points.
c) The x and y-intercepts.
d) The missing coordinates of the points (4, a) & (b, 10) if they lie on this line.

Solution 18.4

a) $m = \dfrac{y_2 - y_1}{x_2 - x_1} = \dfrac{-1 - 3}{5 - 2} = \dfrac{-4}{3} = -\dfrac{4}{3}$.

b) $y = mx + n$, $y = -\dfrac{4}{3}x + n$.

Let's plug the coordinates of any given point into the equation to find n.

Let's plug (2, 3): $3 = -\dfrac{4}{3} \cdot 2 + n$, $3 = -\dfrac{8}{3} + n$, $3 + \dfrac{8}{3} = n$, $n = \dfrac{17}{3}$.

Thus, the equation is $y = -\dfrac{4}{3}x + \dfrac{17}{3}$.

c) To find the x-intercept, replace y with zero and solve for x:
$0 = -\dfrac{4}{3}x + \dfrac{17}{3}$, $\dfrac{4}{3}x = \dfrac{17}{3}$, $4x = 17$, $x = \dfrac{17}{4}$.

So the x-intercept is $(\dfrac{17}{4}, 0)$.

Similarly, to find the y-intercept, replace x with zero and solve y: $y = -\dfrac{4}{3} \cdot 0 + \dfrac{17}{3}$, $y = \dfrac{17}{3}$.

Thus, the y-intercept is $(0, \dfrac{17}{3})$.

Notice that the constant number in the equation is the y-coordinate of the y-intercept.

d) If a point lies on a line, then its coordinates satisfy the equation of that line.

So, for (4, a):
$a = -\dfrac{4}{3} \cdot 4 + \dfrac{17}{3}$, $a = -\dfrac{16}{3} + \dfrac{17}{3}$, $a = \dfrac{1}{3}$ and

for (b, 10): $10 = -\dfrac{4}{3} \cdot b + \dfrac{17}{3}$, $10 - \dfrac{17}{3} = -\dfrac{4}{3} \cdot b$,

$\dfrac{13}{3} = -\dfrac{4}{3} \cdot b$, $13 = -4 \cdot b$, $b = -\dfrac{13}{4}$.

Problem 18.5

Find the exact intersection point of the lines represented by the equations $y = 2x + 1$ and $x - 3y = 6$.

Solution 18.5

Finding the intersection point(s) of two lines is the same as finding the solution(s) to the system of equations of these graphs.

So, we need to solve the system of equations
$\begin{cases} y = 2x + 1 \\ x - 3y = 6 \end{cases}$

Let's solve by substitution.

Substitute $2x + 1$ for y in the second equation:
$x - 3(2x + 1) = 6$, $x - 6x - 3 = 6$, $-5x = 9$,
$x = -\dfrac{9}{5} = -1\dfrac{4}{5} = -1.8$.

Plug the x-value in the first equation:
$y = 2x + 1 = 2 \cdot \left(-\dfrac{9}{5}\right) + 1 = -\dfrac{18}{5} + 1$
$= -\dfrac{13}{5} = -2\dfrac{3}{5} = -2.6$.

Hence, the solution is (−1.8, −2.6), which is the intersection point of the given lines.

Without solving the system of equations, just by looking at the graphs and guessing, it is almost impossible to find the exact coordinates.

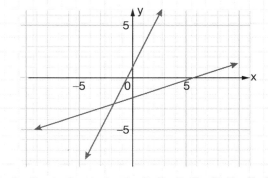

CHAPTER 18 Linear Equations

Problem 18.6
For what values of **a** are the lines represented by
$y = -x + 1$ and $y = ax - 1$

a) Parallel?

b) Intersecting?

c) Coincident (overlapping)?

Solution 18.6
Recall that two lines are parallel if their slopes are equal. So,

a) These lines are parallel if $a = -1$.

b) These lines are intersecting if $a \neq -1$.

c) These lines are never coincident since their y-intercepts are not equal.

Problem 18.7
What is the area of the triangle formed by the lines
$y = 6 - x$, $y = 6 + x$, and $y = 2$?

A) 16   B) 18   C) 19   D) 20   E) 21

Solution 18.6

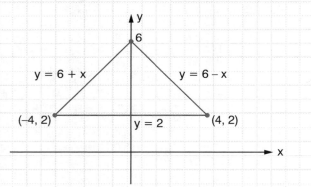

The intersection points are (2, 4), (2, −4) and (0, 6). As drawn in the figure on the right, the height is 4 and the length of the base is 8 in the triangle. Therefore, its are a is $\frac{4 \cdot 8}{2} = 16$.
The answer is A.

Number Match Puzzles

1. Make 3 squares using 3 moves

2. Fix By Moving 1 Matchstick

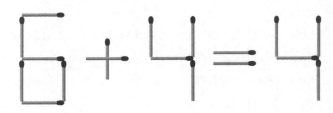

3. Move Only 2 sticks to make a correct equation.

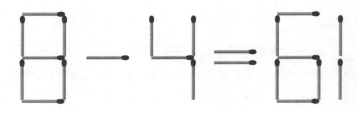

4. What is the biggest number you can make by moving exactly 2 matches?

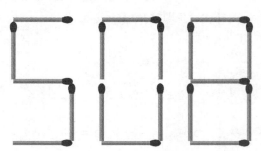

Problem Set 1 — Linear Equations — CHAPTER 18

1. Find the distance between (5, 8) and (5, –5).

2. If point (a, 2) is on the line
   $x + 3y - 2 = 0$, then find a.

3. What is a + b?

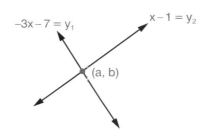

4. Find the y – intercept of the line
   $y + 2x + 5 = 0$

5. Find the x – intercept of the line
   $5y + 6x + 30 = 0$

6. If $y - 2 = 2(x - 3)$
   what is the y – intercept of the line?

7. What is the x – intercept of the line
   $y + 4x = 12$?

8.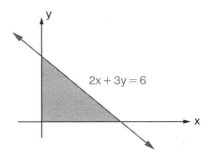

   What is the area of the shaded region?

9.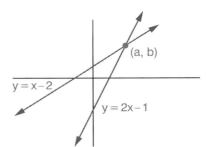

   What is a + b?

10. Solve for x:
    $-2(4 - 3x) - 6x = 10$

11. What is a + b?

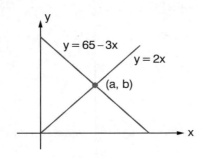

12.
Figure numbers	1	2	3	4	...	21
Number of Tiles	11	17	23	29	...	y

What is y?

13.
IN(x)	−4	−3	−2	−1	10
OUT(y)	−22	−17	−12	−7	z

What is z?

14. Osman wants to rent a boat. The rental shop charges initial fee of $12 plus $20 per hour to rent the boat. If the total cost was $132 for how many hours was the boat rented?

15. You are buying candy bars online. They cost $1.50 each and there is a $3.50 shipping fee. You have $29 to spend.

How many candy bars can you get?

16. Your teacher is giving you a test worth 100 points containing 40 questions. There are two-point and four-point questions on the test. How many of each type of question are on the test?

17.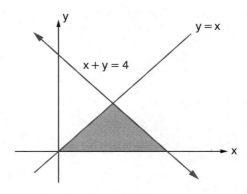

What is the area of shaded region?

18. What is the slope of the line that contains the points (5, 5) and (4, 2)?

19. What is the slope of the line that contains the points (3, 2) and (−8, 2)?

20. Which equation represents the line that passes through the points (1, 6) and (3, 10)?

A) $y = 2x + 4$

B) $y = 2(x - 1) + 6$

C) $y = 2(x - 3) + 10$

Problem Set 2 — Linear Equations — CHAPTER 18

1. Triangle ABC has its vertices at A(0, 0), B(6, 0), and C(3, 6). What is the area of the triangle, in square units?

2. Rectangle ABCD has its vertices at A(0, 0), B(6, 0), C(6, 4), and D(0, 4). What is the area of the rectangle, in square units?

3. What is the area of the shaded region?

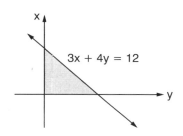

4. What is the slope of the line?

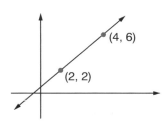

5. The graph of $x + 3y - 2 = 0$ crosses the y-axis at

6. The graph of $y + 2x - 4 = 0$ crosses the x-axis at

7. Find the distance between the points $(-1, 3)$ and $(2, -4)$.

8. Find the y-intercept of the line $y + 2x - 1 = 0$.

9. Find the slope of the line containing the points $(-1, 3)$ and $(2, 4)$.

10. The point of intersection of the lines $x - y = 3$ and $x + y = 1$ is

CHAPTER 18 — Linear Equations — Problem Set 2

11. Write an inequality that represents the graph?

12. Write an inequality that represents the graph?

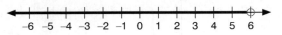

13. Write an inequality that represents the graph?

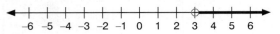

14. Write an inequality that represents the graph?

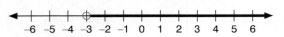

15. Find the equation of line M?

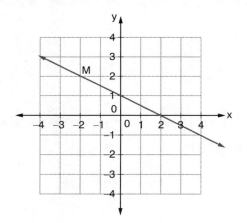

16. Simplify: $4y - y + 10 - 15$

17. What points positioned on the number line best represents the value of S ÷ T?

18. Triangle ABC has its vertices at A(2, 0), B(6, 0) and C(6, 3). The area of the triangle, in square units, is

19. What is the slope of the line $3x + 4y = 15$?

20. Find the equation of the line which passes through the points A(2, 3) and B(4, 9).

CHAPTER 19
Number Systems

Target Concepts and Skills

- [ ] Defining the decimal system.
- [ ] Defining number sets and their connections.
- [ ] Prime numbers and prime factorization.
- [ ] Converting a repeating decimal to a fraction.
- [ ] Rationalizing a denominator

Remark 19.1 – Decimal System (Hindu-Arabic Number System)

The number system that requires ten different numerals (digits: 0,1, 2, 3, 4, 5, 6, 7, 8, 9) to denote numbers is called the decimal system (base ten or positional system). This system also requires a decimal point to represent decimal fractions. Depending upon the position, each digit takes different place values.

Example 19.1

The number 324.15 represents the number

$$\underbrace{3 \cdot 10^2 + 2 \cdot 10^1 + 4 \cdot 10^0}_{\text{Integer part}} + \underbrace{1 \cdot 10^{-1} + 5 \cdot 10^{-2}}_{\text{Fractional part}}$$

Definition 19.2 – Number Sets

1) Natural Numbers:
   $N = \{1, 2, 3, 4, 5, 6, 7, 8, 9, \ldots\}$
2) Whole Numbers:
   $W = \{0, 1, 2, 3, 4, 5, 6, 7, 8, 9, \ldots\}$
3) Integers:
   $Z = \{\ldots -4, -3, -2, -1, 0, 1, 2, 3, 4, 5, 6, 7, 8, 9, \ldots\}$

4) Rational Numbers:
   $Q = \left\{\dfrac{a}{b} \text{ such that a \& b are integers, } b \neq 0\right\}$.
   For example, $\dfrac{2}{3}, -\dfrac{3}{5}, \dfrac{6}{2}$ are rational numbers.

5) Irrational Numbers: Any number that is not rational is called an irrational number.
   So, they cannot be expressed as a ratio like $\dfrac{a}{b}$.
   For example, $\sqrt{2}, \sqrt{5}, \pi$ are irrational numbers.

6) Real Numbers (R): The union of all number sets above is called the set of real numbers. Each point on the number line corresponds to a real number.

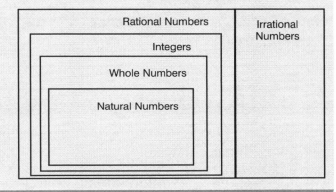

Problem 19.1

Categorize the following numbers based on the smallest set they belong to.

a) 2
b) –5
c) 2.25
d) 2.25252525…(Repeating the same way)
e) $\sqrt{3}$
f) $\sqrt{9}$
g) $\sqrt{18}$

Math Fluency

CHAPTER 19 — Number Systems

Solution 19.1

a) 2 is a natural number.

b) −5 is an integer.

c) $2.25 = \frac{9}{4}$. So, it is a rational number.

d) $2.25252525\ldots = \frac{223}{99}$.
So, it is a rational number.

e) $\sqrt{3} \approx 1.7320508076\ldots$. There is no pattern in the decimal expansion. This means that this number cannot be expressed as a ratio of two integers. So, it is an irrational number.

f) $\sqrt{9} = 3$ is a natural number.

g) $\sqrt{18} = \sqrt{9 \cdot 2} = \sqrt{9} \cdot \sqrt{2}$
$= 3 \cdot \sqrt{2} \approx 3 \cdot 1.4142135624\ldots \approx 4.2426406871\ldots$
There is no pattern in the decimal expansion. So, it is an irrational number.

Notice that any irrational number has no pattern in its decimal expansion.

Example 19.2

Let's convert the following repeating decimal numbers into rational numbers.

a) $3.\overline{4} = 3.444\ldots$
Let $3.444\ldots = x$
Multiply both sides by 10: $34.444\ldots = 10x$
To get rid of the repeating part, subtract side by side: $34.444\ldots - 3.444\ldots = 10x - x$, $31 = 9x$,
$x = \frac{31}{9}$.

b) $5.\overline{42} =$
Let $5.424242\ldots = x$
Multiply both sides by 100: $542.424242\ldots = 100x$
To get rid of the repeating part, subtract side by side: $542.424242\ldots - 5.424242\ldots = 100x - x$,
$537 = 99x$, $x = \frac{537}{99}$.

Notice that depending on the number of repeating digits, in order to eliminate the repeating part, we multiply both sides by an appropriate power of ten.

Problem 19.2

How many integers are there between the following numbers? (No calculator!)

a) 2 & 10

b) $\frac{2}{3}$ & $\frac{10}{7}$

c) $\frac{\sqrt{2}}{3}$ & $\frac{\sqrt{10}}{7}$

d) $\frac{7}{\sqrt{2}}$ & $\frac{10}{\sqrt{10}}$

Solution 19.2

a) Between 2 & 10, there are seven integers: 3, 4, 5, 6, 7, 8, 9.

b) To be able to see the integers between $\frac{2}{3}$ & $\frac{10}{7}$, we should get a common denominator first.
$\frac{2}{3} = \frac{2 \cdot 7}{3 \cdot 7} = \frac{14}{21}$ & $\frac{10}{7} = \frac{10 \cdot 3}{7 \cdot 3} = \frac{30}{21}$.
Thus, there might be some integers falling in the interval: $\frac{14}{21} < \ldots < \frac{30}{21}$.
As many as the number of multiples of 21 between 14 and 30, we have integers between $\frac{14}{21}$ & $\frac{30}{21}$. So, there is just one such integer since $\frac{14}{21} < \frac{21}{21} < \frac{30}{21}$.
This integer is $\frac{21}{21} = 1$.

c) $\frac{\sqrt{2}}{3} = \frac{\sqrt{2} \cdot 7}{3 \cdot 7} = \frac{7\sqrt{2}}{21} = \frac{\sqrt{7^2 \cdot 2}}{3 \cdot 7} = \frac{\sqrt{98}}{21}$ & $\frac{\sqrt{10}}{7}$
$= \frac{\sqrt{10} \cdot 3}{7 \cdot 3} = \frac{3\sqrt{10}}{21} = \frac{\sqrt{3^2 \cdot 10}}{21} = \frac{\sqrt{90}}{21}$.

By the same reasoning as in part (b), we should look for the multiples of 21 between $\sqrt{90}$ and $\sqrt{98}$. Obviously, there is no such multiple of 21. This means that there are no integers between $\frac{\sqrt{2}}{3}$ & $\frac{\sqrt{10}}{7}$.

d) First, we need to rationalize each denominator:
$\frac{3}{\sqrt{10}} = \frac{3 \cdot \sqrt{10}}{\sqrt{10} \cdot \sqrt{10}} = \frac{3\sqrt{10}}{10} = \frac{\sqrt{90}}{10}$ and
$\frac{7}{\sqrt{2}} = \frac{7 \cdot \sqrt{2}}{\sqrt{2} \cdot \sqrt{2}} = \frac{7\sqrt{2}}{2} = \frac{\sqrt{98}}{2}$.

Number Systems

CHAPTER 19

And then, we should get a common denominator:

$$\frac{\sqrt{98}}{2} = \frac{5\sqrt{98}}{10} = \frac{\sqrt{2450}}{10}.$$

So, let's check if there are any multiples of 10 between $\sqrt{90}$ and $\sqrt{2450}$.

$\sqrt{90} < x < \sqrt{2450}$ or $90 < x^2 < 2450$, where x is a multiple of 10.

So, we have $10^2, 20^2, 30^2, 40^2$ which means that there are four integers between $\frac{7}{\sqrt{2}}$ & $\frac{3}{\sqrt{10}}$.

Definition 19.3 – Prime Numbers

A natural number greater than 1 and not a product of two smaller natural numbers is called a prime number.

2, 3, 5, 7, 11, 13, 17, 19, 23, 29, ... are some prime numbers. Although there is no pattern for prime numbers, there are some methods to determine whether a given number is prime. Especially for very large numbers, these methods are extremely useful.

Prime numbers are building blocks for all other natural numbers.

Problem 19.3

Rationalize the denominators of the following fractions.

a) $\dfrac{2}{\sqrt{7}}$

b) $\dfrac{2}{\sqrt{7} - 2}$

c) $\dfrac{2}{\sqrt{7} - \sqrt{3}}$

Solution 19.3

a) $\dfrac{2}{\sqrt{7}} = \dfrac{2 \cdot \sqrt{7}}{\sqrt{7} \cdot \sqrt{7}} = \dfrac{2\sqrt{7}}{7}.$

b) Recall that $(a - b) \cdot (a + b) = a^2 - b^2$.

So, $\dfrac{2}{\sqrt{7} - 2} = \dfrac{2}{\sqrt{7} - 2} \cdot \dfrac{(\sqrt{7} + 2)}{(\sqrt{7} + 2)}$

$= \dfrac{2 \cdot (\sqrt{7} + 2)}{(\sqrt{7} - 2) \cdot (\sqrt{7} + 2)} = \dfrac{2 \cdot (\sqrt{7} + 2)}{(\sqrt{7})^2 - 2^2}$

$= \dfrac{2 \cdot (\sqrt{7} + 2)}{7 - 4} = \dfrac{2\sqrt{7} + 4}{3}.$

c) By the reasoning in part (b), $\dfrac{2}{\sqrt{7} - \sqrt{3}}$

$= \dfrac{2}{\sqrt{7} - \sqrt{3}} \cdot \dfrac{\sqrt{7} + \sqrt{3}}{\sqrt{7} + \sqrt{3}} = \dfrac{2(\sqrt{7} + \sqrt{3})}{(\sqrt{7})^2 - (\sqrt{3})^2}$

$= \dfrac{2(\sqrt{7} + \sqrt{3})}{7 - 3} = \dfrac{2(\sqrt{7} + \sqrt{3})}{4} = \dfrac{\sqrt{7} + \sqrt{3}}{2}.$

Example 19.3

Let's find the prime factorizations (Each factor must be a prime number) for the following numbers.

a) $12 = 2^2 \cdot 3$

b) $96 = 2 \cdot 48 = 2 \cdot 3 \cdot 16 = 2 \cdot 3 \cdot 2^4 = 3 \cdot 2^5$

c) $520 = 2^3 \cdot 5 \cdot 13$

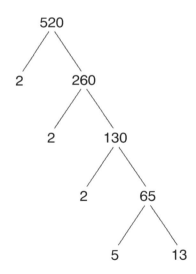

Sets of Numbers in the Real Number System

Reals

A real number is either a rational number or an irrational number.

$-5, 0, \frac{2}{3}, \sqrt{2}, \pi, 4$

Rationals

A rational number is any number that can be put in the form $\frac{p}{q}$ where p and q are integers and q ≠ 0.

$-5, -\frac{2}{3}, 0, \frac{1}{2}, 3.444\ ...$

Irrationals

An irrational number is a nonrepeating, nonterminating decimal.

$\sqrt{2}, \pi, 2.15752\ ..., \sqrt{13}$

Non-Integer Fractions

A non-integer fraction is a fraction whose numerator is *not* a multiple of the denominator.

$\frac{-5}{6}, 0, \frac{2}{3}, \frac{5}{7}, 2\frac{2}{5}$

Integers

The integers consist of the natural numbers, 0, and the opposites of the natural numbers.

$...\ -2, -1, 0, 1, 2, 3, \sqrt{16}\ ...$

$...\ -5, -4, -3, -2, -1$

Whole Numbers

The whole numbers consist of the natural numbers and 0.

0, 1, 2, 3, 4, ...

0

Natural Numbers

The natural numbers are also referred to as the counting numbers.

1, 2, 3, 4, ...

Problem Set 1 — Number Systems — CHAPTER 19

1. x and y are digits and $x + y = 12$.
   What is the largest value of $x \cdot y$?

2. x and y are digits and $x \cdot y = 16$.
   What is the largest value of $x + y$?

3. x and y are digits and $x \cdot y = 12$.
   What is the smallest value of $x + y$?

4. Suppose a, b, and c are positive integers with $a \cdot b = 13$ and $b \cdot c = 12$, what is the value of $a + b + c$?

5. Suppose x and y are whole numbers.
   For how many $x \cdot y$ values $x + y = 5$.

6. Suppose x and y are positive integers and $x = \dfrac{y + 12}{y}$.
   What is the number of distinct values of x?

7. If x is an integer then $4x - 3$ is odd or even?

8. If x is an integer then $x^3 + 2x + 1$ is odd or even?

9. If n is an integer then $n^2 - n$ is odd or even?

10. If $b = 2c$, and $a = 3b$,
    what is the value of $\dfrac{a + b + c}{c}$?

CHAPTER 19 — Number Systems — Problem Set 1

11. How many whole numbers lie in the interval between $\frac{5}{3}$ and 2π?

12. How many prime numbers are there between 10 and 30?

13. When two numbers are added, the result is −15. If one of the numbers is 8, what is the other number?

14. What is the minimum possible product of three different numbers of the set $\{-8, -6, -4, 0, 3, 5, 7\}$?

15. If $0.3\overline{4} + 0.4\overline{3} = \frac{a}{9}$, what is a?

16. How many integers are there between $-\frac{\sqrt{26}}{2}$ and $\sqrt{24}$?

17. How many whole number lie in the interval between $\sqrt{13}$ and 6π?

18. Find the 7th term $2, 2\sqrt{2}, 4, 4\sqrt{2}, ...$

19. The next number in the sequence $2, 2, \frac{8}{3}, 4, \frac{32}{5}$?

20. What is the minimum possible product of three numbers of the set $\{-4, -2, 0, 3, 5, 6\}$?

Problem Set 2 — Number Systems — CHAPTER 19

1. How many numbers use exactly 2 digits?

2. How many integers between $\frac{3}{4}$ and $\frac{16}{3}$?

3. How many integers between $-\frac{16}{3}$ and $\frac{20}{3}$?

4. What is 0.33333... ?
   Express your answer as the simplest fraction.

5. Which of the following is an irrational number?
   A) $\sqrt{36}$ B) $\sqrt{\frac{49}{16}}$ C) $\sqrt{8}$ D) $-\sqrt{16}$

6. Which of the following is on example of an irration number?
   A) 3.5 B) −2 C) π D) $\frac{1}{2}$

Questions 7 – 10

Identify the sets to which each of the following numbers belongs by marking an "X" in the appropriate boxes.

Number	Natural Numbers	Whole Numbers	Integers	Rational Numbers	Irrational Numbers	Real Numbers
$-\sqrt{17}$						
−2						
$-\frac{9}{37}$						
0						
−6.06						
$4.5\overline{6}$						
29						

Math Fluency

CHAPTER 19 — Number Systems — Problem Set 2

11. What is the nature of decimal expansion of irrational numbers?

    A) Terminating

    B) Nonterminating – repeating

    C) Nonterminating – non – repeating

12. Which of the following is an irrational number?

    A) $\sqrt{25}$ B) $\sqrt{2} \times \sqrt{2}$ C) $\sqrt{5}$ D) $\sqrt{4}$

13. When you rationalize the following denominator what is the lowest term of the fraction.

    A) $\dfrac{2\sqrt{5}}{\sqrt{6}}$ B) $\dfrac{6}{\sqrt{3}}$

14. When we multiply $(\sqrt{3} - \sqrt{2})$ and $(\sqrt{3} + \sqrt{2})$ what number we obtain?

15. Rationalize the denominator of the following.

    $\dfrac{6}{\sqrt{5} - \sqrt{2}}$

16. If we express 0.373737... as $\dfrac{a}{b}$ in lowest terms, what is a + b?

17. If we express 1.244444... as $\dfrac{a}{b}$ in lowest terms, what is a + b?

18. a = 2.33333 ...   b = 3.22222 ...

    What is $\dfrac{1}{a} + \dfrac{1}{b}$?

19. What is $\dfrac{0.\overline{5} + 0.\overline{4}}{0.\overline{5} - 0.\overline{3}}$

20. What is the minimum possible product of three different numbers of the set $\{-6, -5, -4, 0, 2, 5, 7\}$?

CHAPTER 20
Data & Statistics

✓ Target Concepts and Skills

- ☐ Defining main measures of central tendency.
- ☐ Finding main measures of central tendency for a given data set.
- ☐ Using various frequency charts to represent different data types.

Definition 20.1 – Measures of Central Tendency

1) A measure that attempts to describe a data set with a single value representing the center of its distribution is called a measure of tendency. There are three primary measures of tendency: the mean, the median, and the mode.
2) The arithmetic average of data values is called the mean of these values.
3) The middle value of data values, when they are arranged in increasing or decreasing order, is called the median.
4) The most commonly occurring value in a data set is called the mode.

Example 20.1

Let's find the mean, median, and mode for the data set $\{4, 5, 5, 10, 8, 16\}$.

$$\text{Mean} = \frac{4+5+5+10+8+16}{6} = 8$$

The median is the middle term when the data values are in increasing/decreasing order. Let us put them in increasing order: 4, 5, 5, 8, 10, 16. There is no exact middle value. So, we take the two values in the middle and find their average.

$$\text{Median} = \frac{5+8}{2} = 6.5$$

Mode = 5 since it appears twice while other values appear just once.

Example 20.2

In the previous example, what if we change 16 to 22? Which of the three measures are affected by this change?

$$\text{Mean} = \frac{4+5+5+10+8+22}{6} = 9$$

$$\text{Median} = \frac{5+8}{2} = 6.5, \quad \text{Mode} = 5.$$

Therefore, only the mean is affected by this change.

Notice that the mean of a data set is very sensitive to any change in data values. However, the mode and the median are not so sensitive.

Definition 20.2 – Range

The range of a data set is the difference between the largest and the smallest values. In the previous example, the range is 12, which is equal to $16 - 4$.

Problem 20.1

To the data set $\{5, 6, 8, 12, 14\}$, what value must be added to get a mean value of 10?

Solution 20.1

Let this value be x. Then,

$$10 = \frac{5+6+8+12+14+x}{6},$$

$$60 = 5+6+8+12+14+x,$$

$$60 = 45 + x, \quad x = 15.$$

Problem 20.2

The mean weight of the twenty students in a classroom is 200 pounds. One student of 180 pounds leaves the classroom. Find the mean weight of the remaining students.

CHAPTER 20 — Data & Statistics

Solution 20.2
Let S be the sum of the weights of the students.
Then, $200 = \dfrac{S}{20}$, $4000 = S$
After one student leaves the classroom:
$M = \dfrac{4000 - 180}{19} = 201.05$ pounds.

Problem 20.3
Find the mean when we combine two data sets with means $M_1 = 20$ & $M_2 = 30$ if they include 10 and 15 values, respectively.

Solution 20.3
Let S_1 and S_2 be the sums of data values in each set. Then, we have $\dfrac{S_1}{10} = 20$ and $\dfrac{S_2}{15} = 30$.

Thus, $S_1 = 10 \cdot 20 = 200$ and $S_2 = 15 \cdot 30 = 450$.

$M_{combined} = \dfrac{S_1 + S_2}{10 + 15} = \dfrac{200 + 450}{25} = \dfrac{650}{25} = 26$.

Definition 20.3 – Frequency Table
1) Frequency is the number of times a specific data value appears in a data set.
2) A table in which data values and their frequencies are listed is called a frequency table.

Example 20.2
For the data set of ages of people in a park
{1,3,3,5,5,5,7,8,9,13,15,17,17,25,25,26},
we can make a frequency table:

Interval	Frequency
1 up to 6	6
6 up to 11	3
11 up to 16	2
16 up to 21	2
21 up to 26	2
26 up to 31	1

Definition 20.4 – Histogram
A histogram is a graphical representation of a grouped frequency distribution with continuous classes.

We can represent the data set in the previous example as a histogram.

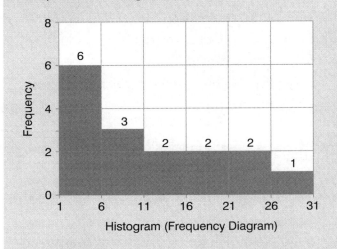

Histogram (Frequency Diagram)

Definition 20.5 – Bar Chart
A bar chart is a graph that represents a categorical variable or ungrouped numeric variable in columns.

Example 20.3
A group of children and their birthplaces are given in the following frequency table.

Country of Birth	Frequency
United States of America	16
Canada	3
Mexico	8
India	10
China	9
Italy	4

Data & Statistics

CHAPTER 20

The following graph represents the same data as a bar chart.

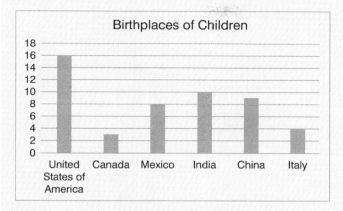

Notice that although a histogram and a bar chart look similar, a histogram is used for continuous data, whereas a bar chart is used for categorical data. Therefore, in a bar chart, there are spaces between columns, but in a histogram, there are no spaces between columns.

Definition 20.6 – Box and Whisker Plot

The box and whisker plot summarizes the data variation using five pieces of information. These pieces are minimum value (q_0 or 0th percentile), first quartile (q_1 or 25th percentile or median of the first half), median (q_2 or 50th percentile), third quartile (q_3 or 75th percentile or median of the second half), and maximum value (q_4 or 100th percentile).

We can represent the data in example 20.2 by using the box and whisker plot as follows:

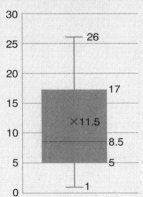

In this graph:
$q_0 = 1$,
$q_1 = 5$,
median = 8.5,
$q_3 = 17$ and
$q_4 = 26$
Mean = 11.5

Definition 20.7 – Pie Chart

A pie chart is a circular statistical graphic that displays the proportion of data values in a data set. A pie chart works best if the sample data only has a few components.

We can display the data given in Example 20.3 by using a pie chart as follows:

Problem 20.4

Find the median of each list of values.

a) 5, 7, 8, 6, 3, 5, 9, 11, 13, 5, 10
b) 6, 9, 13, 15, 17, 21, 19, 18

Solution 20.4

a) First we write the values in ascending order:
3, 5, 5, 5, 6, 7, 8, 9, 10, 11, 13. The median is 7 because 7 is the middle value.

b) In ascending order, the values are:
6, 9, 13, 15, 17, 18, 19, 21
Since there is an even number of values, the median is $\frac{15 + 17}{2} = 16$

Problem 20.5

The average(mean) of 25 numbers is 24, and the average of 15 other numbers is 20.
What is the average of all 40 numbers?

Solution 20.5

The sum of all 40 numbers is
$25 \cdot 24 + 15 \cdot 20 = 960$
So, their average is $\frac{960}{40} = 22.5$

Math Fluency

CHAPTER 20 — Four Fours — Puzzle

Use the digit 4 exactly four times to write number sentences equivalent to the numbers from 1 to 25.

You may use any mathematical operations and symbols (e.g., 4.4, 44, 4^4, 4!, $\sqrt{4}$). Use parentheses as needed to clarify the order of operations.

Answer	Solution 1	Solution 2
1	(4 + 4 − 4) / 4	(4 + 4) ÷ (4 + 4)
2		
3		
4		
5		
6		
7		
8		
9		
10		
11		

Answer	Solution 1	Solution 2
12		
13		
14		
15		
16		
17		
18		
19		
20		
21		
22		
23		
24		
25		

Problem Set 1 — Data & Statistics — CHAPTER 20

Answer question 1–4

Let our data set be {1, 2, 3, 6, 6, 7, 9, 9, 9, 12}

1. What is the mean?

2. What is the median?

3. What is the mode?

4. What is the range?

5. If the average of 30, 20, x, 10 and 40 is 25, what is the value of x?

6. The arithmetic mean of two numbers a and b is 11. If a is 2 more than b. Find a.

7. The average of 6, 7, 13, and x is 9, what is the value of x?

8. What is the range of the following data set? {102, 89, 84, 94, 90, 104, 132}

9. The average ages of 5 people in a room is 20 years. A 40 year old person leaves from the room. What is the average age of 4 remaining people?

10. The mean, median, and unique mode of the positive integers 5, 6, 7, 8, 8, 9, and x are all equal. What is the value of x?

11. The mean age of Sam's 4 friend is 9, and their median age is 8. What is the sum of the ages of Sam's youngest and oldest friends?

12. The average of ten numbers is 20. Subtract 20 from nine of these numbers. After this subtraction, what is the average of ten numbers?

13. The result of a survey of the hair color of 300 people are shown in this circle graph. How many people have blonde hair?

Hair color
black 22%
brown 32%
red 16%
blonde

14. The mean (average) of a set of six numbers is 10. When the number 25 is removed from the set, the mean of the remaining numbers is

15. The mean (average) of five consecutive even numbers is 12. The mean of the smallest and largest of these numbers is

Answer question 16–19

Data value (x)	Frequency (f)
3	1
4	1
5	3
6	7
7	15
8	8
9	5

16. What is the mode?

17. What is the mean?

18. What is the median?

19. What is the range?

20. A set of 14 data is: 6, 8, 7, 7, 5, 7, 6, 8, 6, 9, 6, 7, a, b. The mean and mode of the set are both 7. What is a + b?

Problem Set 2 — Data & Statistics — CHAPTER 20

Use the graph answer question 1 – 4.

A random sample of people were asked "How many times did you eat at a restaurant last week?" A column graph was used to display the results.

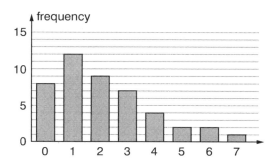

1. How many people were surveyed?

2. Find the mode of the data.

3. How many people surveyed did not eat at a restaurant at all last week?

4. What percentage of people surveyed ate at a restaurant more than three times last week?

5. What value of x makes the mean of the first three numbers in the list equal to the mean of the last four?

    10, 5, x, 7, 9, 12

Use the graph answer question 6 – 9.

A selection of businesses were asked how man employees they had. A column graph was consturcted to display the results.

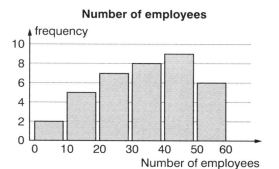

6. How many businesses were surveyed?

7. Find the modal class.

8. Describe the distribution of the data.

9. What percentage of businesses surveyed had less than 30 employees?

Use the graph answer question 10 – 12.

The table shows the number of aces served by tennis players in their first sets of a tournament.

Number of aces	1	2	3	4	5	6
Frequency	4	11	18	13	7	2

10. Mean

11. Median

12. Mode

13. The table alongside shows the results when 3 coins were tossed simultaneously 30 times.

Number of heads	Frequency
0	4
1	12
2	11
3	3
Total	30

What is the mean of the data?

Answer question 14 – 15.

The boxplot below summarizes the point scored by a basketball team.

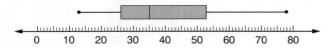

14. What is the median?

15. What is the sum of the minimum and maximum values?

16. (CEMC-2018 - Gauss 8-9)

The mean (average) height of a group of children would be increased by 6 cm if 12 of the children in the group were each 8 cm taller.

How many children are in the group?

17. (UNB-2014 - Gr 9-6)

Consider four numbers, a; b; c and d. The average of a and b is 10. The average of b; c and d is 20. The average of all four numbers is 19.

What is the value of a?

18. Five test scores have a mean of 80, a median of 81, and a mode of 84. What is the sum of two lowest scores?

19. (2015 UK - SMC #5)

The integer n is the mean of the three numbers 17, 23 and 2n. What is the sum of the digits of n?

20. The average (arithmetic mean) of 10 different positive numbers is 10.

What is the product of the smallest and the largest values of these number set?

CHAPTER 21
Sets

Target Concepts and Skills

- [ ] Defining sets and subsets.
- [ ] Defining union and intersection of sets.
- [ ] Defining the difference set.
- [ ] Applying the Inclusion-Exclusion Principle to real-life situations.

Definition 21.1 – Set

A collection of different things is called a set. Each thing in a set is an element of this set. Sets can be represented in various forms like roster form, set builder form, Venn diagram, and descriptive method.

Example 21.1

Roster form: $A = \{1, 2, 3, 4\}$

Set builder form:
$A = \{x \mid x \text{ is a natural number less than 5}\}$

Descriptive method:
$A = \{\text{Natural numbers less than 5}\}$

Venn diagram:

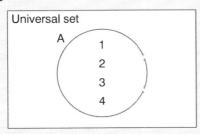

Definition 21.2 – Union & Intersection of Sets

1) The union of two sets A and B is the set that includes all elements that are in **either** A or B. We write $A \cup B$ to represent the union of the sets A and B.

2) The intersection of two sets A and B is the set that includes all elements that are in **both** A and B. We write $A \cap B$ to denote the intersection of the sets A and B.

Example 21.2

Let $A = \{1, 2, 3, 4\}$, $B = \{3, 4, 5, 6, 7\}$. Then,
$A \cup B = \{1, 2, 3, 4, 5, 6, 7\}$ and $A \cap B = \{3, 4\}$.

By the Venn diagram:

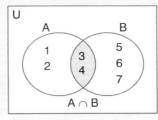 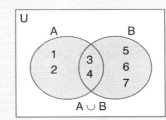

Remark 21.1 – Inclusion-Exclusion Principle

Let $n(A)$ represent the number of elements in set A. Then,

$$n(A \cup B) = n(A) + n(B) - n(A \cap B)$$

Problem 21.1

Find $n(A \cup B)$ and illustrate the relative positions of sets using a Venn diagram if

a) $n(A) = 5$, $n(B) = 7$, $n(A \cap B) = 3$.
b) $n(A) = 5$, $n(B) = 7$, $n(A \cap B) = 0$.
c) $n(A) = 5$, $n(B) = 7$, $n(A \cap B) = 5$.

CHAPTER 21 — Sets

Solution 21.1

Note: In the following figures, the numbers in red represent the number of elements in that region.

a) By the **Inclusion-Exclusion Principle**,
$n(A \cup B) = n(A) + n(B) - n(A \cap B) = 5 + 7 - 3 = 9.$

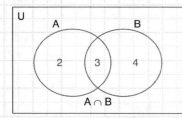

b) $n(A \cup B) = n(A) + n(B) - n(A \cap B) = 5 + 7 - 0 = 12$

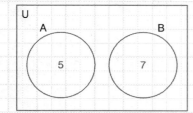

c) $n(A \cup B) = n(A) + n(B) - n(A \cap B) = 5 + 7 - 5 = 7$

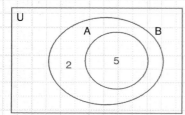

Definition 21.3 – Disjoint Sets

1) If the sets A and B have no elements in common, that is $n(A \cap B) = 0$, they are called disjoint sets. In part (b) of the previous example, sets A and B are disjoint.
2) If all the elements of set A are included in set B, A is called a subset of set B. We denote it as $A \subset B$. In part (c) of the previous example, $A \subset B$.
3) If a set has no elements, it is called an empty set. An empty set is denoted by { } or ∅.

Remark 21.2 – Number of Subsets of a Set

If a set has n elements, the number of its subsets is equal to 2^n.

Example 21.3

The subsets of set A = {1, 2, 3} are
{1}, {2}, {3}, {1,2}, {1,3}, {2,3}, {1,2,3}, { }.
For set A, n = 3. So, there are $2^3 = 8$ subsets.

Definition 21.4 – Difference of Sets

The difference between the two sets A and B is the set that includes all those elements that belong to A **but not** B. We write A – B to denote the difference between sets A and B.

Example 21.4

Let's find the difference between sets
A = {1, 2, 3, 4}, B = {3, 4, 5, 6, 7}.
A – B = {1, 2}, B – A = {5, 6, 7}.
By the Venn diagram:

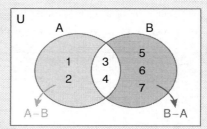

Problem 21.2

A college radio station surveyed 156 incoming first-year students to find out what genres of music they liked. Below are the results for the two genres.

	like classical	like country	like both classical and country
Number of Students	90	80	35

Find the number of students who like
a) Country but not classical
b) Country or classical or both
c) Neither classical nor country.

Solution 21.2

Let's illustrate the given data by constructing a Venn diagram.

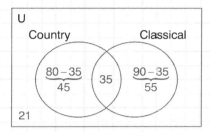

a) Country but not classical means
   Country − Classical = 45

b) Country or classical or both means
   Country ∪ Classical = 45 + 35 + 55 = 135

c) Neither classical nor country means
   Universal − (Country ∪ Cassical)
   = 156 − 135 = 21.

Problem 21.3

How many integers between 10 and 150 inclusive are divisible by

a) 3
b) 5
c) 3 **and** 5?
d) 3 **or** 5?

Solution 21.3

Let the set of numbers (between 10 and 150 inclusive) that are divisible by 3 be T and by 5 be F.

a) We are looking for n(T), which is equal to the number of multiples of 3 between 10 and 150 inclusive. These are 12, 15, ... , 150.
   There are $\frac{150-12}{3} + 1 = 47$ multiples of 3.
   So, n(T) = 47.

b) By the same reasoning in part (a), there are $\frac{150-10}{5} + 1 = 29$ multiples of 5.
   So, n(F) = 29.

c) We are looking for n(T∩F). Divisibility by 3 and 5 means divisibility by 3 · 5 = 15. In other words, we want to find the number of multiples of 15 between 10 and 150. These are 15, 30, ... ,150.
   There are $\frac{150-15}{15} + 1 = 10$ multiples of 15.
   So, n(T∩F) = 10.

d) We are looking for n(T∪F), which is equal to n(T) + n(F) − n(T∩F) by the Inclusion-Exclusion Principle. So, n(T∪F) = n(T) + n(F) − n(T∩F)
   = 47 + 29 − 10 = 66

Problem 21.4

All students at HS high school speak at least one of the foreign languages, French or German. 85% of students speak French, and 75% speak German. What percent of students speak both languages?

Solution 21.4

Let x, y, z, and t be the number of students falling in the described region of the following Venn diagram. Then, we want to find y, the percentage of students who speak both languages.

t = 0 since all students speak at least one foreign language (i.e., there is no student who does not speak any foreign language). This also means that x + y + z = 100.

85% of students speak French. So, x + y = 85 and y + z = 75 since 75% speak German.

By these three equations, we have
z = 100 − (x + y) = 15, x = 100 − (y + z) = 25, and y = 100 − (x + z) = 60.

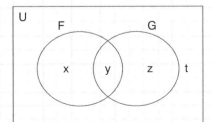

CHAPTER 21 — Table Complete — Puzzle

1. Sharing in a Ratio

a : b	a	b	Difference (a − b)	Total (a + b)	Product (ab)
	14	4			
		35	−14		
3 : 7				80	
		35			
6 : 7	12				
6 : 5	18				
		8		64	
	6	42			

2. Evaluating Expressions

$\dfrac{3x}{9}$	$x + 3$	$3x + 3$	$3(x + 3)$	$\dfrac{x^3}{27}$	$-x^3$	$(-x)^3$	$-(x^3)$
$\dfrac{2x}{6}$	$x + 2$	$2x + 2$	$2(x + 2)$	x^2	$-x^2$	$(-x)^2$	$-(x^2)$
$\dfrac{x}{3}$	$x + 1$	$x + 1$	$1(x + 1)$	x^1	$-x^1$	$(-x)^1$	$-(x^1)$
$\dfrac{0x}{0}$	$\dfrac{x}{3}$	$0x$	$0(x)$	x^0	$-x^0$	$(-x)^0$	$-(x^0)$
$\dfrac{-x}{-3}$	$x - 1$	$-x - 1$	$-1(x - 1)$	x^{-1}	$-x^{-1}$	$(-x)^{-1}$	$-(x^{-1})$

3. Writing Expressions

Variable	1st Operation	2nd Operation	3rd Operation	Expression	When n = 10
n	÷2	×8	+3	$\dfrac{8}{2} + 3$	43
n	÷2	+3	×8		
n	×8	÷2	+3		
n	×8	+3	÷2		
n	+3	÷2	×8		
n	+3	×3	÷2		

Problem Set 1 — Sets — CHAPTER 21

1. If
   A = {a, b, c, d, e}
   B = {a, c, e, f}
   How many elements does (A∩B) have?

2. A = {★, △, □, 5}
   B = {★, 0, 4, □}
   How many elements does (A∪B) have?

3. Suppose A = {x | 3 < x ≤ 10, x ∈ Z}
   a. List the elements of set A.

   b. Find n(A).

4. Find each intersection or union given
   A = {0, 2, 4, 6, 10, 12}
   B = {0, 3, 6, 12, 15}
   C = {1, 2, 3, 4, 5, 6, 7}
   a. A∪C

   b. B∩C

5. Find each intersection or union given
   A = {0, 2, 4, 6, 10, 12}
   B = {0, 3, 6, 12, 15}
   C = {1, 2, 3, 4, 5, 6, 7}
   a. A∩(B∪C)

   b. B∪(A∩C)

6. If n(A) = 14, n(B) = 20, and n(A∩B) = 6, what is n(A∪B)?

7. If n(A) = 20, n(B) = 16, and n(A∪B) = 30, what is n(A∩B)?

8. Sets A and B, shown in the Venn diagram, have the same number of elements. Their union has 199 elements and their intersection has 101 elements. Find the number of elements in A.

   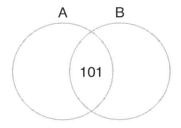

9. Which of the following is equal to
   n(A − B) + n(A∩B) =
   a. n(A)

   b. n(B)

10. Which of the following is an empty set?
    a. Prime numbers up to 10

    b. Even numbers up to 10

    c. Prime numbers divisible by 2

    d. Prime numbers divisible by 3

CHAPTER 21 — Sets — Problem Set 1

11. A = {1, 2, 3} ve A∪B = {1, 2, 3, 4, 5}
    Which of the following is true?
    A) 4 ∈ A   B) 5 ∈ B   C) 1 ∈ (A∩B)   D) 3 ∈ (A∩B)

12. A = {whole numbers divisible by 10 and less than 200}
    B = {whole numbers divisible by 12 and less than 200}
    How many elements does (A∩B) have?

13. Write out all subsets of {1, 2, 3} and {1, 2, 3, 4}
    How many are there?

14. Every student in a school takes at least a math or an art class. There are 100 students in the school and 70 of these students take a math class. Also, exactly 30 students take both a math and an art class.
    How many students take a math class and not an art class?

15. Given n(∪) = 50, n(S) = 30, n(R) = 25, and n(R∪S) = 48, find n(R∩S)

16. How many integers between 1 and 50 inclusive are divisible by 5 or 6?

17. Every student in a class of 28 students has either zero or one history book, zero or one science books, and no other books. Given there are 4 students with neither book, 18 students with a history book, and 12 students with a science book, how many students have exactly one book?

18. There are 28 students in a class. 14 of the are on a soccer team and 12 are on a football team. If 5 students are on neither of these teams, how many students are on both football and soccer teams?

19. All of the 150 students at MT middle school have to take at least one of two language classes, Spanish and French. 90 students take Spanish, and 80 students take French.
    How many students opted to take both?

20. How many of the first 50 positive integers are divisible by 3 or 5, but not both?

CHAPTER 22
BENCHMARK [Chapter 11-21]

1. Solve for the integer values of x.

   $|2x - 1| = 7$

2. If
   $$\frac{2a - b}{3a + 2b} = \frac{2}{5},$$
   What is $\frac{a}{b}$?

3. For real numbers x and y, define
   $x \spadesuit y = (x + y)(x - y)$.
   What is $4 \spadesuit (3 \spadesuit 2)$?

4. f is a function and $f(x) = 4x - 6$.
   What is the value of $f(2) + f(5)$?

5. The mean, median, and mode of the 7 data values x, 7, 9, 10, 8, 3, 5 are all equal to x.
   What is the value of x?

6. The perimeter of a triangle is 36 feet. If the sides are in the ratio 2; 3; 4, find the length of each side of the triangle.

7. If $2x = 3y$
   What is $\frac{4x + 2y}{2x - y}$?

8. The equilateral triangle AFB and the rectangle ABCD have the same perimeter.
   If $AB = 12$ cm, what is the area of rectangle ABCD?

   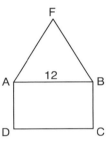

9. If the circumference of a circle is 64π cm, then its area is $x\pi$ cm². What is x?

10. A triangular prism with a volume of 120 cm³ has two edges of the triangular faces measuring 6 cm and 8 cm, as shown. The height of the prism, in cm, is

    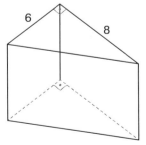

11. What is the largest integer value of a;
    $5 \times (a + 6) < 75$

12. $\sqrt{20 + \sqrt{n}} = 6$
    What is the value of n?

13. $3^{x+1} + 3^{x-2} = 84$
    What is x?

14. If $n(A) = 28$, $n(B) = 40$, and $n(A \cap B) = 12$, what is $n(A \cup B)$?

15. $13 + \dfrac{24}{24 - \dfrac{12}{x + 3}} = 15$
    Find x.

16. Rectangle ABCD has its vertices at A(0, 0), B(6, 0), C(6, 2), and D(0, 2).
    What is the area of the rectangle, in square units?

17. What is the area of the trapezoid?

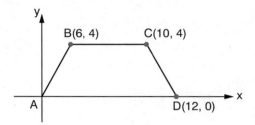

18. If $a = 1.3333...$
       $b = 2.6666...$
    What is $\dfrac{1}{a} + \dfrac{1}{b}$?

19. What is the sum of the mean, median, and mode of the numbers, 3, 4, 0, 4, 2, 5, 0, 4 ?

20. What is the area of the shaded region?

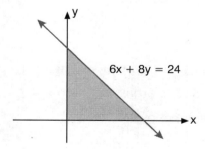

Math Fluency Post-Test & Evaluation

POST-TEST

1. Compute: $88 - 72 \div 4 \times 3$

2. What is the sum of the quotient and remainder when you divide 9660 by 16?

3. What number should go in the blank so that the equation below will be true?

   _____ $\times 100 = 20$

4. What number should go in the blank so that the equation below will be true?

   $8 \div$ _____ $= 32$

5. What is 15% of 80?

6. Find an integer between 100 and 150 that is divisible by 8.

7. Find the least common multiple of 4, 12, and 18.

8. Find the greatest common factor of 32, 48, and 64.

9. Solve for p: $(p - 7) \div 4 = 12$

10. Evaluate $13 \times 103 - 13 \times 3$

POST-TEST

11. Let x, y, and z be integers satisfying:
    $4 < x < y < z < 9$ and $x + z = 12$.
    What is y?

12. Two fractions are equally spaced between $\frac{2}{3}$ and $\frac{7}{3}$. The smaller of the two fraction is

13. If $y = 10 - \frac{10}{2x - 1}$, what is the value of y when $x = \frac{9}{2}$?

14. If $\frac{1 + 2x}{3} = \frac{3 - x}{2}$, what is x?

15. The perimeter of the figure is 30 cm, what is the value of x?

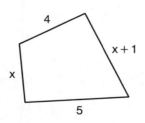

16. $\frac{5}{3} \div \frac{a}{b} = \frac{15}{6}$ is given. What is $\frac{b}{a}$?

17. $\frac{7}{11} \div \left(\frac{7}{11} + \frac{21}{110}\right) = ?$
    Express your answer as lowest term?

18. If the markings on the number line are equally spaced, what is then A?

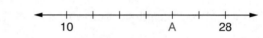

19. What is the sum of the possible values of a if the number below is divisible by 3?
    4725a

20. Suppose f is a linear function and $f(x) = 4x + 6$. What the value of $f(2) + f(-3)$?

21. The perimeter of a triangle is 48 feet. If the sides are in the ratio of 1 : 2 : 3, find the lenght of the longest side?

22. What is the smallest integer value of t;
 $5 \times (t + 4) > 105$

23. If $n(A) = 38$, $n(B) = 50$, and $n(A \cup B) = 80$. What is $n(A \cap B)$?

24. Triangle ABC has its vertices at A(5, 2), B(11, 2), and C(8, 6).
 What is the area of the triangle?

25. What is the sum of the mean, median, and mode of the numbers
 5, 6, 0, 6, 4, 5, 0, 6?

26. What is the value of n if
 $\sqrt{16 + \sqrt{n}} = 5$?

27. The prime factorization of
 $9! = 9 \times 8 \times 7 \times ... \times 1$ is of the form
 $2^a \times 3^b \times 5^c \times 7^d$.
 What is $a + b + c + d$?

28. Determine the quotient when you divide $3\frac{4}{5}$ by $\frac{7}{10}$. Express your answer as a mixed number.

29. If
 $$9 + \cfrac{12}{12 - \cfrac{16}{3x-1}} = 12$$
 What is x?

30. If the circumference of the circle is 36π cm and height of the cylinder is 8, then find the volume.
 Notes: The circumference of the circle is $2\pi r$. The volume of the clynder is $\pi r^2 h$.

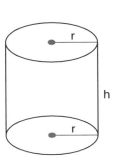

Evaluation — Math Fluency Post-Test

Math Fluency Post-Test & Evaluation

Problem	Topic	My Answer	Correct Answer	Notes
1	Order of operations			
2	Long division			
3	Multiplication			
4	Division			
5	Percent			
6	Divisibility			
7	GCD/LCM			
8	Prime factors			
9	Equations			
10	Distributive property			
11	Integers			
12	Fractions			
13	Arithmetic manipulations			
14	Equations			
15	Geometric equations			
16	Fraction multiplications			
17	Fraction Divisions			
18	Number Lines			
19	Divisibility			
20	Functions			
21	Ratios and Proportions			
22	Inequalities			
23	Sets			
24	Coordinate Geometry			
25	Statistics and Data			
26	Radicals			
27	Prime factorizations			
28	Fraction Divisions			
29	Complex Equations			
30	Geometry			

SOLUTIONS

Pre-Test Solutions	157
Chapter 1 - Problem Set 1	159
Chapter 1 - Problem Set 2	160
Chapter 2 - Problem Set 1	162
Chapter 2 - Problem Set 2	163
Chapter 3 - Problem Set 1	164
Chapter 3 - Problem Set 2	165
Chapter 4 - Problem Set 1	166
Chapter 5 - Problem Set 1	167
Chapter 5 - Problem Set 2	168
Chapter 6 - Problem Set 1	169
Chapter 6 - Problem Set 2	170
Chapter 7 - Problem Set 1	171
Chapter 7 - Problem Set 2	171
Chapter 8 - Problem Set 1	172
Chapter 8 - Problem Set 2	172
Chapter 9 - Problem Set 1	173
Chapter 10 - Benchmark (Chapter 1-9)	174
Chapter 11 - Problem Set 1	175
Chapter 11 - Problem Set 2	176
Chapter 12 - Problem Set 1	177
Chapter 12 - Problem Set 2	178
Chapter 13 - Problem Set 1	179
Chapter 13 - Problem Set 2	179
Chapter 14 - Problem Set 1	180
Chapter 14 - Problem Set 2	180
Chapter 14 - Problem Set 3	181
Chapter 15 - Problem Set 1	182
Chapter 15 - Problem Set 2	182
Chapter 16 - Problem Set 1	184
Chapter 16 - Problem Set 2	184
Chapter 17 - Problem Set 1	185
Chapter 18 - Problem Set 1	186
Chapter 18 - Problem Set 2	187
Chapter 19 - Problem Set 1	189
Chapter 19 - Problem Set 2	190
Chapter 20 - Problem Set 1	192
Chapter 20 - Problem Set 2	193
Chapter 21 - Problem Set 2	195
Chapter 22 - Benchmark (Chapter 11-21)	196
Post-Test Solutions	197

SOLUTIONS — Math Fluency Pre-Test

1. Order of operations:
   $86 - 72 \div 8 \times 3 = 86 - 9 \times 3 = 86 - 27 = 59$

2. Using long division:
   ```
          0503 R 5
      15 )7550
          -0
           75
          -75
            05
           - 0
             50
            -45
              5
   ```
   So, quotient + R = 503 + 5 = 508

3. If a multiplier is greater than the answer, the blank will be a fraction. To find the missing value, divide 90 from both sides and get $\frac{30}{90}$, reduce the fraction and it'll be $\frac{1}{3}$.

4. If the dividend is smaller than the answer, the blank will be a fraction. Since multiplying a number is the same as dividing by its reciprocal, we know that $8 \times 5 = 40$, so the reciprocal of 5 is $\frac{1}{5}$, and the equation would be $8 \div \frac{1}{5} = 40$

5. Finding 15% of 40 is the same as $\frac{15 \times 40}{100}$. The answer here is 6

6. The divisibility rule for 7 is the difference between twice the unit digit of the given number and the remaining part of the given number should be a multiple of 7 or it should be equal to 0. One integer that works is 119:
   Double the unit digit ($9 \times 2 = 18$), Find the different between what remains of the first number and the answer we previously got ($11 - 18 = -7$). -7 is a multiple of 7, so 119 is divisible by 7.

7. Find the factors of the numbers, then find the greatest common factor.
   28: 1, 2, 4, 7, 14, 28
   42: 1, 2, 3, 6, 7, 14, 21, 42
   56: 1, 2, 4, 7, 8, 14, 28, 56
   The GCD of 28, 42, and 56 is 14

8. The prime factorization of $144 = 2^4 \times 3^2$. Hence, the largest prime factor is 3

9. $(x - 9) \div 4 = 12 \rightarrow (x - 9) = 48 \rightarrow x = 57$

10. Use the distributive property of multiplication over addition: $14 \times 8.9 + 86 \times 8.9 = (14 + 86) \times 8.9 = 100 \times 8.9 = 890$

11. The numbers between 5 and 10 can be 6, 7, 8, or 9. If $a + b = 14$, the only two numbers that satisfies the statement is $a = 6$ and $b = 8$. $6 + 8 = 14$, $b = 8$

12. We can make both fractions have the same denominator. To do this, take $\frac{2}{3} \times \frac{4}{4} = \frac{8}{12}$.
    Two fractions that are equally spaced between $\frac{5}{12}$ and $\frac{8}{12}$ would be $\frac{6}{12}$ and $\frac{7}{12}$.
    The larger fraction is $\frac{7}{12}$

13. Replace a with $\frac{4}{3}$, then you'll have
    $15 - \dfrac{15}{3\left(\frac{4}{3}\right) + 1} = 15 - \dfrac{15}{4+1} + 15 - \dfrac{15}{5}$
    $= 15 - 3 = 12$. $b = 12$

14. Multiply both sides by 2 to eliminate the 2 in the denominator on both sides.
    Then you are left with $1 + 3x = 5 - x$. Get x to one side. $1 + 3x = 5 - x \rightarrow 4x = 4 \rightarrow x = 1$

15. Add the sides together and set it equal to 18.
    $3 + 5 + a + 2 + a = 18 \rightarrow 10 + 2a = 18 \rightarrow 2a = 8 \rightarrow a = 4$

PRE-TEST — Math Fluency Pre-Test — SOLUTIONS

16. A hexagon has six sides. Multiply the side length given by 6. Convert $4\frac{3}{4}$ into an improper fraction, which would be $\frac{19}{4}$.
Then multiply by 6. $6 \times \frac{19}{4} = \frac{114}{4} = \frac{57}{2}$

17. To find $\frac{x}{y}$, multiply 5×2 to get x, the numerator, which is 10. Then multiply 6×3 to get y, the denominator, which is 18.
To make it $\frac{x}{y}$, flip the numerator and denominator to get $\frac{18}{10}$. $\frac{18}{10}$ in simplest form is $\frac{9}{5}$.

18. Find out how much distance is between –8 and 4, which is 12. Then count how many spaces there are on the number line, which is 6 (not the tick marks, but the spaces in between).
Then take $12 \div 6 = 2$. Each tick mark goes up by 2. In this case, A = 2.

19. The sum of the digits of the number must be divisible by 3. Possible values of x could be 2, 5, or 8.

20. Plug in -2 for x in the equation, then plug in 4 for x. The two answers you get are $f(-2) = -2$ and $f(4) = 22$. $-2 + 22 = 20$

21. If the sides of the triangle are 2, 3, and 4, the perimeter would be 9. To get from 9 to 36 in perimeter, you have to multiply by 4. If you multiply each side by 4, you get $8 + 12 + 16 = 36$. The longest side is 16.

22. If you plug in 3 for a, you would get $6 \times 8 = 48$, but since the answer has to be lower than 48, the largest value you can use is 2. $6 \times (2 + 5) = 42$

23. For any two finite sets A and B,
$n(A \cup B) = n(A) + n(B) - n(A \cap B)$.
If we plug in the numbers for each part of the equation, we would get $40 + 48 - n(A \cap B) = 70$. Solve, and get $n(A \cap B) = 18$

24. The area of a triangle is (base × height) ÷ 2. Since A and B both have a point at y = 2, the distance between those points is 6, which is the base. The height can be found from the base, which is at 2, to the point C, which is at y = 8. The distance between 2 and 8 is 6, which is the height. Base × height is $6 \times 6 = 36$, $36 \div 2 = 18$

25. The mean is the sum of the numbers divided by how many numbers are in the list, which equals 8. The median is the number in the middle of the list when the list goes from least to greatest, which is 4.5. The mode is the number that appears the most often in the list, which is 6. The sum would be $8 + 6 + 4.5 = 18.5$

26. The $\sqrt{16} = 4$, meaning we have to get x to equal 16. $9 + 7 = 16$, and $\sqrt{49} = 7$. This means x = 49

27. The prime factorization of 8! is $2^7 \times 3^2 \times 5^1 \times 7^1$.
$a + b + c + d = 7 + 2 + 1 + 1 = 11$

28. Convert $4\frac{5}{6}$ into an improper fraction, $\frac{29}{5}$. Then take the reciprocal of $\frac{2}{3}$, which is $\frac{3}{2}$, and multiply the fractions.
$\frac{29}{6} \times \frac{3}{2} = \frac{87}{12}$. Converting it into a mixed number is $7\frac{3}{12}$, which equals $7\frac{1}{4}$.

29. Use the coverup method. $\dfrac{12}{6 - \dfrac{12}{5x+1}} = 3$
$\rightarrow 6 - \dfrac{12}{5x+1} = 4 \rightarrow \dfrac{12}{5x+1} = 2$
$\rightarrow 5x + 1 = 6 \rightarrow x = 1$

30. Find the radius to find the area of the top of the cylinder. If $C = 2\pi r$, then $16\pi = 2\pi r$, and r = 8. The formula would be $\pi 8^2 \times 8 = 512\pi$

SOLUTIONS — Whole Numbers & Operations — CHAPTER 1

Problem Set 1

1. Using the order of operations
   $2 \times 4^2 - (8 \div 2)$
   $= 2 \times 4^2 - 4 = 2 \times 16 - 4 = 32 - 4 = 28$

2. Using the order of operations
   $2 \times 0 \times 1 + 1 = 0 \times 1 + 1 = 0 + 1 = 1$

3. Using the order of operations (From left to right, completing multiplication/division first, then addition/subtraction)
   $2 + 2 \times 2 - 2 \div 2 + 2$
   $= 2 + 4 - 2 \div 2 + 2 = 2 + 4 - 1 + 2 = 7$

4. Using the order of operations
   $-2 \times (6 \div 3)^2 = -2 \times (2)^2 = -2 \times 4 = -8$

5. Using the order of operations for each expression to find the multiple of five (multiplication first, then addition)
   a) $1 \times 2 + 3 + 4 = 2 + 3 + 4 = 9$
   b) $1 + 2 \times 3 + 4 = 1 + 6 + 4 = 11$
   c) $1 + 2 \times 3 \times 4 = 1 + 24 = 25$
   d) $1 \times 2 \times 3 \times 4 = 24$
   C = 25, a multiple of 5

6. Since $\frac{10}{20}$ can be reduced to $\frac{1}{2}$, we need to find what a is so that $8 + a = 10$
   $8 + 2 = 10$
   $a = 2$

7. Using the order of operations for each equation to find which equation is true (multiplication first, then addition)
   a) $1 \times 8 + 8 \times 1 = 18 \rightarrow 8 + 8 = 16$
   b) $0 \times 9 + 9 \times 0 = 18 \rightarrow 0 + 0 = 0$
   c) $2 \times 7 + 7 \times 2 = 28 \rightarrow 14 + 14 = 28$
   d) $3 \times 6 + 6 \times 3 = 18 \rightarrow 18 + 18 = 36$
   C is correct

8. Using associative and commutative properties of multiplication $25 \times (13 \times 4)$
   $= 25 \times (4 \times 13) = (25 \times 4) \times 13 = 100 \times 13$
   $= 1300$

9. Using the order of operations
   $5 - 3 \times 4^3 \div (7 - 1)$
   $= 5 - 3 \times 4^3 \div 6 = 5 - 3 \times 64 \div 6$
   $= 5 - 192 \div 6 = 5 - 32 = -27$

10. Using the order of operations $76 - 72 \div 8 \times 3$
    $= 76 - 9 \times 3 = 76 - 27 = 49$

11. Use long division to find the remainder

    ```
          70510 ' 3
       7 | 493573      | 70,000
           490000      | 70,000
           ------      |   +
             3573      |
             3500      |  500
           ------      |   +
               73      |
               70      |   10
           ------      | ------
                3      | 70510 ' 3
    ```

12. Using the order of operations
    $6 + 3 \times (8 - 3) \div 5$
    $= 6 + 3 \times 5 \div 5 = 6 + 15 \div 5 = 6 + 3 = 9$

13. Using the order of operations
    $16 - 4 \div (1 \div 4) + 1$
    $= 16 - 4 \div \frac{1}{4} + 1 = 16 - 16 + 1 = 1$

14. Using the order of operations
    $80 - 64 \div 8 \times 4$
    $= 80 - 8 \times 4 = 80 - 32 = 48$

15. Find what the left side of the equation equals first
    $10 \times 20 \times 30 \times 40 \times 50 = 12{,}000{,}000$
    Then multiply the numbers on the right side
    $100 \times 4 \times 300 = 120{,}000$
    Divide the value on the left side from the value on the right side to find the missing number
    $12{,}000{,}000 \div 120{,}000 = 100$

CHAPTER 1 — Whole Numbers & Operations — SOLUTIONS

16. Multiples of 5 include any whole number that ends with a 0 or 5. Of these numbers, the even whole numbers can only end in 0. Therefore, the only numbers that are even and multiples of 5 between 1 and 99 are:
    10, 20, 30, 40, 50, 60, 70, 80, 90
    In total, there are nine numbers

17. Using the distributive property of multiplication over addition $81 \times 5^2 + 19 \times 5^2$
    $= 5^2 (81 + 19) = 5^2 (100) = 25 \times 100 = 2500$

18. Using the order of operations
    $-12^2 + 5[8 \div (3 - 1)]$
    $= -12^2 + 5[8 \div 2] = -12^2 + 5(4) = -144 + 5(4)$
    $= -144 + 20 = -124$

19. Find the value of the first part of the equation
    $3 \times 3 \times 5 \times 5 \times 7 \times 9 = 14175$
    Find the value of the second part of the equation
    $3 \times 3 \times 7 \times m \times m = 63 \times m^2$
    Divide the first value by 63
    $14175 \div 63 = 225$
    Take the square root of the answer to find m
    $\sqrt{225} = \pm 15$
    m = 15 or -15

20. A is incorrect because if n = 1
    2023 − 3(1) = 2020
    B is incorrect because if n = 1
    2023 + 1 = 2024
    C is incorrect because if n = 2
    2023(2) = 4046
    D is correct because if n = 1, 2, 3
    2023 + 2(1) = 2025
    2023 + 2(2) = 2027
    2023 + 2(3) = 2029
    Each multiple of 2 that is added to 2023 will keep 2023 an odd number

Problem Set 2

1. Using associative and commutative properties of multiplication $(-2.5 \times 0.73) \times 4$
   $= 0.73 \times (-2.5 \times 4) = 0.73 \times -10 = -7.3$

2. Using distributive property of multiplication over addition $14 \times 8.9 + 86 \times 8.9$
   $= 8.9 (14 + 86) = 8.9 \times 100 = 890$

3. Using distributive property of multiplication over subtraction
   $1513 \times 692 - 1513 \times 691$
   $= 1513 (692 - 691) = 1513 \times 1 = 1513$

4. Any three-digit number multiplied by 1001 will repeat itself in the answer: $111 \times 1001 = 111{,}111$
   Therefore $123{,}123 \div 1001 = 123$

5. Multiply both values to find and fill in the missing numbers
   $879 \times 2 = 1758$; $879 \times 90 = 79110$;
   $879 \times 400 = 315600$
   x = 1; y = 9; z = 1
   1 + 9 + 1 = 11

6. If $21 \times 31 = 651$, then you must add 31 + 21 + 1 to 651 since you are adding a 22 and 32 to the total
   651 + 31 + 21 + 1 = 704

7. Use the distributive property of multiplication over addition
   $4 \times 99 + 3 \times 99 + 2 \times 99 + 99$
   $= 99 (4 + 3 + 2) + 99 = 990$

8. First reduce the numbers by lining up the top half of the expression with the bottom half, then add the remaining numbers

   $175 + 278 + 479$
   $\underline{-75 + 78 + 279}$
   $100 + 200 + 200 = 500$

SOLUTIONS — Whole Numbers & Operations — CHAPTER 1

9. $31^2 = 961$, and $32^2 = 1024$. All numbers that are ≤ 31 will be a square number less than 1000. In total, there are 31 numbers.

10. Find the number of terms in the sequence using the formula:
    $t_n = a + (n - 1)d \rightarrow 100 = 5 + (n - 1)5 \rightarrow$
    $100 = 5n \rightarrow n = 20$
    Use this formula to find the sum:
    $S_n = n((a_1 + a_n)/2)$
    $S_{20} = 20((5 + 100)/2) = 1050$

11. Find the number of terms in the sequence using the formula:
    $t_n = a + (n - 1)d \rightarrow 99 = 18 + (n - 1)9 \rightarrow 99 = 9 + 9n \rightarrow n = 10$
    Use this formula to find the sum:
    $S_n = n((a_1 + a_n)/2)$
    $S_{10} = 10((18 + 99)/2) = 585$

12. Use this formula to find the sum of the numbers in the parenthesis: $S_n = n((a_1 + a_n)/2)$
    $S_{10} = 10((101 + 119)/2) = 1100$,
    then multiply by 4
    $1100 \times 4 = 4400$

13. A is incorrect because the three consecutive numbers closest to reach 14 when added are $3 + 4 + 5 = 12$ and $4 + 5 + 6 = 15$
    B is incorrect because the three consecutive numbers closest to reach 7 are $1 + 2 + 3 = 6$ and $2 + 3 + 4 = 9$
    C is incorrect because the three consecutive numbers closest to reach 26 are $7 + 8 + 9 = 24$ and $8 + 9 + 10 = 27$
    E is incorrect because the three consecutive numbers closest to reach 38 is $11 + 12 + 13 = 36$ and $12 + 13 + 14 = 39$
    D is correct because $8 + 9 + 10 = 27$

14. Find $(1 + 2 + 3 + 4 + 5)^2 = 15^2 = 225$
    List cubed numbers starting at 1^3 and add them together until you reach 225
    $1^3 + 2^3 = 9$
    $1^3 + 2^3 + 3^3 = 36$
    $1^3 + 2^3 + 3^3 + 4^3 = 100$
    $1^3 + 2^3 + 3^3 + 4^3 + 5^3 = 225 \rightarrow n = 5$

15. Any number multiplied by 5 will end in either a 0 or 5. If that same number is also multiplied by 2, it must end in a 0. Therefore, the ones place will have a 0.

16. To maximize this value, the largest number should be the exponent, and the base should be the second largest number. This would mean that $b^c = 3^4 = 81$. If we have $a = 2$, then we would get: $2 \times 3^4 = 162$

17. Using the order of operations
    $(3^3 - 3) \div 4 \times 6 \div 1 = (27 - 3) \div 4 \times 6 \div 1$
    $= 24 \div 4 \times 6 \div 1 = 36$

18. Reduce the equation:
    $(10 \,?\, 5) + 4 - (10 - 9) = 5 \rightarrow (10 \,?\, 5) + 3 = 5$
    Subtract 3 from 5
    $5 - 3 = 2$
    In order to get 2 from 10 and 5, we must divide 10 by 5, so the correct symbol would be $\div$

19. If a and b are two distinct single digits, then the largest digits we can use are 9 and 8. To maximize the expression, we would set a equal to 9 and b equal to 8
    $7(9) + 5(8) = 103$

20. If you take 26×300 and 13×600, you get 7,800 as an answer for both. This leaves $A = 26$ and $B = 13$. $B - A = 13 - 26 = -13$

CHAPTER 2 — Integers & Operations — SOLUTIONS

Problem Set 1

1. Find the solution to 9120 − 9124 = 86. Then do 210 − 86 to find what the box is so both sides equal the same. 210 − 86 = 124

2. 3 × 5 = 15 and 7 × 9 = 63. If you add 15 + 63, you'll get 78. From left to right, the operations would be: × + ×

3. Since the answer is negative and one of the numbers is 11, that means you must add a negative number larger than −11 to get the answer. In this case, 11 + (−37) = −26

4. By placing 3 with y,
$$\frac{3^3 + 3}{3^2 - 3} + \frac{27 + 3}{9 - 3} = \frac{30}{6} = 5$$

5. P added together three times needs to end in 7, 9 + 9 + 9 = 27, so P = 9. That makes the sum 1997. After carrying the 2 from 27 to the tens place, you have 2 + 7 + Q + Q. The sum needs to end in 9, and 2 + 7 + 5 + 5 = 19. This means Q = 5. The sum of 5 + 9 = 14

6. 13 is prime, so a or b will be 1 or 13. 52 can be divided by 13, so b × c = 13 × 4. The common factor, b, is 13. Therefore, a = 1 and c = 4. 1 × 13 × 4 = 52.

7. E is correct. Try examples like 8 − 5 = 3; 12 − 7 = 5; 46 − 19 = 27. An even number minus an odd number will always be odd.

8. y + 3 in the tens and ones place will equal the same number. If y = 7, then 7 + 3 = 10 and x = 0. y − x = 7 − 0 = 7

9. The sum of the first 100 positive multiples is similar to the sum of the first 100 positive integers but with an extra 0. The answer will be the same only with an extra 0: 50,500

10. 153 ÷ 3 = 51. 51 is the middle number. Take 51 − 1 and 51 + 1 to find the consecutive numbers 50, 51, 52. The largest is 52.

11. Use the order of operations:
10 − 6 = 4 → 5 × 4 ÷ 2 = 10

12. Find 10 + 20 = 30. Take 30 − 5 = 25. The box = 25

13. Find 3 + 2 = 5, so A = 5. In the hundreds place, 5 + 4 = 9, so C = 9. In the tens place, B + 5 = 9, so B = 4. A + B + C = 5 + 4 + 9 = 18.

14. In the thousands place, two numbers must equal 2, which is 1 + 1. In the hundreds place, two numbers must equal 0, which is 0 + 0. In the tens place, the smiley face value is 0 and the square value is 1, and 0 + 1 = 1.
In the ones place, if the square equals 1, then we have triangle + 1 = 3, triangle = 2. Square + triangle + smile = 1 + 2 + 0 = 3

15. To get from −3 to 0, we add 3. To get from 0 to 5 we add 5. Add 3 + 5 = 8 degrees Celsius

16. Subtracting +32 is the same as subtracting 32, so take −22 − 32 = −54. Adding +10 means to add positive 10. −54 + 10 = −44

17. Taking the difference means to subtract.
−11 − 9 = −20

18. B is false because the opposite of −13 isn't −13 but positive 13.

19. The additive inverse of −3.5 is 3.5. The additive inverse of 5.3 is −5.3. 3.5 + (−5.3) = 3.5 − 5.3 = −1.8

SOLUTIONS — Integers & Operations — CHAPTER 2

20. Use the sum of an arithmetic sequence for the numbers being added first (50, 46, 42, 38...)

    $S_n = \frac{n}{2}[2a + (n-1)d] =$

    $S_n = \frac{13}{2}[2(50) + (13-1)-4] = 338.$

    Then use it for the numbers being subtracted (48, 44, 40, 36...) $S_n = \frac{n}{2}[2a + (n-1)d] =$

    $S_n = \frac{12}{2}[2(48) + (12-1)-4] = 312.$

    Subtract $338 - 312 = 26$

Problem Set 2

1. Use the order of operations: $4 - 8((-1)^2 - 4(-3))$
   $4 - 8(1 + 12) = 4 - 8(13) = 4 - 104 = -100$

2. Use the order of operations: $5 + (-6)^2 \div (2 \cdot 3^2)$
   $5 + (-6)^2 \div (2 \cdot 3^2) = 5 + 36 \div (2 \cdot 9)$
   $= 5 + 36 \div 18 = 7$

3. $x^4 - 2x = 2^4 - 2(2) = 16 - 4 = 12$

4. $x^2 - 4x = (-2)^2 - 4(-2) = 4 - 8 = 12$

5. $3a^b + 4b^a = 3(2)^3 + 4(3)^2 = 3(8) + 4(9)$
   $= 24 + 36 = 60$

6. Use the order of operations: $(-3) - (3 \times (-4) + 7)$
   $(-3) - (3 \times (-4) + 7) = (-3) - (-12 + 7)$
   $= (-3) - (-5) = 2$

7. $\frac{5x + 2}{x + 2} = \frac{5(2) + 2}{2 + 2} = \frac{12}{4} = 3$

8. $3x^2 - xy^2 = 3(2)^2 - 2(3)^2 = 3(4) - 2(9) = 12 - 18$
   $= -6$

9. $7 \times a + 18 \div (a + b) = 7 \times 2 + 18 \div (2 + 4)$
   $= 14 + 18 \div 6 = 14 + 3 = 17$

10. $10 - 5 \times b \times (10 - a) = 10 - 5 \times 4 \times (10 - 2)$
    $= 10 - 5 \times 4 \times (8) = 10 - 20 \times 8 = 10 - 160$
    $= -150$

11. Reverse the operations: $360 \div 12 = 30$

12. $(4 \times 4) + 4 \times 4 = 32$; $4 \times (4 + 4) \times 4 = 128$;
    $4 \times 4 + (4 \times 4) = 32$. Two numbers, 32 and 128

13. Factor pairs of 36:
    $(1 \times 36)\ (2 \times 18)\ (3 \times 12)\ (4 \times 9)\ (6 \times 6)$
    Of these pairs, adding $4 + 9 = 13$.
    The larger number is 13.

14. Take the square root of 1000, which is ~31.62. This means that any number $\leq 31^2$ will be below 1000. This means there are 30 perfect squares below 1000, not including 1.

15. The number in the tens digits is 2.
    Multiply $6 \times 7 = 42$, then $8 \times 9 = 72$. Now you have $5 \times 42 \times 72$. If you start to multiply the ones places, you get $2 \times 2 \times 5 = 20$, making the 0 in the ones place an the 2 in the tens place.

16. $4^3 + 6^2 = 10^x = 64 + 36 = 10x \rightarrow x = 2$

17. Try $a = 1, b = 3, c = 5, d = 7$: $(c-b)(d-a)$
    $= (5 - 3)(7 - 1) = 12$
    Try $a = 3, b = 5, c = 7, d = 9$: $(c-b)(d-a)$
    $= (7 - 5)(9 - 3) = 12$
    The answer will always be 12.

18. Use the order of operations:
    $-3(5 - 6) - 4(2 - 3) = -3(-1) - 4(-1) = 3 + 4 = 7$

19. Find factors of 15: 1, 3, 5, 15. 15 can be divided by 4 numbers, so x can be 4 distinct values.

20. 8 increases by 16 when tripled.
    $8 \times 3 = 24$, $8 + 16 = 24$

CHAPTER 3 — Primes & Divisibility — SOLUTIONS

Problem Set 1

1. 15 has four positive divisors: 1, 3, 5 15

2. The smallest prime bigger than 17 is 19, because 19 can only be divided by 1 and 19.

3. There are three primes between 40 and 50: 41, 43, 47. Each number can only be divided by 1 and itself.

4. List of perfect cubes under 91 : $1^3 = 1$, $2^3 = 8$, $3^3 = 27$, $4^3 = 64$. $27 + 64 = 91$ → $3^3 + 4^3 = 91$

5. There are 99 integers less than 600 and greater than 500. Since we don't include 500 or 600 in our count, there would only be 99 integers.

6. Take $537 - 342 = 195$. "Inclusive" means to include all numbers in the count, meaning there are actually 196 whole numbers between 342 and 537.

7. Take $104 - 32 = 72$. Take $72 \div 2$ to find the number of even numbers, which is 36 numbers, then add 1 to include all numbers in the count, so there are 37 numbers.

8. We subtract the biggest number by the smallest number to find out how many integers are in between those numbers, but you have to add 1 to include the last or first number in the entire list.

9. Start with taking the highest even number and the lowest even number between 33 and 97, which is 34 and 96. Subtract $96 - 34 = 62$. Take $62 \div 2$ to find the number of even numbers, which is 31. Add 1 to include all the numbers in the count, which is 32.

10. The prime factorization of 28 is 2^2 C 7 → $2^2 = 4$; $4 \times 7 = 28$

11. Find the least common multiple (LCM) of each.
    8: 8, 16, 24, 32, 40, 48, 56, 64, 72, 80
    12: 12, 24, 36, 48, 60, 72, 84, 96
    18: 18, 36, 54, 72
    The LCM of 8, 12, and 18 is 72, which is between 70 & 80.

12. For integers with two digits, there are 3 integers: 33, 66, 99. For three digit integers, this will include any integer with the same three digits: 111, 222, 333, 444, 555, 666, 777, 888, 999. In total, there are 12.

13. List of primes under 21: 2, 3, 5, 7, 11, 13, 17, 19. The two numbers that work are $19 + 2 = 21$. The product of $19 \times 2 = 38$.

14. The prime factors of $2010 = 2 \times 3 \times 5 \times 67$. The sum of $2 + 3 + 5 + 67 = 77$.

15. Taking a number (a) times another number (b) is the same as taking a number (a) divided by the inverse of a number ($\frac{1}{b}$).
    If $8 \times 4 = 32$, then $8 \div \frac{1}{4} = 32$.

16. The divisibility rule for dividing a number by 8 is if the number formed by the last three digits of a number is divisible by 8. Possible answers include: 104, 112, 120, 128, 136, 144

17. Find the LCM of 16 and 20 that is between 200 & 300.
    16 (starting at 10): 160, 176, 192, 208, 224, 240
    20 (starting at 10): 200, 220, 240
    The integer is 240.

18. The prime factorization of $144 = 2^4 \times 3^2$. The largest prime factor is 3.

19. Factors of 48: 1, 2, 3, 4, 6, 8, 12, 16, 24, 48
    Factors of 72: 1, 2, 3, 4, 6, 8, 9, 12, 18, 24, 36, 72
    The number they have in common that's between 10 and 20 is 12.

SOLUTIONS — Primes & Divisibility — CHAPTER 3

20. Find the LCM of 3, 4, and 5
    3: 3, 6, 9, 12, 15, 18, 21, 24, 27, 30, 33, 36, 39, 42, 45, 48, 51, 54, 57, 60
    4: 4, 8, 12, 16, 20, 24, 28, 32, 36, 40, 44, 48, 52, 56, 60
    5: 5, 10, 15, 20, 25, 30, 35, 40, 45, 50, 55, 60
    The LCM of 3, 4, and 5 between 1 and 100 is 60.

Problem Set 2

1. If you take the 3, 4, and 5 out of the ones place and just do 2000 × 2000 × 2000, it will divide evenly by 10 since it ends in zero.
   If you do 3 × 4 × 5 = 60, that also divides evenly by 10, so there is no remainder.

2. Factors of 24: 1, 2, 3, 4, 6, 8, 12, 24.
   1 + 2 + 3 + 4 + 6 + 8 + 12 + 24 = 60

3. Prime factorization of 90: 2 × 3 × 3 × 5
   2 + 3 + 3 + 5 = 13

4. iii is correct because the divisibility rule for 10 is that the last digit must end in 0, and the divisibility rule for 3 is that the sum of the digits of the number must be divisible by 3

5. The sum of the digits must equal a number divisible by 3, so the possible values of m could be 1, 4, and 7. So, the sum is 1 + 4 + 7 = 12.

6. There are only 2 values m could be, because a number is divisible by 5 if it ends in 0 or 5. So the sum of the possible values of m is only 5 slace 0 does not work divisible by 3.

7. If B = 0, 60 can be divided by 4. A can be any number, and if we're trying to find the smallest value of A + B, we can use 0 + 0 = 0.

8. 9 cannot be a + b, since a number is divisible by 18 if it can be divided by 2 and 9.
   If a + b + 4 = 13, the only number that can be c is 5, which doesn't make the number divisible by 2.

9. The sum of the digits must equal 9.
   So, a + b can be 3, 6, 9, 12, and 15.

10. Use the commutative property of multiplication.
    Do 25 × 8 = 200, and 25 × 8 = 200 again.
    Do 200 × 200 = 40,000.
    There are 4 zeros in the product.

11. The remainder is 3. For example, 46 ÷ 6 leaves a remainder of 4, and 47 ÷ 6 leaves a remainder of 5. 46 + 47 = 93. 93 ÷ 6 = 15 with a remainder of 3.

12. m + n could be 4 or 13 for the sum of the digits to be divisible by 9.

13. Find the factors of 60: 1, 2, 3, 4, 5, 6, 10, 12, 15, 20, 30, 60. There are 12 values that x could be.

14. Since 2023 is an odd number, one of the prime numbers must be 2. But 2021 is not a prime number, so there are no ways 2023 can be written as the sum of two prime numbers.

15. $2^4 = 2 \times 2 \times 2 \times 2 = 16$. $5^2 = 25$.
    25 × 16 = 400

16. There are 7: 4, 9, 25, 49, 121, 169, 289. They can each only be divided by 1, their square root, and themselves.

17. Since 61 is odd, one prime number is 2 and the other is 59. The product of 2 × 59 = 118.

18. M = 3 or 9. The sum of the digits have to be divisible by 3, and the last two digits must be a number divisible by 4.

19. B must be 0 if it divides by 20. A can be any number. To find the minimum value, we can use A = 0 and B = 0, 0 + 0 = 0

20. x can equal 4. y must be 0 if it can divide by 4 and 5, and for the number to divide by 3, the sum must be a number divisible by 3.
    5 + 3 + 4 + 0 = 12.

CHAPTER 4 — Least Common Multiple(LCM) & Greatest Common Divisor (GCD) — SOLUTIONS

Problem Set 1

1. Numbers divisible by 15, 12 and another number would have to be a multiple of 15 and 12, so the answer is E) 60

2. Numbers divisible by 14, 10 and another number would have to be a multiple of 14 and 10, so the answer is A) 10

3. GCD (24, 40) = 8   LCM (24, 40) = 120
   $8 \times 120 = 960$. The GCD (24, 40) and the LCM (24,40) equals 960, and $24 \times 40 = 960$

4. There are three distinct prime factors:
   $2 \times 2 \times 3 \times 5$ (2 shows up twice)

5. 12: 12, 24, 36, 48, 60, 72   18: 36, 54, 72
   24: 48, 72   LCM (12, 18, 24) = 72

6. 72: $2^3 \times 3^2$, 80: $2^4 \times 5$
   The common factors here is $2^3 = 8$.

7. 24: $2^3 \times 3$, 30: $2 \times 3 \times 5$, 36: $2^2 \times 3^2$
   Take the base with the largest power and any other integers: $2^3 \times 3^2 \times 5 = 360$

8. 4: 2^2, 12: $2^2 \times 3$, 18: 2×3^2
   Take the base with the largest power and any other integers: $2^2 \times 3^2 = 36$

9. 32: 2^5, 48: $2^4 \times 3$, 64: 2^6
   The common factors are $2^4 = 16$

10. $a \times b$ = GCD $\times$ LCM. If b = 12, then we can set this up as $a \times 12 = 216$. $a = 18$

11. Divisors of 24: 1, 2, 3, 4, 6, 8, 12, 24
    Divisors of 30: 1, 2, 3, 5, 6, 10, 15, 30
    Common factors: 1, 2, 3, 6

12. Since the last digit needs to end in 0 or 5 for it to be divisible by 15, the only options are the integers that end in 0 because you can't divide an integer that ends in 5 by 12. The numbers would be: 120, 180, 240, 300, 360, 420, 480, 540, 600, 660, 720, 780, 840, 900, and 960. There are 15 numbers listed.

13. There are 12 numbers between 1 and 110 that are divisible by 9, and 6 can only be divided by even numbers. Of the 12 numbers listed, half of them are even, so there are 6 numbers that can divided both 6 and 9

14. Multiply the numerator and denominator of
    $\frac{17}{80} \times 4 = \frac{68}{320}$ and $\frac{7}{160} \times 2 = \frac{14}{320}$ to get a common denominator on the bottom, then you'll have $\frac{68}{320} - \frac{14}{320} + \frac{13}{320} = \frac{14}{320} = \frac{67}{320}$, which is its lowest form.

15. The LCM (m, m + 1) = m(m + 1) = m^2 + m. This is because the LCM of two integers that are right next to each other can only have the lowest multiple when they are multiplied together.

16. You can find the GCD (210, 300, 360).
    Use prime factorization. 210: $2 \times 3 \times 5 \times 7$,
    300: $2^2 \times 3 \times 5^2$, 360: $2^3 \times 3^2 \times 5$
    The common factor is $2 \times 3 \times 5 = 30$,
    so the greatest value of x = 30

17. $a \times b$ = LCM $\times$ GCD. a is x in this case.
    LCM = 108, GCD = 9b = 36.
    $x \times 36 = 9 \times 108$. $x \times 36 = 972$. x = 27

18. 16: 2^4, 20: $2^2 \times 5$
    LCM (16, 20) = $2^4 \times 5 = 80 = k$
    LCM (12, 80): 12: $2^2 \times 3$, 80: $2^4 \times 5$
    LCM (12, 80) = $2^4 \times 3 \times 5 = 240$

19. LCM (1, 2, 3, 4, 5, 6) = 6!   To find 6!, find the prime factorization of each integer:
    1 = 1; 2 = 2; 3 = 3; 4 = 2^2; 5 = 5; 6 = 2×3,
    Take the base with the largest power and other remaining integers: $2^2 \times 3 \times 5 = 60$

20. Find the LCM (3, 4, 6) = 12
    A cube would be $12^3 = 1728$.
    Take $3 \times 4 \times 6 = 72$.
    Divide 1728 by 72 to know how many bricks are needed to make a cube. $1728 \div 72 = 24$ bricks to make a 12 $\times$ 12 $\times$ 12 cube.

SOLUTIONS — Fractions & Operations — CHAPTER 5

Problem Set 1

1. D is closest to 0 because it is the smallest fraction that comes after 0.

2. To find x and y, we must multiply the top and bottom of $\frac{1}{15}$ by 4 to find x and then 2 to find y. Multiplying by 4 gives us $\frac{4}{60}$, and multiplying by 2 gives us $\frac{2}{30}$. x + y = 4 + 2 = 6.

3. The reciprocal of –2 is $-\frac{1}{2}$, and the reciprocal of –1 is $-\frac{1}{1}$, or just -1. Therefore, $-\frac{1}{2}$ is greater than –1.

4. $(6 \div -3)(4 - 12) = -2(-8) = 16$

5. B is bigger because multiplying fractions will usually give a smaller answer, in this case it's $\frac{1}{8}$. Dividing fractions will give a larger answer, and here it's 2.

6. B is smaller because $\frac{1}{4} - \frac{1}{5} = \frac{1}{20}$, which is smaller than $\frac{1}{3} - \frac{1}{5}$, which is $\frac{2}{15}$.

7. Multiply the top across: $1 \times 2 \times 3 = 6$. Multiply the bottom across: $2 \times 3 \times 4 = 24$. $\frac{6}{24}$ can reduce to $\frac{1}{4}$.

8. Add the two whole numbers first, $4 + 1 = 5$. Then find a common denominator for the fractions, which is 45. Multiply $\frac{4}{15} \times 3 = \frac{12}{45}$. Add the fractions, $\frac{3}{45} + \frac{12}{45} = \frac{15}{45} = \frac{1}{3}$. The answer is $5\frac{1}{3}$

9. Since the left denominator is multiplied by 9 to get 63, the top must also be multiplied by 9. $3 \times 9 = 27$. x = 27

10. x would be 16, since $\frac{3}{4} + \frac{4}{16} = \frac{3}{4} + \frac{1}{4} = 1$

11. The smallest is $\frac{1}{2}$ because the other fractions have numerators that are above what would equal $\frac{1}{2}$ if you reduced them.

12. The common denominator is 12. Multiply the top and bottom of $\frac{2}{3} \times 4 = \frac{8}{12}$. Multiply the top and bottom of $\frac{1}{4} \times 3 = \frac{3}{12}$. The equation is now $\frac{7}{12} - \frac{8}{12} + \frac{3}{12} = \frac{2}{12} = \frac{1}{6}$

13. The common denominator is 42. Multiply the top and bottom of $\frac{3}{14} \times 3 = \frac{9}{42}$. Multiply the top and bottom of $\frac{5}{7} \times 6 = \frac{30}{42}$. Multiply the top and bottom of $\frac{1}{21} \times 2 = \frac{2}{42}$. The equation is now $\frac{9}{42} - \frac{30}{42} + \frac{2}{42} = -\frac{19}{42}$

14. Reverse the operation to find a. $\frac{3}{25} \times \frac{1}{5} = \frac{3}{125}$. $\frac{3}{125} \times 25 = \frac{75}{125} = \frac{3}{5}$

15. $\frac{17}{4}$ is above 4, because $\frac{16}{4} = 4$, and $\frac{25}{2}$ is less than 13, since $\frac{26}{2} = 13$, so the answer could be B, C, or D

16. Multiply $4 \times \frac{13}{13} = \frac{52}{13}$. $63 - 52 = 11$. x = 11

17. Multiply $\frac{1}{9} \times 2$ on top and bottom and it'll be $\frac{2}{18}$. $\frac{2}{18} + \frac{1}{18} = \frac{3}{18}$ which can reduce down to $\frac{1}{6}$, so x = 6

18. $(7 + 7)(7 + \frac{1}{7}) = 14(\frac{49}{7} + \frac{1}{7}) = 14(\frac{50}{7}) = 100$

19. C is correct because $\frac{13}{4}$ is little bigger than 3 because $\frac{12}{4} = 3$, and $\frac{13}{4}$ goes above that.

20. $(\frac{4}{14} + \frac{20}{10}) \times 10 = (\frac{24}{10})10 = 24$

Math Fluency — 167

CHAPTER 5 — Fractions & Operations — SOLUTIONS

Problem Set 2

1. Finding the lowest common denominator is similar to finding the LCM of the denominators. Here, the LCM is 60, so the lowest common denominator would also be 60.

2. Dividing two fractions is that same as taking one fraction and multiplying it by its reciprocal. You can do $\frac{1}{2} \times 6 = 3$

3. $(3 \times 4) \div (\frac{1}{5} \times \frac{1}{4}) = 12 (\frac{1}{20}) = \frac{12}{20} = \frac{6}{10} = 0.6$

4. Multiply the numerators across: $6 \times 4 \times 7 = 168$. Multiply the denominators across: $8 \times 6 \times 14 = 672$. $\frac{168}{672} = \frac{1}{4}$

5. Multiply the numerator and denominator of the left fraction by 2, which will be $\frac{10}{98}$. $\frac{10}{98} + \frac{3}{98} = \frac{13}{98}$

6. Since we are adding two different fractions, we have to find a common denominator for 5. In this case, we would multiply $\frac{5}{1} \times \frac{5}{5} = \frac{25}{5}$. Take $\frac{25}{5} + \frac{1}{5} = \frac{26}{5}$. This would end up being $\frac{1}{\frac{26}{5}}$, which would be the same as $1 \times \frac{5}{26} = \frac{5}{26}$.

7. Start with the bottom of the fraction first. $2 + \frac{1}{2} = \frac{5}{2}$. Then we have $1 + \frac{1}{\frac{5}{2}}$. This is the same as $1 + (1 \times \frac{2}{5}) = 1\frac{2}{5}$.

8. $\frac{3}{19} \times 100 = \frac{300}{19}$. $\frac{3}{19} \times 81 = \frac{243}{19}$. $\frac{300}{19} - \frac{243}{19} = \frac{57}{19} = 3$

9. We can take each whole number and replace it with the 1 in the fraction to its left. Then we would get $\frac{4}{2}, \frac{16}{8},$ and $\frac{64}{32}$. This would be $2 \times 2 \times 2 = 8$

10. $2 \times 3 = 6$. $\frac{1}{4} \times \frac{1}{9} = \frac{1}{36}$. $6 \times \frac{1}{36} = \frac{6}{36} = \frac{1}{6}$. The reciprocal would be 6

11. Find the common denominator, which is 12. $\frac{1}{2} \times \frac{6}{6} = \frac{6}{12}$. $\frac{1}{4} \times \frac{3}{3} = \frac{3}{12}$. Take $\frac{6}{12} + \frac{3}{12}$. $x = 9$

12. $40 \times \frac{1}{8} = \frac{40}{8} = 5$. $40 \times \frac{1}{5} = \times \frac{40}{5} = 8$, $5 + 8 = 13$

13. $-\frac{1}{9} \div -\frac{5}{18} = -\frac{1}{9} \times -\frac{18}{5} = \frac{18}{45} = \frac{2}{5}$

14. Multiplicative inverse of $-\frac{3}{4} = -\frac{4}{3}$. The multiplicative inverse of $\frac{4}{3} = \frac{3}{4}$. The product would be $\frac{3}{4} \times -\frac{4}{3} = -1$

15. B is bigger because $\frac{1}{3} > \frac{1}{4}$ in the expressions

16. Multiple $\frac{12}{23} \times \frac{10}{10} = \frac{120}{230}$. Add the fractions in the parenthesis and it will be $\frac{121}{230}$. Take $\frac{11}{23}$ multiplied by the reciprocal of the fraction we acquired $\frac{11}{23} \times \frac{230}{121} = \frac{2530}{2789} = \frac{10}{11}$

17. Turn the mixed fraction into an improper fraction: $3\frac{1}{2} = \frac{7}{2}$. Find the common denominator for 8 and 4, which is 8. Take $\frac{3}{4} \times \frac{2}{2} = \frac{6}{8}$. $\frac{3}{8} - \frac{6}{8} = -\frac{3}{8}$. $-\frac{3}{8} \times \frac{7}{2} = -\frac{21}{16}$.

18. $\frac{3}{4} \times \frac{2}{2} = \times \frac{6}{8}$. $1\frac{1}{2} = \frac{3}{2}$. $\frac{3}{2} \times \frac{4}{4} = \frac{12}{8}$. $\frac{6}{8} - \frac{12}{8} + \frac{1}{8} = -\frac{5}{8}$

19. Subtracting a negative is the same as adding. $3 + 1 = 4$. $\frac{5}{6} + \frac{1}{6} = \frac{6}{6} = 1$. $4 + 1 = 5$.

20. The least possible value is 19.
$\frac{20}{19} = 1 + \frac{1}{1 + \frac{a}{b}} \rightarrow \frac{20}{19} - 1 = + \frac{1}{1 + \frac{a}{b}}$
$\rightarrow \frac{20 - 19}{19} = \frac{1}{\frac{b + a}{b}} \rightarrow \frac{1}{19} = 1 \times \frac{b}{b + a}$
$\rightarrow \frac{1}{19} = \frac{b}{b + a} \rightarrow a + b = 19$.

SOLUTIONS   Decimals/Percents & Operations   CHAPTER 6

Problem Set 1

1. $\dfrac{5.2 \times 10}{0.4 \times 10} = \dfrac{52}{4} = 13$

2. $36 \div 1.2 = 36 \div \dfrac{1}{15} = 36 \div \dfrac{6}{5} = 36 \times \dfrac{5}{6} = \dfrac{180}{6} = 30$

3. $100 \div 0.4 = 100 \div \dfrac{2}{5} = 100 \times \dfrac{5}{2} = \dfrac{500}{2} = 250$

4. $0.75 + 1.60 = 2.35$. $20 \times 2.35 = 47$. $x = 47$

5. $10.8 - (-9.7) = 10.8 + 9.7 = 20.5$

6. Three tenths = 0.3.
   Four thousands = 0.004. $0.3 + 0.004 = 0.304$

7. Write 2.5 as a fraction: $\dfrac{25}{10}$. The reciprocal is $\dfrac{10}{25}$.
   To find how much is exceeds, we have to find a common denominator to subtract the fractions. The common denominator is 50. $\dfrac{25}{10} \times \dfrac{5}{5} = \dfrac{125}{50}$.
   $\dfrac{10}{25} \times \dfrac{2}{2} = \dfrac{20}{50}$. $\dfrac{125}{50} - \dfrac{20}{50} = \dfrac{105}{50} = \dfrac{21}{10}$

8. a) It goes over two places values: 159.95
   b) It goes over two places values: 90.63
   c) It goes over three places values: 361.221

9. Turn the fractions into decimals:
   $45 + 0.3 + 0.04 + 0.007 = 45.347$

10. $\dfrac{3}{1000}$ is in the thousandths place, and 8 is in the ones place. In the decimal, 7 is in the hundredths place, so that would be $\dfrac{7}{100}$, and $a = 100$

11. $6 \div 0.3 = 6 \times \dfrac{10}{3} = 20$. $2 \div 0.1 = 2 \times \dfrac{10}{1} = 20$.
    $20 + 20 = 40$

12. Turn the decimals into fractions: $-0.2 = -\dfrac{2}{10}$.
    $-1.6 = -\dfrac{16}{10}$. Find a common denominator for 10 and 8, which is 40. $-\dfrac{2}{10} \times \dfrac{4}{4} = -\dfrac{8}{40}$. $-\dfrac{16}{10} \times \dfrac{4}{4}$
    $= -\dfrac{64}{40}$. $\dfrac{25}{8} \times \dfrac{5}{5} = \dfrac{125}{40}$. Perform the operations:
    $-\dfrac{8}{40} - (-\dfrac{64}{40}) + \dfrac{125}{40} = \dfrac{181}{40}$.

13. $-1.8 = -\dfrac{18}{10}$. $32 \times -\dfrac{10}{18} = -\dfrac{30}{36} = -\dfrac{5}{6}$.

14. $\dfrac{7}{40} = 0.175$

15. $\dfrac{1}{2} = 0.5$. $\dfrac{0.2}{2} = 0.05$. $0.5 + 0.05 = 0.55$

16. $36 \div 1.2 = 36 \div \dfrac{12}{10} = 36 \times \dfrac{10}{12} = 30$.
    $0.04 = \dfrac{4}{100}$. $30 \times \dfrac{4}{100} = \dfrac{120}{100} = 1.2$

17. $3.25 = 3\dfrac{1}{4}$. $1.75 = 1\dfrac{3}{4}$.

18. $0.15 = \dfrac{3}{20}$; $0.3 = \dfrac{3}{10}$.
    $\dfrac{3}{20} \times \dfrac{3}{10} \times \dfrac{10}{9} \times \dfrac{5}{4} = \dfrac{450}{7200} = \dfrac{1}{16}$

19. $3(-0.75 + 0.05) = -2.25 + 0.15 = -2.1$
    $= -\dfrac{21}{10}$. $1.2 = \dfrac{12}{10} = \dfrac{6}{5}$.
    $-\dfrac{21}{10} \div \dfrac{6}{5} = -\dfrac{21}{10} \times \dfrac{5}{6} = -\dfrac{105}{60} = -\dfrac{7}{4}$

20. Start with the denominator of the large fraction. Since it writes 0×5, that equals 0, and $0 + \dfrac{1}{0.5} = \dfrac{1}{0.5}$. Solve the bottom fraction:
    $0.5 = \dfrac{1}{2}$; $1 \div \dfrac{1}{2} = 1 \times \dfrac{2}{1} = 2$. Complete the equation: $0.6 + \dfrac{1}{2} = 0.6 + 0.5 = 1.1$.

CHAPTER 6 — Decimals/Percents & Operations — SOLUTIONS

Problem Set 2

1. By creating a double number line, we can find the value of 1.5 pounds of oranges:

   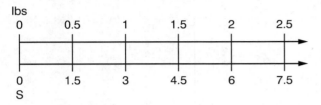

   By going in increments of 0.5 on top, we can find how much 1.5 pounds of oranges is, which is $4.5.

2. $0.1 + 0.2 + 0.3 \times 0.4 = 0.1 + 0.2 + 0.12 = 0.42$

3. $80\% = \frac{80}{100}$; $\frac{80}{100} \times 800 = \frac{64000}{100} = 640$

4. $\frac{4}{100} \times 5 = 15$; $\frac{5x}{100} = 15$; $\frac{x}{20} = 15$; $x = 300$

5. $\frac{8}{100}x = 16$; $\frac{4}{50}x = 16$; $x = \frac{800}{4}$; $x = 200$

6. 100% of 500 is 500. 10% of 500 is:
   $\frac{10}{100} \times 500 = x$; $\frac{1}{10} \times 500 = x$;
   $x = 50$. $500 + 50 = 550$

7. 10% of 10 = $\frac{1}{10} \times 10 = 1$.
   20% of 20 = $\frac{2}{10} \times 20 = 4$. $1 \times 4 = 4$

8. $\frac{3}{10} = 0.3$; $\frac{9}{1000} = 0.009$; $4 + 0.3 + 0.009 = 4.309$

9. Multiply 4×13 first, then 4×0.25, and add the products together.
   $4 \times 13 = 52$, $4 \times 0.25 = 1$. $52 + 1 = \$53$

10. Find a common denominator for the fractions under A and D, which is 12. Multiply $\frac{1}{6} \times \frac{2}{2} = \frac{2}{12}$. Multiply each fraction by $\frac{3}{3}$ to find the points between A and D. $\frac{1}{12} \times \frac{3}{3} = \frac{3}{36}$. $\frac{2}{12} \times \frac{3}{3} = \frac{6}{36}$. A = $\frac{3}{36}$, B = $\frac{4}{36}$, C = $\frac{5}{36}$, D = $\frac{6}{36}$. The value of B is $\frac{4}{36} = \frac{1}{9}$

11. 1 page = 2.5 cents. 2.5 cents × 4 pages = 10 cents. $1 has 10 groups of 10 cents. 10 cents can make 4 pages, 10 groups of 4 pages = 40 pages per $1. 40 pages × $15 = 600 pages

12. 20% of 50 = $\frac{20}{100} \times 50 = x$. $\frac{1000}{100} = 10$.
    20% of what is 40: $\frac{20}{100}x = 40$. $\frac{4000}{20} = 200$.
    $x + y = 10 + 200 = 210$.

13. $\frac{x}{100} \times 40 = 25$; $\frac{40x}{100} = 25$; $\frac{2x}{5} = 25$; $\frac{125}{2} = x$; $x = 62.5$

14. Move the decimals to the right until they are no longer present: $0.02 \rightarrow 2$; $1.25 \rightarrow 125$. Multiply the numbers: $2 \times 125 = 250$. Replace the decimal, and the answer is 0.025.

15. $\frac{18}{100} \times 60 = \frac{1080}{100} = 10.8$. $\frac{27}{100}x = 10.8$; $\frac{1080}{27} = 40$. $x = 40$

16. $\frac{10}{100}x = 5$; $\frac{500}{10} = 50$; $\frac{25}{100} \times 50 = \frac{1250}{100} = 12.5$

17. $\frac{10}{100} \times 200 = \frac{2000}{100} = 20$. $20 - 25 = -5$

18. $\frac{60}{100}x = 30$; $\frac{3000}{60} = 50$. $\frac{50}{100} \times 50 = 25$

19. $0.8B = A$; $\frac{0.8B}{B}$, B's cancel out, so $\frac{A}{B} = 0.8$, or 80%

20. $0.2x = x - 20$; $0 = (1 - 0.2)x - 20$; $20 = 0.8x$; $x = 20 \div 0.8$; $x = 25$

SOLUTIONS — Evaluations & Expressions — CHAPTER 7

Problem Set 1

1. $y = 3x = y = 3 \times 4 = 12$
2. $\dfrac{2+5x}{2+x} = \dfrac{2+5(2)}{2+2} = \dfrac{12}{4} = 3$
3. $4x + 3x - 2x = 7x - 2x = 5x$
4. $5c + 3c + 2d + 8d = 8c + 10d$
5. $x^5 - 2x = 3^5 - 2(3) = 243 - 6 = 237$
6. $3x^y + 4y^x = 3(3)^4 + 4(4)^3 = 243 + 256 = 499$
7. $\dfrac{3x+y}{x-y} = \dfrac{3(12)+(-6)}{12-(-6)} = \dfrac{36-6}{12-6} = \dfrac{30}{18} = \dfrac{5}{3}$
8. $x(x-1)(x-2)(x-3)(x-4)$
   $= 3(3-1)(3-2)(3-3)(3-4)$
   $= 3 \times 2 \times 1 \times 0 \times -1 = 0$
9. Start with the second equation since the value of c is given. $b + 7 = 16$; $b = 9$. $a + 9 = 12$; $a = 3$
10. B is true. Because $3 \times 3 = 9$, and $9 - 1 = 8$
11. $x^2 - xy + 2y^2 = (-1)^2 - 1(-2) + 2(-2)^1$
    $= 1 + 2 - 4 = -1$
12. $p = 4, s = 3, q = 5, r = 2$; $4 \times 3 - 5 \times 2$
    $= 12 - 10 = 2$
13. a) $k - m = -3 - 4 = -7$;
    b) $m - n = 4 - (-6) = 4 + 6 = 10$
14. $n + m - k = -6 + 4 - (-3) = 1$
    $n - k - m = -6 - (-3) - 4 = -7$
15. $2x^2 + 3xy - 4y^2 = 2(2)^2 + 3(2)(-4) - 4(-4)^2$
    $= 8 - 24 - 64 = -80$
16. $-2x^2 - 3x^2 = -2(-4)^2 - 3(-4)^2 = -32 - 48 = -80$
17. $\dfrac{x-2}{2x+7} = \dfrac{-x-2}{2(-3)+7} = \dfrac{-2}{1} = -5$
18. $\dfrac{x-2}{2x+7} = \dfrac{\frac{1}{2}-2}{2\left(\frac{1}{2}\right)+7} = \dfrac{-1\frac{1}{2}}{1+7} = -1\frac{1}{2} \div 8$
    $= -\dfrac{3}{2} \times \dfrac{1}{8} = -\dfrac{3}{16}$
19. The common denominator for 16 and 10 is 80.
    $\dfrac{7}{16x} \times \dfrac{5}{5} = \dfrac{35}{80x}$; $\dfrac{3}{10x} \times \dfrac{8}{8} = \dfrac{24}{80x}$; $\dfrac{35}{80x} - \dfrac{24}{80x} = \dfrac{11}{80x}$
20. Plug in 5 for n in the expression:
    $5^3 + 5 - 1 = 125 + 5 - 1 = 129$

Problem Set 2

1. $5(2 - x) = 5(2) - 5(x) = 10 - 5x$
2. Distribute the negative to x and –2, which would then be $3 - x + 2 = 5 - x$, so the answer is B
3. $(a - (b - c)) - ((a - b) - c) = a - b + c - a + b + c$
   $= c + c = 2c$
4. $4(2 + 3r) - \dfrac{1}{2}(4 + 24r) = 8 + 12r - 2 - 12r = 6$
5. Find a common denominator for the fractions, which is 4. $\dfrac{3y}{1} \times \dfrac{4}{4} = \dfrac{12y}{4}$; $\dfrac{y-8}{2} \times \dfrac{2}{2} = \dfrac{2y-16}{4}$;
   $\dfrac{12y}{4} + \dfrac{2y-16}{4} + \dfrac{6y}{4} = \dfrac{20y-16}{4} = 5y - 4$
6. $2(a - 2b) + 3(-a + 2b) = 2a - 4b - 3a + 6b$
   $= -a + 2b$
7. $r - 3(s - r) + 2s = r - 3s + 3r + 2s = 4r - s$
8. $3(x - y) - 5(y - x) = 3x - 3y - 5y + 5x = 8x - 8y$
9. $\dfrac{p}{2q} \times \dfrac{3}{3} = \dfrac{3p}{6q}$; $\dfrac{p}{3q} \times \dfrac{2}{2} = \dfrac{2p}{6q}$; $\dfrac{3p}{6q} + \dfrac{2p}{6q} = \dfrac{5p}{6q}$
10. $3a + 4b - (-6a - 3b) = 3a + 4b + 6a + 3b = 9a + 7b$
11. $(x + 2y) - (2x + y) = 2y + 2y - 2(2y) + y$
    $= 2y + 2y - 4y + y = -y$
12. $4[x + 3(2x + 1)] = 4(x + 6x + 3) = 4x + 24x + 12$
    $= 28x + 12$
13. $9 + 3[x + (3x + 2)] + 4 = 9 + 3(x + 3x + 2) + 4$
    $= 9 + 3x + 9x + 6 + 4 = 12x + 19$
14. $4 + 10[x + (2x + 3)] + 12x = 4 + 10(x + 2x + 3)$
    $+ 12x = 4 + 10x + 20x + 30 + 12x = 42x + 34$
15. $5 + 2[3 + (2x + 1) + x] - 2$
    $= 5 + 6 + 4x + 2 + 2x - 2 = 6x + 11$
16. $2(a + b - 2c) - 3(a - b - c)$
    $= 2a + 2b - 4c - 3a + 3b + 3c = -a + 5b - c$
17. $a - (a - b - a - c + a) - b + c$
    $= a - a + b + a + c - a - b + c = 2c$
18. $(-8a) + 9a + (-15a) + 4a = -8a + 9a - 15a + 4a$
    $= -10a$
19. C is incorrect because $\dfrac{1}{3}(3x) = \dfrac{3x}{3} = x$, and $\dfrac{2}{3}(9) = \dfrac{18}{3} = 6$, so it would be $x + 6$ instead of $3x + 6$
20. By the guess-check, $x = 3$, $z = 1$, and $y = 6$. So, $x + y + z = 10$.

CHAPTER 8 — Equations — SOLUTIONS

Problem Set 1

1. $3(2x + 1) \to 3(2(-8) + 1) = 3(-16 + 1)$
   $= 3(-16) + 3(1) = -48 + 3 = -45$

2. $\dfrac{x-6}{4} - 4 \to \dfrac{-14-6}{4} - 4 = \dfrac{-20}{4} - 4 = -5 - 4 = -9$

3. $-2m^2 + 10 \to -2(-6)^2 + 10 = -72 + 10 = -62$

4. $6m^2 + 2n^2 \to 6(7)^2 + 2(3)^2 = 6(49) + 2(9)$
   $= 294 + 18 = 312$

5. $(6x)^2 - (\dfrac{x}{5}) \to (6(5))^2 - (\dfrac{5}{5}) = 30^2 - 1 = 900 - 1 = 899$

6. $ab + bc + ac \to 2(5) + 5(-2) + 2(-2)$
   $= 10 - 10 - 4 = -4$

7. $2x - 7 = -2x + 1 \to 4x = 8 \to x = 2$

8. $3x + 4 = x + 8 \to \div 2x = 4 \to x = 2$

9. $5x + 4 - 2x = -(x + 8) \to 3x + 4 = -x - 8$
   $\to 4x = -12 \to x = -3$

10. $-2m + 8 + m + 1 = 0 \to m = 9$

11. No solution: $-(y^2 - 2) = y^2 - 5 - 2y^2$
    $\to -y^2 + 2 = -5 - y^2 \to 0 \neq -7$

12. $m = 8 - 2(p - m) \to m = 8 - 2p + 2m$
    $\to 2p + m = 8 + 2m \to 2p = 8 + m \to p = 4 + \dfrac{m}{2}$

13. $8(3m - 2) - 7m = 0 \to 24m - 16 - 7m = 0$
    $\to 17m = 16 \to m = \dfrac{16}{17}$

14. $\dfrac{6}{x+2} = \dfrac{3}{4} \to x = 6 \therefore \dfrac{6}{8} \div \dfrac{2}{2} = \dfrac{3}{4}$

15. $(x - 3)(x + 4) = x^2 + 4 \to x^2 + x - 12 = x^2 + 4$
    $\to x - 12 = 4 \to x = 16$

16. $4 - 2(3x + 2) = 4x - 10 \to 4 - 6x - 4 = 4x - 10$
    $\to 10x = 10 \to x = 1$

17. $9x - 21 + 9 = 2(5 - x) \to 9x - 12 = 10 - 2x$
    $\to 11x = 22 \to x = 2$

18. $\dfrac{4}{3x+2} = \dfrac{2}{x+3} \to 2(3x + 2) = 4(x + 3)$
    $\to 6x + 4 = 4x + 12 \to 2x = 8 \to x = 4$

19. If 16 is $\dfrac{1}{4}$ of a number, we can multiply 16×3 to find $\dfrac{3}{4}$ of the number. $16 \times 3 = 48$.

20. $\dfrac{x}{4} + \dfrac{7}{16} = 11\dfrac{7}{16} \to \dfrac{x}{4} \times \dfrac{4}{4} = \dfrac{4x}{16} \to \dfrac{4x}{16} + \dfrac{7}{16}$
    $= \dfrac{183}{16} \to 4x + 7 = 183 \to 4x = 176 \to x = 44$

Problem Set 2

1. $4x + 12 = 48 \to 4x = 36 \to x = 9$

2. $2x + 6 \times 1 = 16 \to 2x + 6 = 16 \to 2x = 10 \to x = 5$

3. $3 + 5x = 28 \to 5x = 25 \to x = 5$

4. $2x - 3z = 5y \to 2(11) - 3z = 5(-8)$
   $\to 22 - 3z = 40 \to -3z = 18 \to z = -6$

5. $\dfrac{48}{x} = 16 \to 16x = 48 \to x = 3$

6. $\dfrac{x}{2} - 6 = 4 \to \dfrac{x}{2} = 10 \to 10 \times 2 = x \to x = 20$

7. $\dfrac{w}{5} - 1 = 15 \to \dfrac{w}{5} = 16 \to 16 \times 5 = w \to w = 80$

8. $24 = x - 18 \to x = 42$

9. $2t = s + 4 \to 2(3) = s + 4 \to 6 = s + 4 \to s = 2$

10. $2x - 3(x + 4) = -5 \to 2x - 3x - 12 = -5$
    $\to -x = 7 \to x = -7$

11. $5(n - 2) = 85 \to 5n - 10 = 85 \to 5n = 95 \to n = 19$

12. $4x + 14 = 8x - 48 \to 4x = 62 \to 2x = 31$

13. $7 + 6x = 13 + 9x \to -6 = 3x \to x = -2$

14. Using the commutative property:
    $5\dfrac{2}{3} \times a = \dfrac{3}{5} \times 5\dfrac{2}{3} \to a = \dfrac{3}{5}$

15. $m + 1 = \dfrac{n-2}{3} = 3 \times (m + 1) = (\dfrac{n-2}{3}) \times 3$
    $\to 3m + 3 = n - 2 \to 3m - n = -5$

16. $2(x - 5) = 3(2 - x) \to 2x - 10 = 6 - 3x$
    $\to 5x = 16 \to x = 3.2$

17. $2(x - 5) = -11 \to 2x - 10 = -11 \to 2x = -1$
    $\to x = -\dfrac{1}{2}$

18. $\dfrac{1}{2} + \dfrac{2}{3} + \dfrac{3}{4} + \dfrac{n}{12} = 2 \to \dfrac{1}{2} \times \dfrac{6}{6} = \dfrac{6}{12}$;
    $\dfrac{2}{3} \times \dfrac{4}{4} = \times \dfrac{8}{12}$; $\dfrac{3}{4} \times \dfrac{3}{3} = \times \dfrac{9}{12}$;
    $\dfrac{6}{12} + \dfrac{8}{12} + \dfrac{9}{12} + \dfrac{n}{12} = \dfrac{23+n}{3} \to \dfrac{23+n}{3} = 2 \to n = 1$

19. w has to be less than 28, because $y + z = 28$. If we set $w = 20$, then $x = 25$, $y = 26$, and $z = 2$. As long as $w < 28$, $w + z = 22$

20. First, add $8 + 9 + 4 = 21$, which is the magic sum. Then, find the middle square: $21 - 5 - 9 = 7$. Next, find the diagonal sum from the top right to the bottom left: $21 - 7 - 4 = 10$. After that, find the missing middle value in the top row: $21 - 10 - 8 = 3$. Lastly, find the value of n in the middle column: $21 - 3 - 7 = 11 = n$

SOLUTIONS Algebra & Geometry - 1   CHAPTER 9

Problem Set 1

1. All sides of a square are equal in length, so $28 \div 4 = 7$. Finding the area is length × height. If each side is 7 cm, then length × height = $7 \times 7 = 49$ cm².

2. That the square root of 144 since length × height = area. $\sqrt{144} = 12$; each side length is 12 cm.

3. The sum of the angles of a triangle is 180 degrees. $25 + 70 = 95$. $180 - 95 = 85$ degrees is the third angle.

4. 5cm – 3 cm = 2 cm for the missing lengths in the upper right corner. 6 cm – 2 cm = 4 cm for the missing height.
   6 cm + 5 cm + 4 cm + 2 cm + 2 cm + 3 cm = 22 cm

5. $x + 1 + x + 6 + 10 = 3 + 1 + 3 + 6 + 10 = 23$

6. There are 12 triangles shown in the figure, and 7 of those triangles are shaded. This could be represented as $\frac{7}{12}$

7. Since line PR = 180 degrees, that makes the angle labelled $2x = x + 50$. $x = 50$ degrees

8. First, solve for x so you can find the real lengths of each side of the triangle.
   $7 + x + 4 + 2x + 1 = 36$; $3x + 12 = 36$; $3x = 24$; $x = 8$.
   Plug in 8 for x on the values that are unknown: $x + 4 = 8 + 4 = 12$; $2x + 1 = 2(8) + 1 = 17$.
   The lengths of the triangle are: 7, 12, and 17. The longest side is 17.

9. Find the perimeter of the square: $2.4 + 2.4 + 2.4 + 2.4 = 9.6$ inches. Then, find the area: $2.4^2 = 5.76$ in². $9.6 - 5.76 = 3.84$

10. $x + 1 + x - 1 + x = 21 \rightarrow 3x = 21 \rightarrow x = 7$

11. The area of a triangle is the area of a rectangle divided by 2. If the base of the rectangle is 16, and x remains the same for the height of both the triangle and the rectangle, then y, the width of the triangle, has to be $16 \div 2 = 8$, in order for both areas to be equal.

12. Find the area of 6 × 4 first, which will give the area of the rectangle, which is 24. Divide that in half to find the area of the triangle, which is 12.

13. The volume of a rectangular prism is base × width × height. $4 \times 5 \times x = 60$. $60 \div 5 \div 4 = x$. $x = 3$ cm

14. The perimeter of a rectangle contains two widths of equal size and two lengths of equal size. With this information, we can find an equation: $2W \times 2L = 32$. Put 4 in for W, width, to find L, length. $2(4) \times 2L = 32$; $8 \times 2L = 32$; $2L = 24$; Length = 12 inches

15. The angles of a triangle = 180 degrees. Triangle BCE has 3 equal angles. To find the angle values, take $180 \div 3 = 60$ degrees per angle. On the diagram, point E has congruent angles within each triangle, which both equal 60 degrees. That means triangle ADE has two known angles, 60 degrees and 90 degrees.
    To find x, take $180 - 90 - 60 = x = 30$ degrees

16. The volume of a rectangular block is base × width × height. The base × width = 24 cm². Find the height: $120 \div 24 = 5$ cm is the height

17. $2(5 + n) + 2(5 - n) = 10 + 2n + 10 - 2n = 20$

18. Perimeter of the triangle: $14 + 12 + 12 = 38$ cm. Perimeter of the rectangle:
    $2x + 2(8) = 38$; $2x + 16 = 38$; $2x = 22$; $x = 11$

19. The sides of an equilateral triangle are all equal. Set 2x equal to x + 15 to find x and find the length of one side. $2x = x + 15$; $x = 15$. Plug in 15 to x on any side: $15 + 15 = 30$. If one side is 30, then the whole perimeter is 90

20. Find the width of the rectangle by subtracting the x-value of point Q from the x-value of point P: $26 - 15 = 11$.
    Find the height of the rectangle by subtracting the y-value of point Q from the y-value of point R: $55 - 35 = 20$. Take 11 × 20 to find the area: $11 \times 20 = 220$ units²

CHAPTER 10 — BENCHMARK [Chapter 1-9] — SOLUTIONS

Problem Set 1

1. E is correct. If a = 4 and b = 7, 4 + 7 = 11. Or, if a = 12 and b = 13, 12 + 13 = 25. Only E will result in an odd integer.

2. Order of operations:
   $56 - 96 \div 16 \times 2 = 56 - 6 \times 2 = 56 - 12 = 44$

3. Find a common denominator between $\frac{1}{4}$ and $\frac{5}{8}$, which would be 8. $\frac{1}{4} \times \frac{2}{2} = \frac{2}{8}$. The fractions between $\frac{2}{8}$ and $\frac{5}{8}$ is $\frac{3}{8}$ and $\frac{4}{8}$. The smaller of the two is $\frac{3}{8}$.

4. $\frac{4 \times (0.15 + 0.45)}{1.2} = \frac{4 \times 0.6}{1.2} = \frac{2.4}{1.2} = 2$

5. The common denominator between the two fractions is 10. $-\frac{4}{5} \times \frac{2}{2} = -\frac{8}{10}$. To get from $-\frac{8}{10}$ to 0, would be 8 tenths, and to get from 0 to $\frac{7}{10}$ would be 7 tenths. Altogether, the distance between the two points is 15 tenths, or $\frac{15}{10}$.

6. $5r - 3(s-r) + 2s = 5r - 3s + 3r + 2s = 8r - s$

7. The common denominator between the fractions is 6. $\frac{x}{3} \times \frac{2}{2} = \frac{2x}{6}$; $\frac{x}{2} \times \frac{3}{3} = \frac{3x}{6}$; $\frac{2x}{6} + \frac{3x}{6} - \frac{x}{6} = \frac{4x}{6}$; $= \frac{2x}{3}$.

8. $\frac{1+2x}{3} = \frac{4+x}{2} \to 3(4+x) = 2(1+2x)$
   $\to 12 + 3x = 2 + 4x \to 10 = x$

9. All sides have to be the same length to be a square. Set both sides equal to each other to find the value of n. $6n = 2n + 12 \to 4n = 12 \to n = 3$

10. $5 + 4 + x + 8 + x = 37 \to 17 + 2x = 37$
    $\to 2x = 20 \to x = 10$

11. $65 + n + 5 + n = 180 \to 70 + 2n = 180$
    $\to 2n = 110 \to n = 55$;
    Angle B = 60 degrees

12. The only number that can divide 6, 8, and 12 and is between 100 and 130 is 120.

13. Find the GCD of 32, 48, and 64.
    Prime factorization of 32: 2^5
    Prime factorization of 48: $2^4 \times 3$
    Prime factorization of 64: 2^6
    The GCD is $2^4 = 16$

14. −1 has to go in the bottom left corner, so a = −2 for the left column. b = −2 as well because that's the only number missing in the right column.
    a + b = −2 + −2 = −4

15. $10 - \frac{10}{2\left(\frac{1}{2}\right)+1} = 10 - \frac{10}{1+1} = 10 - \frac{10}{2} = 10 - 5$;
    b = 5

16. $-\frac{4}{5} \div \frac{a}{b} = -\frac{8}{15}$ is the same as $-\frac{4}{5} \times \frac{b}{a} = -\frac{8}{15}$.
    b = 2, a = 3; $\frac{a}{b} = \frac{3}{2}$

17. Find the common denominator for the fractions, which is 10. $\frac{4}{5} \times \frac{2}{2} = \frac{8}{10}$; $1\frac{1}{2} = \frac{3}{2}$; $\frac{3}{2} \times \frac{5}{5} = \frac{15}{10}$;
    $\frac{8}{10} - \frac{8}{10} = x + \frac{15}{10} \to \frac{5}{10} = x + \frac{15}{10} \to x = -\frac{10}{10}$

18. To rent for 2 days would be $20 × 2 = $40.
    To travel 70 miles would be $0.25 × 70 = $17.50.
    Altogether, it would be $40 + $17.50 = $57.50

19. 20% of 40 = 40 × .2 = 8; 40 = 20% of 200.
    8 + 200 = 208

20. For the equation to be true, a = 2, b = 8, and c = 4 → 921 − 458 = 463.
    a + b + c = 2 + 8 + 4 = 14

SOLUTIONS — Equations & Inequalities — CHAPTER 11

Problem Set 1

1. Like terms can be combined;
   $\frac{x + 32 + (12 - x)}{15} + 3 = \frac{44}{15} + 3$
   $\rightarrow \frac{44}{15} + \frac{45}{15} = \frac{89}{15}$.

2. Multiply both sides by 9; $9 \cdot \frac{27}{3} = 9 \cdot \frac{x}{9} \rightarrow 81 = x$.

3. Subtract 2 from each side; $\frac{5}{x} + 2 - 2 = \frac{7}{2} - 2$
   $\rightarrow \frac{5}{x} = \frac{7}{2} - \frac{4}{2} \rightarrow \frac{5}{x} = \frac{3}{2}$.
   Cross multiply; $10 = 3x$.
   Divide each side by 3; $\frac{10}{3} = \frac{3x}{3}$. So, $x = \frac{10}{3}$.

4. $\frac{(10)(6)}{3} + 3^2 = \frac{x}{4} \rightarrow \frac{60}{5} + 9 = \frac{x}{4} \rightarrow 12 + 9 = \frac{x}{4}$
   $\rightarrow 21 = \frac{x}{4}$. Multiply each side by 4; $84 = x$.

5. Combine like terms; $-112 + x = -14$.
   Add 112 to each side; $x = 98$.

6. Combine like terms; $2.35 + 10h = 2.72$.
   Subtract 2.35 from each side $10h = 0.37$.
   Divide each side by 10; $h = 0.037$.

7. Subtract x from each side and add 4 to each side;
   $\frac{2}{9}x - x = 3 \rightarrow \frac{2}{9}x - \frac{9}{9}x = 3 \rightarrow -\frac{7}{9}x = 3$.
   Multiply each side by 9; $-7x = 27$.
   Divide each side by -7, $x = -\frac{27}{7}$.

8. se the distributive property of multiplication over addition; $2x + 2 - 4 = 6 \rightarrow 2x - 2 = 6$. Add each side 2; $2x = 8$. Divide each side by 2; $x = 4$.

9. To solve for each variable in this system of equations, start with the third equation; $3x + 1 = 10$. Subtract from each side 1; we get $3x = 9$. Divide each side by 3, so $x = 3$. Replace x by 3 in $6y + x - 4 = 11$; $6y + 3 - 4 = 11 \rightarrow 6y - 1 = 11$. Add each side 1; $6y = 12$. Divide each side by 6, and we get $y = 2$. Replace x by 3 and y by 2 in $z + 2x - y = 10$; $z + 2.3 - 2 = 10 \rightarrow z + 6 - 2 = 10$ $\rightarrow z + 4 = 10$ Subtract 4 from each side $z = 6$. So, there is one solution: (3, 2, 6).

10. Cross multiply; $2x - 5 = 77$. Add each side 5; $2x = 82$. Divide each side by 2; $x = 41$.

11. Cross multiply; $2 \cdot (2x + 1) = 1 \cdot (3x - 6)$.
    Use the distributive property of multiplication over addition on both sides; $4x + 2 = 3x - 6$.
    Subtract 3x and 2 from each side; $x = -8$.

12. Use the distributive property of multiplication over subtraction; $\frac{84}{3} - \frac{7x}{3} = 1 \rightarrow \frac{84 - 7x}{3} = 1$.
    Cross multiply; $84 - 7x = 3$;
    Subtract 84 from each side; $-7x = -81$.
    Divide each side by -7; $x = \frac{81}{7}$.

13. Add all equations side-by-side; $2x + 2y + 2z = 24$.
    Divide each side by 2, $x + y + z = 12$.
    Replacing $y + z$ by 7 in equation '$x + y + z = 12$'.
    So, $x + 7 = 12 \rightarrow x = 5$.

14. Add all equations side-by-side, $2x + 2z = 16$.
    Divide each side by 2; $x + z = 8$.

15. Replace b with 4a in equation '$2a + 3b = 28$';
    $2a + 3.4a = 28 \rightarrow 2a + 12a = 28 \rightarrow 14a = 28$.
    Divide each side by 14, $a = 2$.

16. This is a step-by-step fill-in-the-blank process.
    $23 + \dfrac{48}{26 - \dfrac{12}{x + 3}} = 25 \rightarrow 23 + 2 = 25$.
    So; $\dfrac{48}{26 - \dfrac{12}{x + 3}}$ is equal to 2. Therefore,
    $26 - \dfrac{12}{x + 3} = 24$, which means that $\dfrac{12}{x + 3} = 2$.
    Cross multiply; $12 = 2x + 6$.
    Subtract 6 from each side; $6 = 2x$.
    Divide each side by 2; $3 = x$.

17. This is a step-by-step fill-in-the-blank process.
    $109 + \dfrac{50}{23 + \dfrac{30}{13 + \dfrac{x + 4}{4}}} = 111 \rightarrow 109 + 2 = 111$.
    So, $\dfrac{50}{23 + \dfrac{30}{13 + \dfrac{x + 4}{4}}} = 2$. Therefore,
    $23 + \dfrac{30}{13 + \dfrac{x + 4}{4}} = 25$. So, $\dfrac{30}{13 + \dfrac{x + 4}{4}} = 2$.

CHAPTER 11 — Equations & Inequalities — SOLUTIONS

Therefore, $13 + \frac{x+4}{4} = 15$, which means $\frac{x+4}{4} = 2$. Cross multiply; $x + 4 = 8$. Subtrct 4 from each side; $x = 4$

18. This is a step-by-step fill-in-the-blank process. $3 + \frac{4}{4 + \frac{6}{x}} = 5 \rightarrow 3 + 2 = 5$. So, $\frac{4}{4 + \frac{6}{x}} = 2$. Therefore, $4 + \frac{6}{x} = 2$. Subtract 4 from each side; $\frac{6}{x} = -2$. Cross multiply; $6 = -2x$. Divide each side by -2, $-3 = x$.

19. Cross multiply, $x + 1 = 2x$. Subtract x from each side; $1 = x$.

20. Add $\frac{3}{4}$ to each side; $\frac{x}{2} = \frac{9}{8} + \frac{3}{4} \rightarrow \frac{x}{2} = \frac{9}{8} + \frac{6}{8}$ $\rightarrow \frac{x}{2} = \frac{15}{8}$. Cross multiply; $8x = 30$. Divide each side by 8; $x = \frac{15}{4}$.

Problem Set 2

1. $\frac{8+4}{4-2} \rightarrow \frac{12}{6} \rightarrow 6$.

2. Integer values of x are $-4, -3, -2, -1, 0, 1, 2, 3$. So, there are eight values satisfying this inequality.

3. Divide all sides by 2; $a + 6 > 15$. Subtract 6 from all sides; $a > 9$. So, $a = 10$ is the smallest integer value.

4. Divide all sides by 5; $a + 6 < 10$. Subtract 6 from each side; $a < 4$. So, $a = 3$ is the largest integer value satisfying the inequality.

5. Multiply 2 and $(x-1)$. Then, $2x - 2 \geq +3$. Add 2 to each side; $2x \geq 5$. Divide each side by 2; $x \geq \frac{5}{2}$. So, $x = 3$ is the smallest integer value satisfying the inequality.

6. Cross multiply; $x + 3 = -28$. Subtract 3 from each side; $x = -31$.

7. Subtract 5 from each side; $-6x \geq -24$. Divide each side by -6, $x \leq 4$. The positive integer values of x are 1, 2, 3, and 4. So, the sum of positive integer values of x is 10.

8. Integer values of x are $-4, -3, -2, -1, 0, +1$. So, the sum of all integer values of x is -9.

9. Multiply each side by 3; $2x + 1 > 12$. Subtract 1 from each side; $2x > 11$. Divide each side by 2; $x > 112$. So, $x = 6$ is the smallest integer value of x satisfying the inequality.

10. Add all inequalities side-by-side; $-8 < x + y < 10$. The values of $x + y$ are $-6, -5, -4, -3, -2, -1, 0, 1, 2, 3, 4, 5, 6, 7, 8$. Why? So, there are 15 values.

11. The values of x are $-2, -1, 0, 1, 2, 3$. So, there are 6 values of x satisfying the inequality.

12. Multiply each side by 5; $-10 < 3x - 1 \leq 35$. Add 1 to each side; $-9 < 3x \leq 36$. Divide each side by 3; $-3 < x \leq 12$. The values of x are $-2, -1, 0, 1, 2, 3, 4, 5, 6, 7, 8, 9, 10, 11$, and 12. So, there are 15 integer values of x.

13. Subtract 2 from each side; $-12 < 6x \leq 30$. Divide each side by 6; $-2 < x \leq 5$. The values of x are $-1, 0, 1, 2, 3, 4$, and 5. So, there are 7 values of x.

14. $4 = \sqrt{16}$. So, $\sqrt{11} < \sqrt{16}$. So, 4 makes the inequality true.

15. Subtract 1 from each side; $2 < \frac{x}{2}$. Multiply each side by 2; $4 < x$. So, $x = 5$ is the smallest value of x.

16. $x - 9 = 20$ or $x - 9 = -20$. So, $x = 29$ or $x = -11$. The sum of x values is $29 + (-11) = 18$.

17. $x + 14 = 5$ or $x + 14 = -5$. So, $x = -9$ or $x = -19$. The sum of s values is $(-9) + (-19) = -28$.

18. $x - 6 = 2x + 4$ or $x - 6 = -2x - 4$. So, $x = -10$ or $x = \frac{2}{3}$. The largest value of x is $\frac{2}{3}$.

19. Multiply each side by 2; $6 \leq 3x + 3 \leq 12$. Subtract 3 from each side; $3 \leq 3x \leq 9$. Divide each side by 3; $1 \leq x \leq 3$. The values of x are 1, 2, 3. So, the sum of all possible integer values of x is 6.

20. $5 - 3t \geq 17 + 3t$. Add each side $3t$; $5 \geq 17 + 6t$. Subtract 17 from each side; $-12 \geq 6t$. Divide each side by 6; $-2 \geq t$. So, $t = -2$ is the largest t value satisfying the inequality.

SOLUTIONS — Ratios & Proportions — CHAPTER 12

Problem Set 1

1. Find a common denominator for 10 and 15, which is 30. $\frac{x}{10} \times \frac{3}{3} = \frac{3x}{30}$; $\frac{6}{15} \times \frac{2}{2} = \frac{12}{30}$; $\frac{3x}{30} = \frac{12}{30}$. $x = 4$, so the missing value is 4

2. Divide 200 by 16, which is 12.5. Then, multiply 37 by 12.5, which is 462.5. This would give us the correct ratio between the fractions.

3. Find a common denominator for 100 and 8, which is 200. $\frac{x}{100} \times \frac{2}{2} = \frac{2x}{100}$; $\frac{7}{8} \times \frac{25}{25} = \frac{175}{100}$; $\frac{2x}{100} = \frac{175}{200}$. $x = 87.5$, so the missing value is 87.5

4. If 3 pounds = $7.50, if we work backwards from 3 pounds, 2 pounds would be $5.00, 1 pound would be $2.50, and 0 pounds would be $0. It goes up by $0.25 per pound. $10 would be 4 pounds.

5. The ratio from the small triangle can be written as $\frac{3}{4}$. The ratio for the larger triangle can be written as $\frac{6}{x}$. To get the numerator from 3 to 6, it was multiplied by 2. The denominator would be multiplied by 2 as well. $4 \times 2 = 8$. However, the base already has a 4 included, so $x = 4$ to get 8

6. $\dfrac{A + \frac{3}{7}A}{A - \frac{3}{3}A} = \dfrac{\frac{10A}{7}}{\frac{4A}{7}} = \frac{10}{4} = \frac{5}{2}$

7. $2(2m + 3) = 7(3m - 4)$; $4m + 6 = 21m - 28$; $17m = 34$; $m = 2$

8. B is the better. If B was 3 pounds of sugar for $3, then A would be 1 pound of sugar for $2.50, which is only $0.50 less than 3 pounds.

9. It would be in region I because if A is (10, 20), then (9, 20) is going to be on the same like as (10, 20), just a little over to the left.

10. Using the double number line method, starting at 15 pages per .5 minutes, means we go up by .5 minutes and add 15 pages each time. By the time we get to 3 minutes, it would print 90 pages.

11. Cross multiply: $2(2a - b) = 2a$, $4a - 2b = 2a$ $2a = 2b$, $a = b$. Therefore $\frac{a}{b} = 1$.

12. We can look at these ratios as Student A: $\frac{90 \text{ meters}}{15 \text{ seconds}}$ and Student B: $\frac{80 \text{ meters}}{12 \text{ seconds}}$. Use a common denominator to see how far each student would run if they ran the same amount of time. $\frac{90 \text{ meters}}{15 \text{ seconds}} \times \frac{4}{4} = \frac{360 \text{ meters}}{60 \text{ seconds}}$; $\frac{80 \text{ meters}}{12 \text{ seconds}} \times \frac{5}{5} = \frac{400 \text{ meters}}{60 \text{ seconds}}$. This shows Student B would run 400 meters in 60 seconds, which is more than Student A.

13. If 8 cm = 48 kilometers on a map, 1 cm = 6 kilometers since $8 \times 6 = 48$. $20 \times 6 = 120$ kilometers for 20 cm

14. $\frac{x + y}{y - x} = \frac{2 + 3}{3 - 2} = \frac{5}{1} = 5$

15. $\frac{4 + 20 + x}{3} = \frac{16 + y}{2} \to 2(24 + x) = 3(y + 16)$; $48 + 2x = 3y + 48 \to 2x = 3y$; $\frac{2}{3} = \frac{y}{x}$

16. $z = 10$. Since $\frac{5}{2} = 2.5$, $x \times 2.5$ must equal a whole number, and this only works for even numbers. If we take $4 \times 2.5 = 10$, then our ratio is 4 : 8 : 10, which adds up to 22 for the perimeter.

CHAPTER 12 — Ratios & Proportions — SOLUTIONS

17. To find this answer, the 4 and 7 must be multiplied by the same number and added to get a number between 250 and 350. If you multiply both by 31, you get 124 : 217. Added together is 341.

18. Each fraction must equal the same number. If a = 15, b = 9 and c = 6, the equation would be 15 + 9 + 2(6) = 36. a = 15

19. a : b = 3 : 4 = 9 : 12; b : c = 3 : 5 = 12 : 20; a : c = 9:20

20. $\frac{a+b-c}{b} = \frac{6c+2c-c}{2c} = \frac{7c}{2c} = \frac{7}{2}$

Problem Set 2

1. 63 ÷ 7 = 9; 9 × 3 = 27

2. 12 ÷ 4 = 3; 18 ÷ 3 = 6

3. 12 ÷ 4 = 3; 18 ÷ 3 = 6

4. Use the cover-up method: $\frac{z+1}{10} = -3$. $\frac{-31+1}{10} = -3$; −3 + 6 = 3; z = −31

5. 20 ÷ 5 = 4; 3 × 4 = 12; M = 12. 15 ÷ 12 = 1.25; 20 × 1.25 = 25. N = 25 → 12 + 25 = 37

6. $\frac{x+3}{4} = \frac{x+8}{5}$; 4(x − 8) = 5(x + 3); 4x − 32 = 5x + 15; x = −47   2 × −47 = −94

7. $\frac{1}{6}$ of 12 = $\frac{1}{6}$ × 12 = 2. $\frac{1}{12}$ of 24 = 2.

8. $\frac{1}{n+3} = \frac{1}{7}$; n = 4. $\frac{1}{n^2+9} = \frac{1}{4^2+9} = \frac{1}{16+9} = \frac{1}{25}$

9. $\frac{5}{x+2} = \frac{4}{x}$ → 5x = 4(x + 2) → 5x = 4x + 8 → x = 8

10. 25 ÷ 5 = 5; 2 × 5 = 10; q = 10

11. $\frac{x+3}{18} = \frac{x-5}{17}$ → 17(x + 3) = 18(x − 5); 17x + 51 = 18x − 90; 141 = x

12. $\frac{12}{x-2} = \frac{32}{x+8}$ → 12(x + 8) = 32(x − 2); 12x + 96 = 32x − 64; 20x = 160; x = 8

13. $\frac{a+b}{a-b} = \frac{4}{1}$ → 4(a − b) = a + b; 4a − 4b = a + b; 3a = 5b; $\frac{a}{b} = \frac{5}{3}$

14. $\frac{x+3y}{x-y} = \frac{3}{1}$ → 3(x − y) = x + 3y; 3x − 3y = x + 3y; 2x = 6y; $\frac{x}{y} = \frac{6}{2}$

15. $\frac{4a-b}{3a+2b} = \frac{2}{3}$ → 2(3a + 2b) = 3(4a − b); 6a + 4b = 12a − 3b; 6a = 7b; $\frac{a}{b} = \frac{7}{6}$

16. 3x = 4y. x = $\frac{4y}{3}$; $\frac{\frac{4y}{3}+2y}{3\frac{4y}{3}-y} = \frac{\frac{10y}{3}}{\frac{9y}{3}} = \frac{10}{9}$

17. 50 : 200 → 1 : 4

18. 6 × 7.5 = 45; 8 × 7.5 = 60; 60 − 45 = 15. x = 45

19. (3 : 4 : 5) × 5 = 15 : 20 : 25 → 15 + 20 + 25 = 60

20. To find this answer, the 4 and 7 must be multiplied by the same number and added to get a number between 25 and 35. If you multiply both by 3, you get 12 : 21, and 12 + 21 = 33 students.

SOLUTIONS — Operations & Functions — CHAPTER 13

Problem Set 1

1. $4\triangle 9 \rightarrow 4 + 9 - 4(9) = 13 - 36 = -23$
2. $6 * 7 \rightarrow 6 \times 7 - 2(6) - 2(7) = 42 - 12 - 14 = 16$
3. $a\triangle 3 = a \times 3 + a + 3 = 39$; $3a + a + 3 = 39$; $4a + 3 = 39$; $4a = 36$; $a = 9$
4. $4 * -2 \rightarrow 4 - 2 + 4 \times -2 = -2 + -8 = -10$
5. $a\square b = 4a - 3b$; $4\square x = 1$; $4\square x = 4(4) - 3(x) = 1$; $16 - 3x = 1$; $-3x = -15$; $x = 5$
6. $a\bigcirc b = \dfrac{a \times b}{a + b}$; $\dfrac{1}{2}\bigcirc a = \dfrac{1}{4}$; $\dfrac{1}{2}\bigcirc a = \dfrac{\frac{1}{2} \times a}{\frac{1}{2} + a} = \dfrac{1}{4}$; $\dfrac{1}{2} \times \dfrac{1}{2} = \dfrac{1}{4}$; $\dfrac{1}{2} + \dfrac{1}{2} = 1$; $a = \dfrac{1}{2}$
7. $<28> = 1 + 2 + 4 + 7 + 14 = 28$.
8. $?(4, 4)) = 4 - \dfrac{1}{4} = \dfrac{15}{4}$
   $?(4, \dfrac{15}{4}) = 4 - \dfrac{1}{15/4} = 4 - \dfrac{15}{4} = \dfrac{1}{4}$
9. $f(x) = 4x + a \rightarrow f(2) = 4(2) + a = 6$; $8 + a = 6$; $a = -2$
10. $f(x) = 2x + n \rightarrow f(8) = 2(8) + n = 20$; $16 + n = 20$; $n = 4$. $f(4) = 2(4) + 4 = 12$
11. Replace x with a and y with 2 $\rightarrow$ $3(a) + 2 - 12 = 0$; $3a - 10 = 0$; $3a = 10$; $a = 3.33$
12. $f(n) = 4n + 1$; $f(15) = 4(15) + 1 = 61$
13. $a_n = a_1 + f \times (n - 1) \rightarrow a_n = 7 + 10(51 - 1) = 507$
14. $5h + 8 \rightarrow 5(6) + 8 = 38$
15. $y = mx + 6 \rightarrow 6 = 24m + 6$; $m = 0$
16. $a@b = 3 + ab + a + 2b$; $x@2 = 16$; $x@2 = 3 + x(2) + x + 2(2) = 16$; $x@2 = 7 + 3x = 16$; $3x = 9$; $x = 3$
17. $2@4 = \dfrac{2}{2} + 4 = 5$; $6@2 = \dfrac{6}{2} + 2 = 5$; $2@4 - 6@2 = 0$
18. $f(0) = \dfrac{3(0) + 1}{0 - 2} = -\dfrac{1}{2}$; $f(3) = \dfrac{3(3) + 1}{3 - 2} = 10$;
    $f(0) + f(3) = -\dfrac{1}{2} + 10 = 9\dfrac{1}{2}$
19. By input-output connection we can find the formula $f(x) = 3x + 1$. $f(50) = 3(50) + 1 = 151$
20. $a * a = a^2 - a$, then $a * (a^2 - a)$
    $= a^2 - (a^2 - a) = a^2 - a^2 + a = 4$ $a = 4$.

Problem Set 2

1. Since the output for any given number is $4x + 7$, replace x for 3; $4(3) + 7$; $y = 19$
2. $f(2) = 8(2) - 5 = 11$
3. $3 * 5 = \dfrac{3 + 5}{2} = 4$
4. $6\otimes 4 = \dfrac{6 + 4}{6 - 4} = \dfrac{10}{2} = 5$
5. D is correct because if you add 6 to any input value, the output will be that number plus 6
6. $f(-4) = 2(-4) = -8$
7. $\dfrac{-2}{4} + (-2)(4) = -8\dfrac{1}{2}$
8. $2* = \dfrac{1}{2}$; $4* = \dfrac{1}{4}$; $\dfrac{1}{2} + \dfrac{1}{4} = \dfrac{2}{4} + \dfrac{1}{4} = \dfrac{3}{4}$
9. $f(1) = 4(1) - 6 = -2$; $f(3) = 4(3) - 6 = 6$; $f(1) + f(3) = -2 + 6 = 4$
10. $f(3) = 2(3) + 4 = 10$
11. $g(5) = 2(5) - 3 = 7$
12. $g(3) = 2(3) - 5 = 1$; $h(3) = 4(3) + 5 = 17$; $g(3) = h(3) = 1 - 17 = -16$
13. $x\spadesuit y = (x + y)(x - y)$; $3\spadesuit(4\spadesuit 5)$
    $= 3\spadesuit((4 + 5)(4 - 5)) = -9$;
    $3\spadesuit -9 = (3 + -9)(3 - (-9)) = -6(12) = -72$
14. $5x - 1$; Example for $x = 2$: $5(2) - 1 = 9$
15. $C(4) = 5(4) + 8 = \$28$
16. $f(2): 2(2) + a = 2$; $4 + a = 2$; $a = -2$
17. $3(a) + 12 + 3(2a) + 12 = 42$; $3a + 12 + 6a + 12 = 42$; $9a = 18$; $a = 2$
18. B is correct because if you multiply any x-value by 1.5, it will equal that number multiplied by 1.5. Example for $x = 3$: $1.5(3) = 4.5$
19. $3\otimes a = 3a + 3 - a$; $a\otimes 5 = a(5) + a - 5$; $3a + 3 - a = 5a + a - 5$; $2a + 3 = 6a - 5$; $8 = 4a$; $a = 2$
20. $f(b) + f(3b) = 2b + 4 + 2(3b) + 4 = 40$; $2b + 4 + 6b + 4 = 40$; $8b + 8 = 40$; $8b = 32$; $b = 4$

CHAPTER 14 — Exponents & Radicals — SOLUTIONS

Problem Set 1

1. $9 \times 9 \times 9 = 9^3$; $9 + 9 + 9 = 27$
   $\rightarrow 9^3 \times 27 = 19{,}683$

2. $2^5 - 2^4 = 2^{4+1} - 2^4 = 2^4 \times 2^1 - 2^4 = 2^4(2-1)$
   $= 24 \times 1 = 16$

3. a) $x \times x \times x \times x \times x \times x = x^6$
   b) $4 \times 4 + n \times n = 4^2 + n^2 = 16 + n^2$

4. $5^2 = 25$; $2^3 = 8$; $25 + 8 + 7 = 40$

5. $A \times A \times A = 12^3$. $A = 12$; $7 \times 7 = 7^2$.
   $B = 2 \rightarrow A + B = 12 + 2 = 14$

6. If a base number has an even exponent, the number will be positive. If it is odd, it will be negative. $(-1)^6 = 1$. $(-2)^2 = -2 \times -2 = 4$. $(-3)^1 = -3$. $(-1)^7 = -1$. $A = 1 + 4 = 5$; $B = -3 + -1 = -4$; $A + B = 5 - 4 = 1$

7. $4^{x+1} = 64$; $4^{x+1} = 4^3$; $x + 1 = 3$; $x = 2$

8. $5^{x+4} = 1$; $5^0 = 1$; $x + 4 = 0$; $x = -4$

9. $2^{11} + 2^{11} = 2 \times 2^{11}$; $4^4 + 4^4 = 2 \times 4^4 = \dfrac{2 \times 2^{11}}{2 \times 4^4}$
   $= \dfrac{2^{11}}{4^4} = \dfrac{2^{11}}{(2^2)^4} = \dfrac{2^{11}}{2^8} = 2^{11-8} = 2^3 = 8$

10. $7^{x-2} = 1$; $7^0 = 1$; $x - 2 = 0$; $x = 2$

11. $2^1 = 2$, $2^2 = 4$, $2^3 = 8$, $2^4 = 16$, $2^5 = 32$
    $3^1 = 3$, $3^2 = 9$, $3^3 = 27$
    $2^4 + 3^3 = 43$; $x + y = 4 + 3 = 7$

12. $9x = (3^2)^x = 3^{2x} = 3^{x^2} = (3^x)^2 = 2^2 = 4$

13. $2^{x-1} = \dfrac{2^x}{2} = 5 \rightarrow 2^x = 10 \rightarrow 4^x = 100$

14. This equality happens only
    $3x + y - 3 = 0$ and $x - y - 5 = 0$
    $3x + y = 3$ and $x - y = 5$. By solving them we get $x + y = 2 + (-3) = -1$

15. $5 \times 5 \times 5 \times 5 \times 5 = 5^5$; $5^2 + 5^2 + 5^2 + 5^2 + 5^2$
    $= 5(5^2) = \dfrac{5^5}{5 \times 5^2} = \dfrac{5^5}{5^3} = 5^2 = 25$

16. $3^{x-2} = \dfrac{3^x}{3^2}$; $3^x + \dfrac{3^x}{3^2} = 30$; $3^x\left(1 + \dfrac{1}{9}\right) = 30$;
    $3^x \times \dfrac{10}{9} = 30$; $3^x = 27$; $x = 3$

17. $1111^5 + 1111^5 = 2 \times 1111^5$; $1111^4 \times 1111^4$
    $= 2 \times 1111^4$; $\dfrac{2 \times 1111^5}{2 \times 1111^4} = \dfrac{1111^5}{1111^4} = 1111^{5-4}$
    $= 1111^1 = 1111$

18. By distributing $2^{10} \cdot 2^{-9} - 2^{10} \cdot 2^{-8} + 2^{10} \cdot 2^{-7}$
    $= 2^1 - 2^2 + 2^3 = 2 - 4 + 8 = 6$.

19. $2^{x+2x+3x} = 2^{2+3+7} = 2^{6x} = 2^{12} = x = 2$.

20. Since $4^4 = 4 \times 4 \times 4 \times 4$, ¼ of these numbers is $4^3 = 64$.

Problem Set 2

1. $\sqrt{81} = \sqrt{9^2} = 9$

2. $\sqrt{b} = 5$; $5^2 = 25$

3. $3^2 = 9$; $4^2 = 16$; $\sqrt{9 + 16} = \sqrt{25} = 5$

4. $\sqrt{0.16} = 0.4$; $\sqrt{0.36} = 0.6$; $0.4 + 0.6 = 1$

5. Work from right to left:
   $\sqrt{81} = 9$; $\sqrt{7 + 9} = \sqrt{16} = 4$;
   $\sqrt{8} + 2 \times 4 = \sqrt{8} + 8 = \sqrt{16} = 4$

6. $\sqrt{25} = 5$; $\sqrt{49} = 7$; $\sqrt{16} = 4$; $5 + 7 - 4 = 8$

7. $\sqrt{25} = 5$; $\sqrt{36} = 6$; $x + 5 = 6$; $x = 1$

8. $11^2 = 121$; $9 + 4y = 121$; $4y = 112$; $y = 28$

9. $\sqrt{4} = 2$. $\sqrt{7} + 2 = \sqrt{9} = 3$. $\sqrt{13} + 3 = \sqrt{16} = 4$

10. $\sqrt{81} = 9$. $\sqrt{16} = 4 \rightarrow \sqrt{n} = 5 \rightarrow n = 25$

11. Perfect cubes: $1^3 = 1$; $2^3 = 8$; $3^3 = 27$; $4^4 = 64$
    Only $\sqrt{1}$ and $\sqrt{64}$ have square roots that are integers: 1 & 8

SOLUTIONS — Exponents & Radicals — CHAPTER 14

12. Find 4^2 first. $4^2 = 16$. Add 1 to 16 to find what x would be: $16 + 1 = 17$, $x = 17$

13. $\sqrt{0.09} = \sqrt{0.3^2} = 0.3$; $\sqrt{0.16} = \sqrt{0.4^2} = 0.4$; $0.3 + 0.4 = 0.7$

14. $\sqrt{98}$ is a little bit less than $\sqrt{100}$, which equals 10. $\sqrt{50}$ is a little bit more than $\sqrt{49}$, which is 7. This would be close to $10 - 7 = 3$.

15. $n = \frac{1}{6}$; $1 \div \frac{1}{6} = 1 \times 6 = 6$

16. $-\sqrt{23}$ is a little bit less than $-\sqrt{25}$, which is -5.

17. $\sqrt{x^3 - 2^y} = \sqrt{5^3 - 2^2} = \sqrt{125 - 4} = \sqrt{121} = 11$

18. $\sqrt{18} = \sqrt{9} \times \sqrt{2} = 3\sqrt{2}$; $\sqrt{12} = \sqrt{4} \times \sqrt{3} = 2\sqrt{3}$; $\sqrt{24} = \sqrt{4} \times \sqrt{6} = 2\sqrt{6}$.
$\frac{3\sqrt{2} \times 2\sqrt{3}}{2\sqrt{6}} = \frac{6\sqrt{6}}{2\sqrt{6}} = 3$

19. $\frac{\sqrt{0.016} \times \sqrt{0.009}}{\sqrt{0.1}} = 0.7$

20. $\sqrt{80}$ is close to $\sqrt{81} = 9$. $\sqrt{120}$ is close to $\sqrt{121} = 11$. Since these numbers would be greater than $\sqrt{80} + \sqrt{120}$, take one digit smaller than $\sqrt{81} + \sqrt{121} = 9 + 11 = 20$. One less is 19.

Problem Set 3

1. $5^0 = 1$; $3^2 = 9$; $4^3 = 6^4$; $5^1 = 5$; $1 \times 9 + 64 - 5 = 68$

2. $\sqrt{5^2 + 12^2} = \sqrt{169} = 13$

3. The exponents are added when multiplying the base, so $x + 2x = 12$; $3x = 12$; $x = 4$

4. $5^2 = 25$. $\sqrt{n}$ must equal 25 because $20 + 5 = 25$. $\sqrt{25} = 5$, so $n = 25$

5. $\frac{4^{20}}{4} = 4^{20-1} = 4^{19} = 2^{38}$.

6. $\frac{a^2}{x} \div \frac{x}{a^2} = \frac{a^2}{x} \times \frac{a^2}{x} = \frac{a^4}{x^2}$

7. $\frac{(x^9)(x^6)}{x^3} = \frac{x^{15}}{x^3} = x^{12}$

8. $\sqrt{0.49} = 0.7$; $\sqrt{0.09} = 0.3$; $0.7 + 0.3 + 13 = 14$

9. Find $26^2 = 676$; Take $676 \div 121$ to find x: ~5.587

10. $5^2 = 25$. Take $25 - 4 = 21$; $a = 21$

11. $3^4 = 81$; $3^1 = 3$; $81 + 3 = 84$.
 $x + 2 = 4$ and $x - 1 = 1$; $x = 2$

12. This equality happens only
 $x + 4 = x + y + 8 = 0$ $x = -4$ and $y = -4$.

13. Since the expressions are equal, set the exponents equal to each other to find
 x: $x + 4 = 2x - 1 \rightarrow 4 = x - 1 \rightarrow 5 = x$

14. $10^{10} = 10$ billion. Half of 10 billion is 5 billion

15. $5x - 6 = x^2 \rightarrow -x^2 + 5x - 6 = 0$
 $\rightarrow -1(x^2 - 5x + 6) = 0 \rightarrow -1(x - 3)(x - 2) = 0$
 $\rightarrow x = 2$ and $x = 3$ works for x in this equation.

16. $\sqrt{40} = \sqrt{4} \times \sqrt{10} = 2\sqrt{10}$; $(\sqrt{5} + \sqrt{2})^2 = 7 + 2\sqrt{10}$
 $\rightarrow 2\sqrt{10} - (7 + 2\sqrt{10}) = 2\sqrt{10} - 7 - 2\sqrt{10} = -7$

17. $\sqrt{2} \times \sqrt{2} \times \sqrt{2} = \sqrt{2^3}$; $\sqrt{2} + \sqrt{2} = 2\sqrt{2} \rightarrow \frac{\sqrt{2^3}}{2\sqrt{2}} = 1$

18. $\sqrt{60} = 2\sqrt{3}\sqrt{5}$; $\sqrt{12} = \sqrt{4} \times \sqrt{3} = 2\sqrt{3}$
 $\rightarrow \frac{2\sqrt{3}\sqrt{5} \times 2\sqrt{3}}{\sqrt{15}} = 4\sqrt{3}$

19. $(\sqrt{3x + 1}) - 3 = 7$; $\sqrt{3x + 1} = 10$; $3x + 1 = 10^2$; $3x + 1 = 100$; $3x = 99$; $x = 33$

20. $1 = \frac{16}{16}$; $\sqrt{\frac{16}{16} + \frac{9}{16}} = \sqrt{\frac{25}{16}} + \frac{5}{4} \rightarrow$
 $\left(\sqrt{\frac{11}{4}} + \frac{5}{4}\right) = \sqrt{\frac{16}{4}} = 2$

CHAPTER 15 — Geometry Basics — SOLUTIONS

Problem Set 1

1. By adding all sides: $7 + 3 + 7 + 3 = 10$. The perimeter is 20 cm.

2. 3x, 6x, and 90° add up to 180°. So, $3x + 6x = 90°$, $9x = 90°$, and $x = 10°$

3. The sum of all three angles is 180°. $90 + x + x + 40 = 180°$. $\Rightarrow 2x = 50 \Rightarrow x = 25°$.

4. The sum of two interior angle is equal to one exterior angle. So, $x = 40 + 40$ (interior angle of 140°). Therefore, $x = 80°$.

5. The sum of the area of the square ($3 \times 3 = 9$) and the area of triangle ($\frac{3 \times 3}{2} = 4.5$) is $9 + 4.5 = 13.5$.

6. $60° + x° = 90° \Rightarrow x = 30°$.

7. The shaded area is $\frac{7 \times 4}{2} = 14$.

8. Perimeter $= 100 = x + 18 + x + 18$ $\Rightarrow 2x + 36 = 100 \Rightarrow 2x = 64 \Rightarrow x = 32$.

9. If the area is 25 square meters, then one side is 5 meters. The perimeter is $4 \times 5 = 20$.

10. The unshaded area is the whole area minus the shaded area. $(4x)^2 - (y)^2 = 16x^2 - y^2$

11. The perimeter of the triangle is $3 \times 8 = 24$. The perimeter of the rectangle is $AD + 8 + AD = BC + 8 = 24$. So, $AD = BC = 4$. So, the area of the triangle is $4 \times 8 = 32$.

12. The area of square B is 400 cm². One side of the square is 20 cm. Therefore, the perimeter of square B is 80 cm.

13. The shaded area is the area of the rectangle minus the total areas of corner triangles. $9 \times 7 - 4 \times 2 \times 22 = 63 - 8 = 55$.

14. By using two similar triangles, $\frac{3}{x} = \frac{10}{x+5} + 5$ $\rightarrow 10x = 3x + 15 \rightarrow 7x = 15 \rightarrow x = 15/7$.

15. Let x be length of an unknown side of the triangle. $36 = x + 12 + x + 12 \rightarrow 12 = 2x \rightarrow x = 6$. Therefore, the area is $12 \times 6 = 72$.

16. 1 meter = 100 cm. 36 meters is 3600 centimeters.

17. By using two similar triangles, $\frac{4}{x} = \frac{12}{x+10}$ $\rightarrow 12x = 4x + 40 \rightarrow 8x = 40 \rightarrow x = 5$.

18. By the Pythagorean theorem, $x^2 = 8^2 + 10^2 \Rightarrow x = \sqrt{164} = 2\sqrt{41}$.

19. This is a counting problem. The total number of squares is $3^2 + 2^2 + 1^2 = 14$. The total number of rectangles is 22. Therefore, the answer is 36.

20. The dimensions of the shaded area are 6 and 4. The area of the rectangle is $6 \times 4 = 24$.

Problem Set 2

1. The sum is 1800. So, $2x + 3x + 4x = 1800$ $\rightarrow 9x = 1800 \rightarrow x = 200$. Three angles are 40, 60, and 80.

2. The sum of two interior angle is equal to one exterior angle. So, $120 = 2x + 3x$. So, $5x = 180$. Therefore, $x = 36°$. The measure of angle BDC $2x = 72°$.

SOLUTIONS   Geometry Basics   CHAPTER 15

3. A + 30° + 30° = 180° → A = 120°.

4. We need to find two legs' lengths. The length of the side opposite to 30 is one half of the length of the hypotenuse. So it is 4 cm. The other side is $4\sqrt{3}$. The perimeter is $8 + 4 + 4\sqrt{3} = 12 + 4\sqrt{3}$.

5. The perimeter of an equilateral triangle is 3x one side length, minimum = 3 × 1 = 3 and maximum = 3 × 1.4 = 4.2. Therefore, the maximum integer value is 4.

6. The length of the side opposite to 30 is one half of the length of the hypotenuse. So it is 6 cm. The other side is $6\sqrt{3}$. The perimeter is $12 + 6\sqrt{3} + 12 + 6\sqrt{3} = 24 + 12\sqrt{3}$.

7. Similarly (#6), one side which is hypotenuse should be 6 cm. So, the perimeter is 18 cm.

8. Two equal lengths is $\sqrt{2}$. So, the length of the hypotenuse is $\sqrt{2} \times \sqrt{2} = 2$. DC = EA = 1, which is half of the length of the hypotenuse. Therefore, the perimeter of the rectangle is $1 + 2 + 1 + 2 = 6$ inches.

9. Since the triangle is an isosceles, AB = BC = 40. So, the distance between the vertex C and the line AB is BC=40. Then, HC = $\frac{40}{2}\sqrt{3} = 20\sqrt{3}$

10. The area is $\frac{4 \times 6}{2} = 12$

11. If we draw the heigh of triangle with base 24. There is a right triangle with two legs of 5 and 12. So, the length of the hypotenuse is 13 (5–12–13 tringle by the Pythagorean theorem). The perimeter of the triangle is $13 + 13 + 24 = 50$.

12. Let $h\sqrt{3}$ be the height of the equilateral triangle, and h is half the length of one of its sides. So, one side is $3 + 3 = 6$. The perimeter is $3 \times 6 = 18$.

13. We can use the formula for the area of an equilateral triangle: Area = $\frac{a^2\sqrt{3}}{4}$ where a is the length of one of the sides of the equilateral triangle. Therefore, the area of an equilateral triangle with a side of 12 cm is $36\sqrt{3}$ square centimeters.

14. The area of ABC = $\frac{6^2\sqrt{3}}{4} = 9\sqrt{3}$ and the area of DEF = $\frac{8^2\sqrt{3}}{4} = 16\sqrt{3}$. The ratio is 9:16.

15. $w + 2w + w + 2w = 30 \to 6w = 30 \to w = 5$. Therefore, the area is $5 \times 10 = 50$.

16. If the length of the diagonal is $4\sqrt{2}$ then the side length is 4. Therefore, the area is 16.

17. By the similarity, $\frac{4}{2} = \frac{x}{4} \to 2x = 16 \to x = 8$.

18. By the Pythagorean theorem, $8^2 + 15^2 = 64 + 225 = AC^2 = ?$. The area of the rectangle is 289.

19. By the Pythagorean theorem and the area of equilateral triangles,
Area ABE + Area BCD = Area FAC (Why ?) →
So, the area of the equilateral triangle BCD is $225 - 49 = 175$

20. By using two similar triangles,
$\frac{2}{3} = \frac{x}{18} \to 3x = 36 \to x = 12$.

Math Fluency

CHAPTER 16 — Coordinate Geometry — SOLUTIONS

Problem Set 1

1. $(0, 0)$ is on lies on both the x– and y– axes.

2. $d = \sqrt{(0-0)^2 + (7-(-4))^2} = \sqrt{0 + 11^2}$
   $d = \sqrt{121} = 11$.

3. $d = \sqrt{(-4-5)^2 + (1-1)^2} = \sqrt{81 + 0}$
   $d = \sqrt{81} = 9$.

4. The midpoint is $\left(\dfrac{4+6}{2}, \dfrac{3-1}{2}\right) = (5, 1)$.

5. The height of the triangle is 4.
   The area is $\dfrac{\text{Base} \times h}{2} = \dfrac{10 \times 4}{2} = 20$.

6. Area $\triangle OKT = \dfrac{OK \times TK}{2} = \dfrac{4 \times 4}{2} = 8$.

7. Area $\triangle OLS = \dfrac{OL \times SL}{2} = \dfrac{8 \times 5}{2} = 20$.

8. Area $\triangle OMR = \dfrac{MR \times OM}{2} = \dfrac{6 \times 9}{2} = 27$.

9. The midpoint is $\left(\dfrac{5-1}{2}, \dfrac{3-1}{2}\right) = (2, 1)$.

10. The midpoint is $\left(\dfrac{0-5}{2}, \dfrac{-2+1}{2}\right) = \left(-2, -\dfrac{1}{2}\right)$.

11. Reflection in the x-axis $(3, -4)$

12. $D(-2, -3)$

13. $E(2, 3)$

14. Distance $AC = 2 + 2 = 4$

15. $P(-1, 3)$

16. $H(9, -1)$

17. The midpoint is $\left(\dfrac{2+8}{2}, \dfrac{5+11}{2}\right) = (5, 8)$.

18. The midpoint is $\left(\dfrac{3+1}{2}, \dfrac{8-4}{2}\right) = (2, 2)$.

19. Area $= \left(\dfrac{AD + BC}{2}\right) \times h = \left(\dfrac{20+10}{2}\right) \times 8 = 120$.

20. $d = \sqrt{(4-0)^2 + (3-0)^2} = \sqrt{4^2 + 3^2} = \sqrt{25} = 5$

Problem Set 2

1. $d = \sqrt{(3-1)^2 + (6-3)^2} = \sqrt{4 + 9} = \sqrt{13}$

2. $d = \sqrt{(-1-2)^2 + (-3-4)^2} = \sqrt{9 + 49} = \sqrt{58}$

3. $d = \sqrt{(5-3)^2 + (-2-(-2))^2} = \sqrt{4 + 0} = 2$

4. $d = \sqrt{(5-2)^2 + (4-(-2))^2} = \sqrt{9 + 36} = \sqrt{45}$
   $= 3\sqrt{5}$

5. $d = \sqrt{(5-(-4))^2 + (-2-(-6))^2}$
   $d = \sqrt{81 + 16} = \sqrt{97}$

6. $d = \sqrt{(4-4)^2 + (-3-2)^2} = \sqrt{0^2 + 25} = 5$

7. $d_{AB} = \sqrt{(5-2)^2 + (1-(-1))^2} = \sqrt{9+4} = \sqrt{13}$
   $d_{AC} = \sqrt{(2-0)^2 + (5-2)^2} = \sqrt{4+9} = \sqrt{13}$
   $d_{BC} = \sqrt{(5-0)^2 + (2-1)^2} = \sqrt{25+1} = \sqrt{26}$
   It is an isosceles triangle.

8. $A(1, 2)$ and $B(5, 4)$. $M\left(\dfrac{1+5}{2}, \dfrac{2+4}{2}\right) = M(3, 3)$.

9. $C(-3, 5)$ and $B(-1, -1)$.
   $N\left(\dfrac{-3-1}{2}, \dfrac{5-1}{2}\right) = N(-2, 2)$.

10. $B(x, y)$. $3 = \dfrac{-1+x}{2} \Rightarrow x = 7$
    $4 = \dfrac{4+y}{2} \Rightarrow y = 4$ $B(7, 4)$.

11. C is the midpoint. $C\left(\dfrac{4-2}{2}, \dfrac{-7-3}{2}\right) = C(1, -5)$.

12. The midpoint AC and DB(x, y).
    $\left(\dfrac{-3+0}{2}, \dfrac{4-2}{2}\right) = \left(\dfrac{x+1}{2}, \dfrac{y+3}{2}\right)$
    $\Rightarrow x = -4 \quad y = -1$

13. $x = 2$ is passing $(2, 2)$ and $(2, -2)$.

14. $y = -2$ is passing $(2, -2)$ and $(-2, -2)$.

15. $d_{DC} = \sqrt{(2-0)^2 + (6-(-2))^2} = \sqrt{4+64} = \sqrt{68}$
    $d_{BC} = \sqrt{(2-(-2))^2 + (-3-(-2))^2} = \sqrt{16+1} = \sqrt{17}$
    Area $= 2\sqrt{17} \cdot \sqrt{17} = 34$.

16. Area $=$ Base $\times h = 8 \times (6-2) = 8 \times 4 = 32$

17. $(2000, 2000-3) = (2000, 1997)$

18. $120 = 10 \times SR \Rightarrow SR = 12$. $P = 3 + 12 = 15$

19. $E\left(\dfrac{1+5}{2}, 8\right) = E(3, 8)$
    $DE = 2 = GF = AG$ (isosceles)
    $DG = 8 - 3 = 5$ Area $= 5 \times 3 = 15$

20. Area DAGF $= \dfrac{3 \times 3}{2} = 4.5$.

SOLUTIONS — Geometry 3-D — CHAPTER 17

Problem Set 1

1. The area of the floor is finding the area for the bottom face. The width is 8 ft and the length is 6 ft. 8 ft × 6 ft = 48 ft²

2. The perimeter is the lengths of the sides of the floor added together. There are two widths of 8 ft each, and two lengths of 6 ft each.
   8 + 8 + 6 + 6 = 28 ft

3. There are six surfaces total.
   Two are length × width, two are length × height, and two are width × height.
   L × W = 6 × 8 = 48 ft²; 48 × 2 = 96 ft²;
   L × H = 6 × 4 = 24 ft²; 24 × 2 = 48 ft²;
   W × H = 8 × 4 = 32 ft²; 32 × 2 = 64 ft²
   → 96 + 48 + 64 = 208 ft²

4. Volume = length × width × height
   → 6 × 8 × 4 = 192 ft³

5. The volume of a triangle = area of base × height. First, find the missing side length with the Pythagorean Theorem.
   $3^2 + x^2 = 5^2$; $9 + x^2 = 25$; $x^2 = 16$; $x = 4$.
   The area of the triangle is (length × width) ÷ 2;
   (4 × 3) ÷ 2 = 12 ÷ 2 = 6 ft². Multiply the area of the base by the height. 6 ft² × 4 = 24 ft³

6. There are six surfaces total.
   Two are length × width, two are length × height, and two are width × height.
   L × W = 4x × 3x = 12x ft²; 12x × 2 = 24x ft²;
   L × H = 4x × 3x = 12x ft²; 12x × 2 = 24x ft²;
   W × H = 3x × 3x = 9x ft²; 9x × 2 = 18x ft²
   → 24x + 24x + 18x = 66x ft²

7. $V = \pi r^2 \times h$ → r = 10, because the radius is half the diameter. $\pi r^2 = \pi \times 10^2 = 314.159$ cm²; 314.159 × 30 = 9,424.78 cm³

8. Cubes have the same length, width, and height. If one length of Cube A is 4, then the volume is 4 × 4 × 4 = 64 cm³. The volume of Cube B is 6 × 6 × 6 = 216 cm³. Cube A divided be Cube B = 64 ÷ 216 = $\frac{8}{27}$ cm³

9. There are six surfaces:
   10 × 4, 10 × 4, 10 × 6, 10 × 6, 6 × 4, 6 × 4.
   40 + 40 + 60 + 60 + 24 + 24 = 248 units²

10. The area of a circle is πr^2. Set $\pi r^2 = 64\pi$ → $\pi 8^2$. If the radius is 8, the diameter is 16.

11. The area of a triangle is (base × height) ÷ 2. The base of the triangle is 5 + 5 = 10. The height is the same length as the radius given, which is 5.
    10 × 5 = 50; 50 ÷ 2 = 25 units²

12. Take the cubed root of 125 to find what one length is: 5 cm. To find the area of one face, take 5 × 5 = 25 cm²

13. To find the area of a sector use:
    $A = \frac{120}{360} \times 9\pi = \frac{1}{3} \times 9\pi = 9.425$ units²

14. The circumference is $2\pi r = 20$ → $\pi r = 10$
    → 10 ÷ π = 3.18 cm.

15. The area of a circle is πr^2. If the diameter is 6, the radius is 3. πr^2 → $\pi 3^2 = 9\pi$ ft²

16. If the circumference is 36π, that can be rewritten as $2\pi \times 18$. The radius would be 18. The area of circle would be $\pi \times 18^2$ → $A = 324\pi$ cm²

17. If one face area is 16, then one length is 4, since 4 × 4 is 16. To find the area, take $4^3 = 64$ units³

18. Since all surface area are the same size and there are 6 sides on a cube, take 96 ÷ 6 = 16. Each surface has an area of 16 cm². That means each side length is 4 because 4 × 4 is 16 cm². The volume is $4^3 = 64$ cm³.

19. The area of a triangular prism is the base × height. The base is the area of a triangle, which is the base of the triangle times the height, divided by 2. 6 × 8 = 48; 48 ÷ 2 = 24. If the base is 24 cm², then we take 24h = 240 → h = 10 cm

20. The full volume is 6 × 18 × 4 = 432 cm³. To find the volume of the water, take
    $432 \times \frac{1}{3} = 144$ cm³

CHAPTER 18 — Linear Equations — SOLUTIONS

Problem Set 1

1. For two points (5, 8) and (5, -5) distance;
$\sqrt{(8-(-5))^2 + (5-5)^2} = 13$.

2. If the point (a, 2) is on the line, replace x by a and replace y by 2. So, $a + 6 - 2 = 0 \rightarrow a = -4$

3. Solve the system of equations to find the intersection points; $-3x - 7 = y$, $x - 1 = y$. Let's solve by substitution. Substitute $x - 1$ for y in first equation; $-3x - 7 = x - 1 \rightarrow -4x = 6$ $\rightarrow x = -\frac{3}{2} = -1.5$. Plug the x-value in the second equation; $-1.5 - 1 = y \rightarrow -2.5 = y$.
So, the intersection point is $(a, b) = (-1.5, -2.5)$.
Therefore, $a + b = (-1.5) + (-2.5) = -4$.

4. For $x = 0$, $y = -5$. So, $(0, -5)$ is the y-intercept of the line.

5. For $y = 0$, $x = -5$. So, $(-5, 0)$ is the x-intercept of the line.

6. For $x = 0$, $y = 2$. So, $(0, 2)$ is the y-intercept of the line.

7. For $y = 0$, $x = 3$. So, $(3, 0)$ is the x-intercept of the line.

8. Let's find the coordinates for the linear function.
For $x = 0$, $y = 2$. So, the first pair is (0, 2).
For $y = 0$, $x = 3$. So, the second pair is (3, 0). As drawn in the figure, the height is 2, and the length of the base is 3 in the triangle.
Therefore, the area of the triangle is $\frac{2 \cdot 3}{2} = 3$.

9. Solve the system of equations to find the intersection points; $y = x - 2$, $y = 2x - 1$. Let's solve by substitution. Substitute x-2 for y in the second equation; $x - 2 = 2x - 1 \rightarrow x = -1$. Plug the x-value in the first equation; $y = -1 - 2 \rightarrow y = -3$. So, the intersection point is $(a, b) = (-1, -3)$. Therefore, $a + b = (-1) + (-3) = -4$.

10. $-2(4 - 3x) - 6x = 10 \rightarrow -8 + 6x - 6x = 10$
$\rightarrow -8 \neq 10$ (False statement) No solution.

11. Solve the system of equations to find the intersection points; $y = 65 - 3x$, $y = 2x$. Let's solve by substitution. Substitute 2x for y in the first equation; $2x = 65 - 3x \rightarrow 5x = 65 \rightarrow x = 13$. Plug the x-value in the second equation; $y = 2 \cdot 13$ $\rightarrow y = 26$. So, the intersection point is $(a, b) = (13, 26)$. Therefore, $a + b = 13 + 26 = 39$.

12. We can use pairs of x (figure numbers) and y (numbers of tiles) in the graph to find the slope m for the equation $y = mx + n$. (1, 11) and (2, 17) are two pairs that satisfied the equation. So, $m = 17 - 11 / 2 - 1 = 6$. Thus, the equation is $y = 6x + n$. Let's plug the coordinates of any given point into the equation to find n; $11 = 6 \cdot 1 + n \rightarrow n = 5$.
Therefore, the equation is $y = 6x + 5$.
Hence, for $x = 21$, $y = 6 \cdot 21 + 5 \rightarrow y = 131$.

13. We can use pairs of IN(x) and OUT(y) (numbers of tiles) in the graph to find the slope m for the equation $y = mx + n$. (-4, -22) and (-3, -17) are two pairs that satisfied the equation. So, $m = -17 - (-22) / -3 - (-4) = 5$. Thus, the equation is $y = 5x + n$. Let's plug the coordinates of any given point into the equation to find n; $-22 = 5 \cdot (-4) + n \rightarrow n = -2$. Therefore, the equation is $y = 5x - 2$. Hence, for IN(x) = 10, Out (y) = -48. So, $z = -48$.

SOLUTIONS — Linear Equations — CHAPTER 18

14.

Hours(x)	0	1	2	...	x
Cost(y)	12	32	52	...	132

Let's make a graph from the given information. We can use pairs of hours(x) and cost(y) in the graph to find the slope m for the equation $y = mx + n$. (0, 12) and (1, 32) are two pairs that satisfied the equation. So, $m = 32-12 / 1-0 = 20$. Thus, the equation is $y = 20x + n$. Let's plug the coordinates of any given point into the equation to find n; $12 = 20 \cdot 0 + n \rightarrow n = 12$. Therefore, the equation is $y = 20x + 12$. Hence, $132 = 20 \cdot x + 12 \rightarrow x = 6$. 6 hours was the boat rented.

15.

Candy(x)	0	1	2	...	x
Cost(y)	3.5	5	6.5	...	29

Let's make a graph from the given information. We can use pairs of Candy(x) and cost(y) in the graph to find the slope m for the equation $y = mx + n$. (0, 3.5) and (1, 5) are two pairs that satisfied the equation. So, $m = \frac{5-3.5}{1-0} = 1.5$. Thus, the equation is $y = 1.5x + n$. Let's plug the coordinates of any given point into the equation to find n; $3.5 = 1.5 \cdot 0 + n \rightarrow n = 3.5$. Therefore, the equation is $y = 1.5x + 3.5$. Therefore, $29 = 1.5x + 3.5 \rightarrow x = 17$. I get 17 candy bars.

16. Let x be the number of 2-point question and y be the number of 4-point question.
Then, $x + y = 40$, $2x + 4y = 100$. Solve the first equation for y; $y = 40 - x$. Substitute $y = 40 - x$ in second equation; $2x + 4 \cdot (40 - x) = 100$
$\rightarrow 2x + 160 - 4x = 100 \rightarrow 60 = 2x \rightarrow 30 = x$.
Substitute $x = 30$ in first equation; $30 + y = 40$
$\rightarrow y = 10$. So, there are 30 two-point and 10 four-point questions on the test.

17. Solve the system of equations to find the intersection points; $y = x$, $x + y = 4$. Let's solve by substitution. Substitute $y = x$ for y in the second equation; $x + x = 4 \rightarrow 2x = 4 \rightarrow x = 2$.
Plug the x-value in the first equation; $y = 2$.
So, the intersection point is (2, 2). For $x + y = 4$, if $y = 0$, then $x = 4$. So, one vertex of the triangle is at the origin (0,0), and the other vertexes of the triangle are at (2, 2) and (0,4). As drawn in the figure, the height is 2, and the length of the base is 2 in the triangle. Therefore, the area of the triangle is $\frac{2 \cdot 2}{2} = 4$.

18. $m = \frac{5-2}{5-4} \rightarrow 3$. So, $m = 3$.

19. $m = \frac{2-2}{3-(-8)} \rightarrow 0$. So, $m = 0$.

20. $m = \frac{10-6}{3-2} \rightarrow 4$.
So, $m = 2$. $y = mx + n \rightarrow y = 2x + n$. Let's plug the coordinates of the given point into the equation to find n; $6 = 2 \cdot 1 + n \rightarrow 4 = n$. Thus, the equation is $y = 2x + 4$.

Problem Set 2

1. One vertex of the triangle is at the origin (0, 0), which we can take as a reference. One vertex is at (6, 0). It lies on the x-axis. This gives us the length of the base, which is 6. The third vertex (0, 3) lies on the y-axis. This gives us the height of the triangle, which is 3. The area of the triangle is $\frac{6 \cdot 3}{2} = 9$.

CHAPTER 18 — Linear Equations — SOLUTIONS

2. Rectangle ABCD has its vertices at A (0,0), B (6,0), C (6, 4) and D (0, 4). This gives us the length of the bases, which are 6 and 4.
   The area of the rectangle is 4 · 6 = 24.

3. Let's find the coordinates for the linear function. For x = 0, y = 3. So, the first pair is (0, 3). For y = 0, x = 4. So, the second pair is (4, 0). As drawn in the figure, the height is 3, and the length of the base is 4 in the triangle. Therefore, the area of the triangle is $\frac{4 \cdot 3}{2} = 6$.

4. $m = \frac{6-2}{4-2} \to 2$. So, m = 2.

5. For x = 0, y = $\frac{2}{3}$.
   So, the graph crosses the y-axis at (0, $\frac{2}{3}$)

6. For y = 0, x = 2.
   So, the graph crosses the x-axis at (2, 0).

7. For two points (–1, 3) and (2, –4) distance;
   $\sqrt{(-4-3)^2 + (2-(-1))^2} = 58$.

8. For x = 0, y = 1.
   So, the graph crosses the y-axis at (0, 1).

9. $m = \frac{4-3}{2-(-1)} \to \frac{1}{3}$. So, m = $\frac{1}{3}$.

10. Add two equations
    x – y = 3
    x + y = 1
    ─────────
    2x = 4 ⇒ x = 2 and y = –1
    The intersection point is (2, –1).

11. x < 3 is the inequality that represents the graph.

12. x < 6 is the inequality that represents the graph.

13. 3 < x is the inequality that represents the graph.

14. –3 < x is the inequality that represents the graph.

15. (2, 0) is the x-intercept of the line, and (0, 1) is the y-intercept of the line. So, the slope of the line is m = $-\frac{1}{2}$. Thus, the equation is y = $-\frac{1}{2}$x + n. Let's plug the coordinates of any given point into the equation to find n; $0 = -\frac{1}{2} \cdot 2 + n \to n = 1$.
    Therefore, the equation is y = $\frac{1}{2}$x + 1.

16. Combine the like terms; 3y –5.

17. S could be $\frac{15}{10}$ = 1.5 and T could be $\frac{16}{10}$ = 1.6. So, S ÷ T is little less than 1 which point R is the best representation on the number line.

18. Triangle ABC has its vertices at A (2, 0), B (6, 0) and C (6, 3). Therefore, the height is 3, and the length of the base is 4 in the triangle.
    Therefore, the area of the triangle is $\frac{3 \cdot 4}{2} = 6$.

19. For x = 0, y = $\frac{15}{4}$. So, the first pair is (0, $\frac{15}{4}$).
    For y = 0, x = 5. The second pair is (5,0).
    Therefore, m = $\frac{\frac{15}{4} - 0}{0 - 5} \to m = -\frac{3}{4}$

20. We need to find the slope for y = mx + n. So, $m = \frac{9-3}{4-2} \to m = 3$. Therefore, y = 3x + n. Let's plug the coordinates of any given point into the equation to find n; 3 = 3·2 + n → n = –3. Hence, the equation is y = 3x – 3.

SOLUTIONS — Number Systems — CHAPTER 19

Problem Set 1

1. The possible combinations of (x, y) are (0, 12), (1, 11), (2, 10), (3, 9), (4, 8), (5, 7) and (6, 6) for x + y + 12. When the sum of two numbers is given, the max product is when both x and y are of the same numeric value. Hence, the largest value of x · y is 6 · 6 = 36.

2. The possible combinations of (x, y) are (1, 16), (2, 8), and (4, 4) for x · y = 16. Therefore, the largest value of x + y is 1 + 16 = 17.

3. The possible combinations of (x, y) are (1, 12), (2, 6), and (3, 4). Therefore, the smallest value of x + y is 3 + 4 = 7.

4. a · b = 13, since 13 is the prime number, the pair of (a, b) can be (1, 13) or (13, 1). If c is 13, it does not satisfy b · c = 12.
   Therefore, a = 13 and b = 1. Since b = 1, then c = 12. Hence, a + b + c → 13 + 1 + 12 = 26.

5. The possible combinations of (x, y) are (0, 5), (1, 4), and (2, 3). For x · y → 5 · 0 = 5, 1 · 4 = 4, 2 · 3 = 6. Therefore, there are 3 values for x · y

6. To simplify, $x = 1 + \frac{12}{2}$. So, the possible combinations of (x, y) are (13, 1), (7, 2), (5, 3), (7, 4), (8, 6) and (13, 12). Therefore, there are 6 distinct values of x.

7. If x is an integer, then 4x is an even integer. The subtraction of an odd number and an even number is always odd. Therefore, 4x − 3 is an odd number.

8. If x is an even number, then x^3 and 2x are an even number. So, $x^3 + 2x + 1$ is an odd number since the sum of an odd number and an even number is always odd. Moreover, if x is an odd number, then x^3 is an odd number while 2x is an even number. So, $x^3 + 2x$ is an odd number since the sum of an odd number and an even number is always odd. Also, $x^3 + 2x + 1$ is an even number since the sum of an odd number is always an even number. Therefore, if x is an even number, then $x^3 + 2x + 1$ is odd, and if x is an odd number, then $x^3 + 2x + 1$ is even.

9. If n is an even number, then n^2 is even. So, $n^2 - n$ is an even number since the sum of two even numbers is always even. If n is an odd number, then n^2 is odd. So, $n^2 - n$ is an even number since the sum of two odd numbers is always even. Therefore, $n^2 - n$ is always even.

10. Replace b by 2c in a = 3b; a = 3 · 2c
    → a = 6c. Replace the b by 2c and a by 6c in
    $\frac{a + b + c}{c}$; $\frac{6c + 2c + c}{c} = \frac{9c}{c} \rightarrow 9$.

11. $\frac{5}{3} < \ldots < 2\pi$ ($\pi \cong 3.14$) $\rightarrow 1.\overline{6} < \ldots < 6.28$.
    Whole numbers lie in the interval are 2, 3, 4, 5 and 6. There are 5 whole numbers.

12. 10 < ..... < 30. Prime numbers are 11, 13, 17, 19, 23, and 29 between 10 and 30. There are 6 prime numbers.

13. When two numbers are added, the result is −15. So, x + y = −15. One of them is 8 so, 8 + y = −15 → y = −23.

CHAPTER 19 — Number Systems — SOLUTIONS

14. The minimum possible product of three different numbers of the set is the product of the set $\{-8, 5, 7\}$. So, $-8 \cdot 5 \cdot 7 = -280$.

15. Let's convert the repeating decimal numbers into rational numbers; $0.3\overline{4} = \frac{31}{90}$ and $0.4\overline{3} = \frac{39}{90}$. So, $\frac{31}{90} + \frac{39}{90} = \frac{a}{9} \rightarrow \frac{70}{90} = \frac{a}{9}$ Cross multiplication; $70 \cdot 9 = 90 \cdot a \rightarrow 7 = a$.

16. To be able to see the integer between $-\frac{\sqrt{26}}{2} < \ldots < \sqrt{24}$, we should get a common denominator. So, multiply each side by 2, $-\sqrt{26} < \ldots < \sqrt{24}$. Therefore, $-5, -4, -3, -2, -1, 0, 1, 2, 3,$ and 4 are integers between $-\frac{\sqrt{26}}{2}$ & $\sqrt{24}$. Hence, there are 10 integers.

17. $\sqrt{13} < \ldots < 6\pi$ ($\pi \cong 3.14$) $\rightarrow \sqrt{13} < \ldots < 18.64$. So, $4, 5, 6, 7, 8, \ldots 17, 18$ are whole numbers lie in the interval. Therefore, there are 15 whole numbers.

18. Multiply $\sqrt{2}$ to obtain the following terms. So, 5th term is $4\sqrt{2} \sqrt{2} = 8$, 6th term is $8\sqrt{2}$, and 7th term is $8\sqrt{2} \sqrt{2} = 16$

19. $2, 2, \frac{8}{3}, 4, \frac{32}{5} \rightarrow \frac{2}{1}, \frac{4}{2}, \frac{8}{3}, \frac{16}{4}, \frac{32}{5}$. The sequence that follows here is $\frac{2^n}{n}$ (n: number of term). Therefore, the next number in the sequence is 6th term. So, $\frac{2^6}{6} \rightarrow \frac{64}{6}$.

20. The minimum possible product of three different numbers of the set is the product of the set $\{-4, 5, 6\}$. So, $-4 \cdot 5 \cdot 6 = -120$.

Problem Set 2

1. The two-digit numbers are between 10 to 99. The two-digit numbers have nine groups, i.e., 10 to 19, 20 to 29, 30 to 39, 40 to 49, 50 to 59, 60 to 69, 70 to 79, 80 to 89 and 90 to 99. Each group has 10 numbers. The total number of two-digit numbers is 90.

2. To be able to see the integer between $\frac{3}{4}$ & $\frac{16}{3}$, We should get a common denominator first. $\frac{3}{4} = \frac{3 \cdot 3}{4 \cdot 3} = \frac{9}{12}$ & $\frac{16}{3} = \frac{16 \cdot 4}{3 \cdot 4} = \frac{64}{12}$. Thus, there might be some integers falling in the interval; $\frac{9}{12} < \ldots < \frac{64}{12}$. As many as the number of multiples of 12 between 9 and 64. So, there are five integers $\frac{9}{12} < (\frac{12}{12}, \frac{24}{12}, \frac{36}{12}, \frac{48}{12}, \frac{60}{12}) < \frac{64}{12}$.

3. $-\frac{16}{3} < \ldots < \frac{20}{3}$. As many as the number of multiples of 3 between -16 and 20. So, there are eleven integers $-\frac{16}{3} < (-\frac{15}{3}, -\frac{12}{3}, -\frac{9}{3}, -\frac{6}{3}, -\frac{3}{3}, \frac{3}{3}, \frac{6}{3}, \frac{9}{3}, \frac{12}{3}, \frac{15}{3}, \frac{18}{3}) < \frac{20}{3}$.

4. $0.3333333\ldots$ $0.\overline{3}$. Let's convert the repeating decimal numbers into rational numbers. Let $0.33333\ldots = x$. Multiply both sides by 10; $3.333\ldots = 10x$. To get rid of the repeating par, subtract side by side; $3.3333\ldots - 0.3333\ldots = 10x - x$, $3 = 9x \rightarrow \frac{3}{9} \rightarrow \frac{1}{3}$.

5. $\sqrt{36} = 6 \rightarrow$ whole numbers, $\sqrt{\frac{49}{16}} = \frac{7}{4} \rightarrow$ rational numbers, $-\sqrt{16} = -4 \rightarrow$ integer number. So, $\sqrt{8} = 2\sqrt{2} \rightarrow$ irrational numbers.

6. $3 \cdot 5 \rightarrow$ rational numbers, $-2 \rightarrow$ integer numbers, $\frac{1}{2} \rightarrow$ rational numbers. So, $\pi \rightarrow$ irrational number.

SOLUTIONS — Number Systems — CHAPTER 19

7. See the table

8. See the table

9. See the table

10. See the table

Number	Natural Numbers	Whole Numbers	Integers	Rational Numbers	Irrational Numbers	Real Numbers
$-\sqrt{17}$					X	X
-2			X	X		X
$-\dfrac{9}{37}$				X		X
0		X	X	X		X
-6.06				X		X
$4.5\overline{6}$				X		X
29	X	X	X	X		X

11. The decimal expansion of an irrational number is non-terminating and non-repeating.

12. $\sqrt{25} = 5 \to$ whole number, $\sqrt{2} \times \sqrt{2} = \sqrt{4} = 2 \to$ whole number, $\sqrt{4} = 2 \to$ whole number. So, $\sqrt{5} \to$ an irrational number.

13. a. $\dfrac{2\sqrt{5}}{\sqrt{6}} = \dfrac{2\sqrt{5} \cdot \sqrt{6}}{\sqrt{6} \cdot \sqrt{6}} = \dfrac{2\sqrt{30}}{6} = \dfrac{\sqrt{30}}{3}$

    b. $\dfrac{6}{\sqrt{3}} = \dfrac{6 \cdot \sqrt{3}}{\sqrt{3} \cdot \sqrt{3}} = \dfrac{6\sqrt{3}}{3} = \dfrac{\sqrt{3}}{2}$

14. Recall that $(a - b) \cdot (a - b) = a^2 - b^2$. So, $(\sqrt{3} - \sqrt{2}) \cdot (\sqrt{3} - \sqrt{2}) \to 3 - 2 = 1$.

15. Recall that $(a - b) \cdot (a + b) = a^2 - b^2$. So,
$\dfrac{6}{\sqrt{5} - \sqrt{2}} \cdot \dfrac{\sqrt{5} + \sqrt{2}}{\sqrt{5} + \sqrt{2}} = \dfrac{6 \cdot (\sqrt{5} + \sqrt{2})}{(\sqrt{5} - \sqrt{2}) \cdot (\sqrt{5} + \sqrt{2})}$
$= \dfrac{6\sqrt{5} + 6\sqrt{2}}{3} = 2\sqrt{5} + 2\sqrt{2}$

16. $0.373737\ldots = 0.\overline{37}$. Let's convert the repeating decimal numbers into rational numbers. Let $0.373737\ldots = x$. Multiply both sides by 100; $37,3737\ldots = 100x$. To get rid of the repeating part, subtract side by side; $37 \cdot 373737.. - 0.373737\ldots = 100x - x$, $37 = 99x \to \dfrac{37}{99}$. Then, $\dfrac{a}{b} = \dfrac{37}{99}$. So, $a + b \to 37 + 99 = 136$.

17. $1.244444\ldots = 1.2\overline{4}$. Let's convert the repeating decimal numbers into rational numbers. $1.24444\ldots = x$. Multiply both sides by 100; $124.444\ldots = 100x$. To get rid of the repeating part, subtract side by side; $124.4444.. - 12.4444\ldots = 100x - 10x$, $112 = 90x \to \dfrac{112}{90} = x \to \dfrac{56}{45} = x$. Then, $\dfrac{a}{b} = \dfrac{56}{45}$. So, $a + b \to 101$.

18. $a = 2.\overline{3}$ and $b = 3.\overline{2}$. Let's convert the repeating decimal numbers into rational numbers; $a = \dfrac{7}{3}$ and $b = \dfrac{29}{9}$. Then, $\dfrac{1}{a} + \dfrac{1}{b}$
$\to \dfrac{1}{7/3} + \dfrac{1}{29/9} = \dfrac{3}{7} + \dfrac{9}{29} = \dfrac{3 \cdot 29}{7 \cdot 29} + \dfrac{9 \cdot 7}{29 \cdot 7}$
$\to \dfrac{87}{203} + \dfrac{63}{203} = \dfrac{150}{203}$.

19. $\dfrac{0.\overline{5} + 0.\overline{4}}{0.\overline{5} - 0.\overline{3}}$. Let's convert the repeating decimal numbers into rational numbers; $0.\overline{5} = \dfrac{5}{9}$, $0.\overline{4} = \dfrac{4}{9}$ and $0.\overline{3} = \dfrac{3}{9}$.
Then, $\dfrac{\dfrac{5}{9} + \dfrac{4}{9}}{\dfrac{5}{9} - \dfrac{3}{9}} \to \dfrac{\dfrac{9}{9}}{\dfrac{2}{9}} \to \dfrac{9}{9} \cdot \dfrac{9}{2} = \dfrac{9}{2}$.

20. $-6 \times 5 \times 7$ gives the possible minimum value. So, the answer is -210.

CHAPTER 20 — Data & Statistics — SOLUTIONS

Problem Set 1

1. Add all of the values in the data set together to get 64. Divide by the number of data entries, 10, to get the mean or average of 6.4.

2. Numbers in order from least to greatest, the middle two numbers are 6 and 7. The median is the between these two numbers: $(6 + 7) \div 2 = 6.5$.

3. The most frequent value is 9, there are three of them present in the data set, while no other value shows up three or more times.

4. $12 - 1 = 11$

5. $(30 + 20 + x + 10 + 40) \div 5 = 25$. Multiply both sides by 5: $30 + 20 + x + 10 + 40 = 125$. Simplify the equation to: $100 + x = 125$. Subtract 100 from both sides, $x = 25$.

6. $\frac{a+b}{2} = 11$ is the equation for the mean of a and b. The second equation is $b + 2 = a$ because a is 2 more than b. Substitution can then take place by placing $b+2$ in place of a in the first equation: $\frac{(b+2)+b}{2} = 11$. Multiply both sides by 2: $(b+2)+b = 22$. Combine like terms on the left side: $2b + 2 = 22$. Subtract 2 from both sides: $2b = 20$. Divide both sides by 2: $b = 10$. Place 10 in for b in the second equation: $b + 2 = a$ → $10 + 2 = 12$. A = 12.

7. $\frac{6+7+13+x}{2} = 9$. Multiply both sides by 4: $6 + 7 + 13 + x = 36$. Simplify left side: $26 + x = 36$. Subtract 26 from both sides: $x = 10$.

8. The maximum value is 132. The minimum value is 84. $132 - 84 = 48$.

9. The average of the first 5 people is 20, so the following equation can be set up: $\frac{a+b+c+d+e}{2} = 20$. Multiply both sides by 5 to reveal that when the first 5 ages are added together, they total 100.
100 − the 40 year old = 60 years left for the 4 other people. $a + b + c + d = 60$. Divide both sides by 4 to find the average of the remaining 4 to be 15 years old.

10. The only possibility for a unique mode is 8, leaving the value of x to either be 8 or a new number not already present in the set. This means that the median is also 8, but to make that true, the value of x has to be larger than 9 (to keep 8 in the middle). The mean also has to equal 8, so to find x find the average of all seven integers: $\frac{5+6+7+8+9+x}{2} = 8$. Multiply both sides by 7: $5 + 6 + 7 + 8 + 8 + 9 + x = 56$. Simplify the left side: $43 + x = 56$. Subtract 43 from both sides: $x = 13$.

11. The average of four unknown numbers is 9: $\frac{a+b+c+d}{2} = 9$. Multiply both sides by 4: $a + b + c + d = 36$. To make the median age 8: $\frac{b+c}{2} = 8$. Multiply both sides by 2: $b + c = 16$. Substitute this in $a + b + c + d = 36$, leaving $a + 16 + d = 36$. Subtract 16 from both sides: $a + d = 20$.

12. Represent the ten numbers with ten variables: $\frac{a+b+c+d+e+f+g+h+i+j}{10} = 20$.
Multiply both sides by 10:
$a + b + c + d + e + f + g + h + i + j = 200$.
To subtract 20 from nine of the numbers:
$20 \times 9 = 180$. Subtract 180 from the right side (200): $a + b + c + d + e + f + g + h + i + j = 20$.
To find the average, divide both sides by 10:
$\frac{a+b+c+d+e+f+g+h+i+j}{10} = 2$.

SOLUTIONS — Data & Statistics — CHAPTER 20

13. Add all percentages in the pie graph together: $32 + 22 + 16 = 70\%$. Leaving 30% to have blonde hair. 30% of 300 = 90 people.

14. Average the six numbers: $\frac{a+b+c+d+e+f}{10} = 10$. Multiply both sides by 6: $a+b+c+d+e+f = 60$, meaning the six numbers total 60 when added together. Subtract 25 from 60 to find that the remaining five numbers total 35. To find the average of the five numbers, divide both sides by 5: $\frac{a+b+c+d+e}{10} = 7$.

15. $\frac{8+10+12+14+16}{10} = 12$. Average of the largest (16) and smallest (8): $\frac{8+16}{2} = 12$.

16. The number 7 has the highest frequency or shows up the most in the data set at 15 times.

17. Each data value needs to get multiplied by the frequency in which it shows up in the data set. Add those values up: $\frac{3+4+15+42+105+64+45}{40}$. There are 40 total values in this data set (add up the numbers in the frequency column). Simplify the top of the fraction: $\frac{278}{40} = 7$.

18. When all 40 values are written out, the middle values are both 7s.

19. Maximum value - minimum value is $9 - 3 = 6$.

20. To make the mode 7, value $a = 7$ because out of the twelve numbers given, four of them are 6s and four of them are 7s, so either a or b has to be a 7. Set up an equation to find the mean of the rest of the values and b: $\frac{5 + (6 \times 4) + (7 \times 5) + (8 \times 2) + 9 + b}{14}$. Multiply both sides by 14 and simplify the top of the fraction: $89 + b = 98$. Subtract 89 from both sides: $b = 9$. Finally, $a + b = 7 + 9 = 16$.

Problem Set 2

1. The bars on the graph read from left to right: 8, 12, 9, 7, 4, 2, 2, 1. When added together, the number of people surveyed is 45.

2. 1 day. 12 people responded saying 1 day, which can be seen as the tallest bar on the graph.

3. The first bar on the left shows 8 people who ate 0 days.

4. 20%. Since it is more than 3 days: $4 + 2 + 2 + 1 = 9$ people. To find the percentage, take these 9 people and put it into a fraction over the total people found in problem #1: $\frac{9}{45} = 0.2$. Multiply by 100 to get a percentage: 20%.

5. $x = 24$. Set the average of the first three values (10, 5, and x) equal to the average of the last four (x, 7, 9, and 12): $\frac{10 + 5 + x}{10} = \frac{a+b+c+d+e}{10}$. Cross multiply the two fractions: $4(10 + 5 + x) = 3(x + 7 + 9 + 12)$. Simplify both sets of parentheses: $4(15 + x) = 3(x + 28)$. Distribute: $60 + 4x = 3x + 84$. Subtract 3x from both sides and 60 from both sides, leaving $x = 24$.

6. 37. The bars on the graph read from left to right: 2, 5, 7, 8, 9, 6. When added together, the number of businesses surveyed is 37.

7. 50 employees. 9 businesses responded saying 50 employees, which can be seen as the tallest bar on the graph.

8. The majority of the data lies in the 30, 40, and 50 graphs, but overall the data is pretty evenly distributed except the 10 employees.

CHAPTER 20 — Data & Statistics — SOLUTIONS

9. Only two bars on the graph are below 30 employees: 5 and 2. Add these values together to get 7. To find the percentage, take these 7 businesses and put it into a fraction over the total businesses found in problem #6: $\frac{7}{37} = 0.19$. Multiply by 100 to get a percentage: 19%.

10. Each "Number of aces" needs to be multiplied by the frequency in which it shows up in the data set. Add those values up and divide by the total number of values in the frequency row (55):
$\frac{4 + 22 + 54 + 52 + 35 + 12}{55} = \frac{179}{55} = 3.25$.

11. When all 55 values are written out, the middle values are both 3s.

12. The value with the highest frequency in the table is 3 with a frequency of 18.

13. Each "Number of heads" value needs to be multiplied by the frequency in which it shows up in the data set. Add those values up and divide by the total: $\frac{0 + 12 + 22 + 9}{30} = \frac{40}{30} = 1.43$.

14. The line in the middle of the box on the box and whisker plot signifies where the median is located, which on this graph is above the value 35.

15. The two dots or whiskers on the box and whisker plot signify the maximum value and the minimum value, which on this graph are 78 and 13. Thus, 78 − 13 = 65.

16. In this problem N = number of kids and A = average height. First, the 12 children that are 8 cm taller, adds 96 to the original average of the problem: $\frac{N \times A}{N}$.
Making the problem now: $\frac{(N \times A) + 96}{N}$.
This is set equal to the average height plus 6: $\frac{(N \times A) + 96}{N} = A + 6$. Multiply both sides by N:
$(N \times A) + 96 = N(A + 6)$.
Distribute: $N \times A + 96 = N \times A + 6N$.
Divide both sides by $N \times A$: $96 = 6N$.
Divide both sides by 6: N = 16.

17. a = 16. To start, $\frac{a + b}{2} = 10$. Multiply both sides by 2: a + b = 20. Then, $\frac{b + c + d}{3} = 20$. Multiply both sides by 3: b + c + d = 60. Set up the final fraction of the average of all four numbers: $\frac{a + b + c + d}{4} = 19$. Multiply both sides by 4: a + b + c + d = 76. Substitute b + c + d in this equation with 60 from before: a + 60 = 76. Subtract 60 from both sides: a = 16.

18. a + b = 151. Starting with making the mode 84, both a and b have to be new values (not 84 or 81). To make the median 81, both values have to be less than 81 to keep it in the center of the data set. Lastly, to make the mean 80 set up the following equation: $\frac{a + b + 81 + 84 + 84}{5} = 80$. Multiply both sides by 5: a + b + 81 + 84 + 84 = 400. Simplify the left side: a + b + 249 = 400. Lastly, subtract 249 from both sides, leaving a + b = 151.

19. The mean of the three numbers can be set up as follows: $\frac{17 + 23 + 2n}{30} = n$. Multiply both sides by 3: 17 + 23 + 2n = 3n. Subtract 2n from both sides and simplify the addition on the left side: 40 = n. Add the digits of n together: 4 + 0 = 4.

20. If the 10 numbers are represented by variables, it can be written:
$\frac{a + b + c + d + e + f + g + h + i + j}{10} = 10$.
Multiply both sides by 10:
a + b + c + d + e + f + g + h + i + j = 100.
If the first nine variables are numbers 1-9, when added together:
1 + 2 + 3 + 4 + 5 + 6 + 7 + 8 + 9 = 45.
100 − 45 = 55, meaning the largest value j can be is 55. If j = 55, then the smallest value is 1. The product of the smallest and largest values is 55 × 1 = 55

SOLUTIONS — Sets — CHAPTER 21

Problem Set 1

1. $A \cap B = \{a, c, e\}$. Three elements.

2. $A \cup B$ {★, 0, 4, □, △, 5}. Six elements.

3. a. $A \cup B = \{4, 5, 6, 7, 8, 9, 10\}$
   b. $n(A) = 7$

4. a. $A \cup C = \{0, 1, 2, 3, 4, 5, 6, 7, 10, 12\}$
   b. $B \cap C = \{3, 6\}$

5. a. $B \cup C = \{0, 1, 2, 3, 4, 5, 6, 7, 12, 15\}$. So, $A \cap (B \cup C) = \{0, 2, 4, 6, 12\}$.
   b. $A \cap C = \{2, 4, 6\}$. So, $B \cup (A \cap C) = \{0, 2, 3, 4, 6, 12, 15\}$.

6. $n(A \cup B) = n(A) + n(B) - n(A \cap B)$
   $= 14 + 20 - 6 = 28$

7. $n(A \cup B) = n(A) + n(B) - n(A \cap B)$
   $30 = 20 + 16 - n(A \cap B)$, $n(A \cap B) = 6$.

8. Let $n(A - B) = x$. Then $n(B - A) = x$, and $n(A \cup B) = 2x + 101$.
   So, $2x + 101 = 199$, $2x = 98$, $x = 49$. $n(A) = 49 + 101 = 150$.
   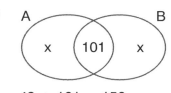

9. $n(A - B) + n(A \cap B) = n(A)$
   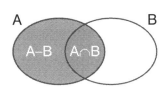

10. a. $\{2, 3, 5, 7\}$ c. $\{2\}$
    b. $\{2, 4, 6, 8, 10\}$ d. This is an empty set.

11. $5 \in B$ is true.

12. $n(A \cap B) = 3$. Because $A \cap B = \{60, 120, 180\} = $ {whole numbers divisible by 10 and 12 and less than 200} = {common multiples of 10 and 12 and less than 200}

13. Subsets of $\{1, 2, 3\}$ are { }, {1}, {2}, {3}, {1, 2}, {1, 3}, {2, 3}, {1, 2, 3}. There are $2^3 = 8$ subsets. Similarly, $\{1, 2, 3, 4\}$ has $2^4 = 16$ subsets.

14. $n(M \cup A) = n(M) + n(A) - n(M \cap A)$
    $100 = 70 + n(A) - 30$
    $n(A) = 60$
    $n(M - A) = n(M \cup A) - (A)$
    $= 100 - 60 = 40$
    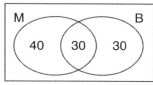

15. $(30 - x) + x + (25 - x) = 48$
    $55 - x = 48$
    $x = 7$.
    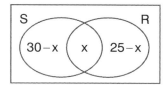

16. Divisible by 5 or 6 means divisible by 5, or by 6 or by 5 and 6. Let $F = \{5, 10, 15, 20, \ldots, 50\}$, $S = \{6, 12, 18, \ldots, 48\}$ $F \cap S = \{30\}$.
    Thus, $n(F \cup S) = n(F) + n(S) - n(F \cap S)$
    $= 10 + 8 - 1 = 19$.

17. We can illustrate this situation:
    $4 + (18 - x) + x + (12 - x) = 28$
    $34 - x = 28$ $x = 6$
    So,
    $n(H - S) + n(S - H)$
    $= 12 + 6 = 18$
    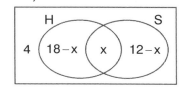

18. We can illustrate the situation:
    $5 + (14 - x) + x + (12 - x) = 28$
    $31 - x = 28$
    $x = 3$
    So,
    $n(S \cap F) = 3$
    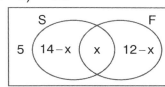

19. $(90 - x) + x + (80 - x) = 150$
    $170 - x = 150$
    $x = 20$
    So,
    $n(S \cap F) = 20$
    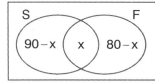

20. Let $T = \{3, 6, 9, \ldots, 48\}$, $F = \{5, 10, 15, \ldots, 50\}$
    Then,
    $n(T) = \dfrac{48 - 3}{3} + 1 = 16$
    $n(F) = \dfrac{50 - 5}{5} + 1 = 10$

    $T \cap F = \{15, 30, 45\}$ (Divisible by both 3 and 5).
    So, $n(T - F) + n(F - T) = 13 + 7 = 20$.

CHAPTER 22 — BENCHMARK [Chapter 11-21] — SOLUTIONS

Problem Set 1

1. By definition, we have $2x - 1 = -7$ or $2x - 1 = 7$. So, $x = -3$ or $x = 4$.

2. After cross-multiplying the given equation, we have $10a - 5b = 6a + 4b$, $4a = 9b$, $\dfrac{a}{b} = \dfrac{9}{4}$.

3. $3 \spadesuit 2 = (3 + 2) \cdot (3 - 2) = 5 \cdot 1 = 5$.
   So, $4 \spadesuit (3 \spadesuit 2) = 4 \spadesuit 5$
   $= (4 + 5) \cdot (4 - 5) = 9 \cdot (-1) = -9$.

4. $f(2) = 2$, $f(5) = 14$. Thus, $f(2) + f(5) = 2 + 14 = 16$.

5. The mean is $\dfrac{x + 7 + 9 + 10 + 8 + 3 + 5}{10}$.
   So, $7x = x + 42$, $6x = 42$, $x = 7$. When we put the numbers in increasing order 3, 5, 7, 7, 8, 9, 10, we see the median = mode = mean = 7.

6. Let the side lengths equal to $2a$, $3a$, and $4a$. Then $9a = 36$, $a = 4$. So, side lengths are 8, 12, and 16 feet.

7. Let $x = 3a$, where $a \ne 0$. Then $y = 2a$.
   Thus, $\dfrac{4x + 2y}{2x - y} = \dfrac{12a + 4a}{6a - 2a} = \dfrac{16a}{4a} = 4$.

8. $P_{AFB} = 3 \cdot 12 = 36$, and $P_{ABCD} = 24 + 2x$, where x is the width of the rectangle.
   So, $36 = 24 + 2x$, $x = 6$.
   Thus $A_{ABCD} = 12 \cdot 6 = 72$ cm².

9. Circumference $= 2\pi r = 64\pi$, $\pi r = 32\pi$, $r = 32$.
   Area $= \pi r^2 = \pi \cdot 32^2 = 1024\pi$.
   So, $x\pi = 1024\pi$, $x = 1024$.

10. Volume $= \dfrac{6 \cdot 8}{2} \cdot h = 24h = 120$. So, $h = 5$ cm.

11. Dividing both sides by 5: $a + 6 < 15$, $a < 9$. So, the largest integer value of a is 8.

12. Squaring both sides, we get: $20 + \sqrt{n} = 36$, $\sqrt{n} = 16$. Squaring both sides again, we get $n = 256$, which satisfies the original equation.

13. We can rewrite the equation as $3 \cdot 3^x + \dfrac{3^x}{9} = 84$,
    $3^x \cdot \left(3 + \dfrac{1}{9}\right) = 84$, $3^x \cdot \left(\dfrac{28}{9}\right) = 84$,
    $3^x = 84 \cdot \dfrac{9}{28}$, $3^x = 3 \cdot 9$, $3^x = 3^3$, $x = 3$.

14. $n(A \cup B) = n(A) + n(B) - n(A \cap B)$. So, $n(A \cup B) = 28 + 40 - 12 = 56$.

15. By the cover-up method: $\dfrac{24}{24 - \dfrac{12}{x + 3}} = 2$,
    $24 - \dfrac{12}{x + 3} = 12$, $\dfrac{12}{x + 3} = 12$, $x + 3 = 1$, $x = -2$.

16. Notice that the length $AB = 6$ and the width $BC = 2$. Then, Area $= 6 \cdot 2 = 12$ square units.

17. Area $= \dfrac{AD + BC}{2} \cdot h = \dfrac{12 + 4}{2} \cdot 4 = 32$.

18. Notice that
    $a = 1.333\ldots = \dfrac{4}{3}$ and $b = 2.666\ldots = 2a = \dfrac{8}{3}$.
    Thus, $\dfrac{1}{a} + \dfrac{1}{b} = \dfrac{1}{4/3} + \dfrac{1}{8/3} = \dfrac{3}{4} + \dfrac{3}{8}$
    $= \dfrac{6}{8} + \dfrac{3}{8} = \dfrac{9}{8}$.

19. Let's put them in increasing order: 0, 0, 2, 3, 4, 4, 4, 5. So, median $= \dfrac{3 + 4}{2} = 3.5$,
    mean $= \dfrac{22}{8} = 2.75$, mode $= 4$.
    Thus, mean + median + mode $= 10.25$.

20. Notice that the x-intercept is $(4, 0)$, and the y-intercept is $(0, 3)$. So, Area $= \dfrac{4 \cdot 3}{2} = 6$.

| SOLUTIONS | Math Fluency Post-Test | POST-TEST |

1. $= 88 - 18 \times 3 = 88 - 54 = 34$

2.
```
       603
   16 ) 9660
      - 96
        060
       - 48
         12
```
   So, $Q + R = 603 + 12 = 615$.

3. Let's do the reverse operation, which is division, and let's divide both sides by 100:

   $$\frac{a \times \cancel{100}^{1}}{\cancel{100}_{1}} = \frac{20}{100}, \quad a = \frac{20}{100} = \frac{1}{5}.$$

4. Let's write it using fractions
   $\frac{8}{a} = 32, \quad a \cdot \frac{8}{a} = a \cdot 32, \quad 8 = 32a$
   $\frac{1}{32} \cdot 8 = \frac{1}{32} \cdot 32a, \quad \frac{8}{32} = a, \quad a = \frac{1}{4}$

5. $x = \frac{15}{100} \cdot 80 = \frac{3}{20} \cdot 80 = \frac{3 \cdot 80}{20} = 3 \cdot 4 = 12.$

6. In other words, a multiple of 8 between 100 and 150.
   $100 < 8x < 150, \quad \frac{100}{8} < x < \frac{150}{8}$
   $12\frac{1}{2} < x < 18\frac{3}{4}$. So, $x = 13, 14, 15, 16, 17, 18$.
   Thus, that number might be 104, 112, 120, 128, 136, or 144

7. $\left.\begin{array}{l} 4 = 2^2 \\ 12 = 2^2 \cdot 3 \\ 18 = 2 \cdot 3^2 \end{array}\right\}$ LCM(4, 12, 18) $= 2^2 \cdot 3^2 = 36$
   We take the largest power of each prime factor and multiply.

8. $\left.\begin{array}{l} 32 = 2^5 \\ 48 = 2^4 \cdot 3 \\ 64 = 2^6 \end{array}\right\}$ GCF(32, 48, 64) $= 2^4 = 16$
   We take the smallest power of each prime factor and multiply.

9. $\frac{p-7}{4} = 12, \quad p - 7 = 12 \cdot 4, \quad p - 7 = 48, \quad p = 55$

10. Factor out 13: $13 \times 103 - 13 \times 3 = 13(103 - 3)$
    $= 13 \cdot 100$
    $= 1300$

11. Only possible case is $x = 5$ and $z = 7$ since $x + z = 12$. So, $y = 6$.

12.
    $\frac{7}{3} - \frac{2}{3} = 3a, \quad \frac{5}{3} = 3a, \quad a = \frac{5}{9}$ So,
    $\frac{2}{3} + a = \frac{2}{3} + \frac{5}{9} = \frac{6}{9} + \frac{5}{9} = \frac{11}{9}$ is the smaller one.

13. $y = 10 - \dfrac{10}{2 \cdot \frac{9}{2} - 1} = 10 - \dfrac{10}{9 - 1} = 10 - \dfrac{10}{8}$
    $= 10 - \dfrac{5}{4} = \dfrac{40}{4} - \dfrac{5}{4} = \dfrac{35}{4}.$

14. Cross multiply: $(1 + 2x) \cdot 2 = 3 \cdot (3 - x)$
    $2 + 4x = 9 - 3x \quad 7x = 7 \quad x = 1$

15. $30 = x + 4 + ?? + 5$
    $30 = 2x + 10 \quad 20 = 2x \quad x = 10$

16. $\frac{5}{3} \div \frac{a}{b} = \frac{5}{3} \cdot \frac{b}{a}$ So, $\frac{5}{3} \cdot \frac{b}{a} = \frac{15}{6}$,
    $\dfrac{\cancel{3}^1}{\cancel{5}_1} \cdot \dfrac{\cancel{5}^1}{\cancel{3}_1} \cdot \dfrac{b}{a} = \dfrac{3}{5} \cdot \dfrac{\cancel{15}^1}{\cancel{6}_2}, \quad \dfrac{b}{a} = \dfrac{3}{2}$

Math Fluency Post-Test — SOLUTIONS

17. $\dfrac{7}{11} \div \left(\dfrac{7}{11} + \dfrac{7}{11} \cdot \dfrac{3}{10}\right) = \dfrac{7}{11} \div \dfrac{7}{11}\left(1 + \dfrac{3}{10}\right)$

$= \dfrac{7}{11} \div \dfrac{7}{11} \cdot \dfrac{13}{10} = \dfrac{7}{11} \cdot \dfrac{11}{7} \cdot \dfrac{13}{10} = \dfrac{13}{10}$

18.

$A = 10 + \dfrac{28-10}{6} \cdot 4$

$= 10 + \dfrac{18}{6} \cdot 4 = 10 + 3 \cdot 4 = 22$

19. 4725a is divisible by 3 if the sum of its digits is a multiple of 3. So, $4 + 7 + 2 + 5 + a = 3k$ where k is an integer. $18 + a = 3k$.
Thus, $18 + a$ can be equal to 18, 21, 24, 27 i.e., $a = 0, 3, 6,$ or 9.

20. $f(2) = 4^2 + 6 = 8 + 6 = 14$
$f(-3) = 4 \cdot (-3) + 6 = -12 + 6 = -6$
Thus, $f(2) + f(-3) = 14 + (-6) = 8$.

21. Let the side lengths be x, 2x, 3x. Then,
$48 = x + 2x + 3x$, $48 = 6x$, $x = 8$.
Thus, the longest side is $3x = 3 \cdot 8 = 24$ feet.

22. Let's isolate t: $\dfrac{5 \times (t+4)}{5} > \dfrac{105}{5}$, $t + 4 > 21$
$t > 17$. Thus $t_{min} = 18$

23. $n(A \cup B) = n(A) + n(B) - n(A \cap B)$
$80 = 38 + 50 - n(A \cap B)$. $n(A \cap B) = 8$.

24. Base $= 11 - 5 = 6$
Height $= 6 - 2 = 4$
Area $= \dfrac{b \cdot 4}{2} = 12$.

25. Mean $= \dfrac{5 + 6 + 0 + 6 + 4 + 5 + 0 + 6}{8} = \dfrac{32}{8} = 4$
Median $= 0, 0, 4, 5, 5, 6, 6, 6 \rightarrow \dfrac{5+5}{2} = 5$
Mode $= 6$
Thus, $4 + 5 + 6 = 15$

26. $\left(\sqrt{16 + \sqrt{n}}\right)^2 = 5^2$, $16 + \sqrt{n} = 25$, $\sqrt{n} = 9$
$(\sqrt{n})^2 = 9^2$, $n = 81$.
Plugging 81 in the original equation indicates that 81 is the solution.

27. $9! = 9 \times 8 \times 7 \times 6 \times 5 \times 4 \times 3 \times 2 \times 1$
$= 3^2 \cdot 2^3 \cdot 7 \cdot 2 \cdot 3 \cdot 5 \cdot 2^2 \cdot 3 \cdot 2 \cdot 1$
$= 2^7 \cdot 3^4 \cdot 5^1 \cdot 7^1$
So, $a = 7, b = 4, c = 1, d = 1$ and
$a + b + c + d = 13$.

28. $3\dfrac{4}{5} = \dfrac{19}{5}$ $\dfrac{19}{5} \div \dfrac{7}{10} = \dfrac{19}{5} \cdot \dfrac{10}{7} = \dfrac{19 \cdot 10}{7 \cdot 5}$
$= \dfrac{19 \cdot 2}{7} = \dfrac{38}{7} = 5\dfrac{3}{7}$

29. $\dfrac{12}{12 - \dfrac{16}{3x-1}} = 3$, $12 - \dfrac{16}{3x-1} = 4$, $\dfrac{16}{3x-1} = 8$,
$3x - 1 = 2$ $3x = 3$, $x = 1$.

30. $2\pi r = 36\pi$, $r = \dfrac{36\pi}{2\pi} = 18$ cm
$V = \pi \cdot r^2 \cdot h = \pi \cdot 18^2 \cdot 8 = 2592\pi$ cm^3

Pre-Test

1. 59 2. 508 3. 1/3 4. 1/5 5. 6 6. 105, 112, 119, 126, 133, 140, 147 7. 14 8. 3 9. 57 10. 890 11. 8
12. 7/12 13. 12 14. 1 15. 4 16. 57/2 17. 9/5 18. 2 19. 8 20. 20 21. 16 22. 2 23. 18 24. 18 25. 18.5
26. 49 27. 11 28. $7\frac{5}{6}$ 29. 1 30. 512π

CHAPTER 1 - Problem Set 1

1. 28 2. 1 3. 7 4. –8 5. C 6. 2 7. C 8. 1300 9. –27 10. 49 11. 3 12. 9 13. 1 14. 48 15. 10 16. 9
17. 2500 18. –124 19. –15,15 20. 100

CHAPTER 1 - Problem Set 2

1. -7.3 2. 890 3. 1513 4. 123 5. 11 6. 704 7. 990 8. 500 9. 31 10. 1050 11. 585 12. 4400 13. 27 14. 5
15. 0 16. 162 17. 36 18. ÷ 19. 103 20. -13

CHAPTER 2 - Problem Set 1

1. 124 2. × + × 3. -26 4. 5 5. 14 6. 52 7. 27 8. 7 9. 50500 10. 52 11. 10 12. 25 13. 18 14. 3 15. 8
16. -44 17. -20 18. 13 19. -1.8 20. 26

CHAPTER 2 - Problem Set 2

1. -100 2. 7 3. 12 4. 12 5. 12 6. 2 7. 3 8. -6 9. 17 10. -150 11. 30 12. 32, 128 13. 13 14. 31 15. 2
16. 2 17. 12 18. 7 19. 7 20. 24

CHAPTER 3 - Problem Set 1

1. 4 2. 19 3. 3 4. 3, 4 5. 99 6. 196 7. 37 8. n-m+1 9. 32 10. 28 11. 72 12. 12 13. 38 14. 77 15. 32
16. 104, 112, 120, 128, 136, 144 17. 240 18. 3 19. 12 20. 60

CHAPTER 3 - Problem Set 2

1. 0 2. 60 3. 13 4. III 5. 1, 4, 7 6. 5 7. 0 8. 9 9. 9 10. 4 11. 3 12. 4, 13 13. 12 14. 0 15. 400 16. 7
17. 118 18. 3, 9 19. 0 20. 12

CHAPTER 4 - Problem Set 1

1. E 2. A 3. 960 4. 3 5. 72 6. 8 7. 360 8. 36 9. 16 10. 18 11. 4 12. 15 13. 12 14. 67/320 15. $m^2 + m$
16. 30 17. 27 18. 240 19. 60 20. 24

CHAPTER 5 - Problem Set 1

1. D 2. 6 3. A 4. 16 5. B 6. B 7. 1/4 8. $5\frac{1}{3}$ 9. 27 10. 16 11. 1/2 12. 1/6 13. –19/42 14. 3/5 15. B, C, D
16. 11 17. 6 18. 100 19. 13/4 20. 24

CHAPTER 5 - Problem Set 2

1. 60 2. 3 3. 0.6 4. 1/4 5. 13/98 6. 5/26 7. $5\frac{2}{5}$ 8. 3 9. 8 10. 1/6 11. 9 12. 13 13. 2/5 14. –1 15. B
16. 10/11 17. –21/16 18. –5/8 19. 5 20. 19

Math Fluency

CHAPTER 6 - Problem Set 1

1. 13 2. 30 3. 250 4. 47 5. 20.5 6. 0.304 7. 21/10 8. 159.95- 90.63- 361.221 9. 45.347 10. 100 11. 40
12. 181/40 13. -5/6 14. 0.175 15. 0.55 16. 1.2 17. $1\frac{3}{4}$ 18. $\frac{1}{16}$ 19. -7/4 20. 1.1

CHAPTER 6 - Problem Set 2

1. 4.5 2. 0.42 3. 640 4. 300 5. 200 6. 550 7. 4 8. 4.309 9. 53 10. 1/9 11. 600 12. 210 13. 62.5 14. 0.025
15. 40 16. 12.5 17. -5 18. 25 19. 0.8 20. 25

CHAPTER 7 - Problem Set 1

1. 12 2. 3 3. 5x 4. 8c+10d 5. 237 6. 499 7. 5/3 8. 0 9. 3 10. 8 11. −1 12. 2 13. a. −7 b. 10 14. −7
15. −80 16. −80 17. −5 18. −3/16 19. 80 20. 129

CHAPTER 7 - Problem Set 2

1. 10−5x 2. B 3. 2c 4. 6 5. 5y−4 6. 2b−a 7. 4r−s 8. 8x−8y 9. 5p/6q 10. 9a+7b 11. −y 12. 28x+12
13. 12x+19 14. 42x+34 15. 6x+11 16. −a+5b−c 17. 2c 18. −10a 19. C 20. 10

CHAPTER 8 - Problem Set 1

1. −45 2. −9 3. −62 4. 312 5. 899 6. −4 7. 2 8. 2 9. −3 10. 9 11. ∅ 12. $4+\frac{m}{2}$ 13. $\frac{16}{17}$ 14. 3/4 15. 16
16. 1 17. 2 18. 4 19. 48 20. 44

CHAPTER 8 - Problem Set 2

1. 9 2. 5 3. 5 4. −6 5. 3 6. 20 7. 80 8. 42 9. 2 10. −7 11. 19 12. 31 13. −2 14. 3/5 15. −5 16. 3.2
17. −1/2 18. 1 19. 22 20. 11

CHAPTER 9 - Problem Set 1

1. 49 2. 12 3. 85 4. 22 5. 23 6. 7/12 7. 50 8. 17 9. 3.84 10. 7 11. 8 12. 12 13. 3 14. 12 15. 30 16. 5
17. 20 18. 11 19. 90 20. 220

CHAPTER 10 - BENCHMARK (Chapter 1-9)

1. E 2. 44 3. 3/8 4. 2 5. 3/2 6. 8r−s 7. 2x/3 8. 10 9. 3 10. 10 11. 60 12. 120 13. 16 14. −4 15. 5 16. 3/2
17. −1 18. 57.50 19. 208 20. 14

CHAPTER 11 - Problem Set 1

1. 89/15 2. 81 3. 10/3 4. 84 5. −14 6. 0.0037 7. −27/7 8. 6 9. (3,2,6) 10. 41 11. −8 12. 81/7 13. 5 14. 8
15. 2 16. 3 17. 4 18. -3 19. 1 20. 15/4

CHAPTER 11 - Problem Set 2

1. 6 2. 8 3. 10 4. 3 5. 3 6. −31 7. 10 8. -9 9. 6 10. 15 11. 6 12. 15 13. 7 14. 4 15. 5 16. 18 17. −28
18. 2/3 19. 6 20. −2

CHAPTER 12 - Problem Set 1

1. 4 2. 462.5 3. 87.5 4. 10 5. 4 6. 5/2 7. 2 8. B 9. A 10. 90 11. 1 12. A 13. 20 14. 5 15. 2/3 16. 22 17. 341 18. 15 19. 9/20 20. 7/2

CHAPTER 12 - Problem Set 2

1. 27 2. 6 3. 6 4. −31 5. 37 6. −94 7. 2 8. 1/25 9. 8 10. 10 11. 141 12. 8 13. 5/3 14. 3 15. 7/6 16. 10/9 17. 1:4 18. 45 19. 60 20. 1/2

CHAPTER 13 - Problem Set 1

1. −23 2. 16 3. 9 4. −10 5. 5 6. 1/2 7. 28 8. $\frac{1}{4}$ 9. −2 10. 12 11. 10/3 12. 61 13. 507 14. 38 15. 0 16. 3 17. 0 18. $9\frac{1}{2}$ 19. 151 20. 4

CHAPTER 13 - Problem Set 2

1. 19 2. 11 3. 4 4. 5 5. D 6. −8 7. $-8\frac{1}{2}$ 8. 3/4 9. 6 10. 10 11. 7 12. −16 13. −72 14. 9 15. 28 16. −2 17. 2 18. 4.5 19. 2 20. 4

CHAPTER 14 - Problem Set 1

1. 19.683 2. 16 3. a. x^6 b. $16+n^2$ 4. 40 5. 14 6. 1 7. 2 8. −4 9. 8 10. 2 11. 7 12. 4 13. 100 14. −1 15. 25 16. 3 17. 1111 18. 6 19. 2 20. 64

CHAPTER 14 - Problem Set 2

1. 9 2. 25 3. 5 4. 1 5. 4 6. 8 7. 1 8. 28 9. 4 10. 25 11. 1&8 12. 17 13. 0.7 14. 3 15. 6 16. −5 17. −5 18. 3 19. 0.7 20. 19

CHAPTER 14 - Problem Set 3

1. 68 2. 17 3. 13 4. 25 5. 2^{38} 6. $\frac{a^4}{x^2}$ 7. x^{12} 8. 14 9. 676/121 10. 21 11. −4 12. 5 13. 5 14. 5×10^9 15. 2&3 16. −7 17. 1 18. $4\sqrt{3}$ 19. 33 20. 2

CHAPTER 15 - Problem Set 1

1. 20 2. 10 3. 25 4. 80 5. 13.5 6. 30 7. 28 8. 14 9. 32 10. $16x^2-y^2$ 11. 32 12. 80 13. 55 14. 15/7 15. 72 16. 3600 17. 5 18. $2\sqrt{41}$ 19. 36 20. 24

CHAPTER 15 - Problem Set 2

1. 40, 60, and 80. 2. 72 3. 120 4. $12+4\sqrt{3}$ 5. 4 6. $24+12\sqrt{3}$ 7. 18 8. 6 9. $20\sqrt{3}$ 10. 12 11. 50 12. 18 13. $36\sqrt{3}$ 14. 9:16 15. 50 16. 16 17. 8 18. 289 19. 175 20. 12

CHAPTER 16 - Problem Set 1

1. (0,0) 2. 11 3. 9 4. (5,1) 5. 20 6. 8 7. 20 8. 27 9. (2,1) 10. (−2,−1/2) 11. (3,−4) 12. (−2,−3) 13. (2,3) 14. 4 15. (−1,3) 16. (9,−1) 17. (5,8) 18. (2,2) 19. 120 20. 5

CHAPTER 16 - Problem Set 2

1. $\sqrt{13}$ 2. $\sqrt{58}$ 3. 2 4. $3\sqrt{5}$ 5. $\sqrt{97}$ 6. 5 7. $\sqrt{26}$ 8. (3,3) 9. (−2,2) 10. (7,4) 11. (1,−5) 12. −4, −1 13. (2,2) and (2,−2) 14. (2,−2) and (−2,−2) 15. 34 16. 32 17. (2000, 1997) 18. 15 19. 15 20. 4.5

CHAPTER 17 - Problem Set 1

1. 48 2. 28 3. 208 4. 192 5. 24 6. 66 7. 3000π 8. 8/27 9. 248 10. 16 11. 25 12. 25 13. 3π 14. 3.18 15. 9π 16. 324π 17. 64 18. 64 19. 10 20. 144

CHAPTER 18 - Problem Set 1

1. 13 2. –4 3. –4 4. –5 5. –5 6. 2 7. 3 8. 3 9. –4 10. Ø 11. 39 12. 131 13. –48 14. 6.6 15. 17 16. 10 17. 4 18. 3 19. 0 20. All

CHAPTER 18 - Problem Set 2

1. 9 2. 24 3. 6 4. 2 5. (0,2/3) 6. (2,0) 7. 58 8. (0,1) 9. 1/3 10. (2,–1) 11. X<3 12. X<6 13. X>3 14. X>–3 15. $y=-\frac{1}{2}x+1$ 16. 3y–5 17. R 18. 6 19. –3/4 20. y=3x–3

CHAPTER 19 - Problem Set 1

1. 36 2. 17 3. 7 4. 26 5. 3 6. 6 7. Odd 8. Even 9. Even 10. 9 11. 5 12. 6 13. –23 14. –280 15. 7 16. 10 17. 15 18. 16 19. 32/3 20. –120

CHAPTER 19 - Problem Set 2

1. 90 2. 5 3. 11 4. 1/3 5. C 6. C 7. Table. 8. Table. 9. Table. 10. Table. 11. C 12. C 13. A. $\frac{\sqrt{30}}{3}$ B. $\frac{\sqrt{3}}{2}$ 14. 1 15. $2\sqrt{5}+2\sqrt{2}$ 16. 136 17. 101 18. 150/203 19. 9/2 20. –210

CHAPTER 20 - Problem Set 1

1. 6.4 2. 6.5 3. 9 4. 11 5. 25 6. 12 7. 10 8. 48 9. 15 10. 13 11. 20 12. 2 13. 90 14. 7 15. 12 16. 7 17. 7 18. 7 19. 6 20. 16

CHAPTER 20 - Problem Set 2

1. 45 2. 1 3. 8 4. 20% 5. 24 6. 37 7. 37 8. 10 9. 19% 10. 3.25 11. 3 12. 3 13. 1.43 14. 35 15. 65 16. 16 17. 16 18. 151 19. 4 20. 55

CHAPTER 21 - Problem Set 1

1. 3 2. 6 3. A. {4,5,6,7,8,9,10}. B.7 4. a. AuC={0,1,2,3,4,5,6,7,10,12} b. BnC={3,6} 5. a. An(BuC)={0,2,4,6,12} b. Bu(AnC)={0,2,3,4,6,12,15} 6. 28 7. 6 8. 150 9. n(A) 10. a. {2,3,5,7} b. {2,4,6,8,10} c {2} d. This is an empty set 11. 5∈B 12. 3 13. 16 14. 40 15. 7 16. 19 17. 18 18. 3 19. 20 20. 20

CHAPTER 22 - BENCHMARK (Chapter 11-21)

1. 4 2. 9/4 3. –9 4. 16 5. 7 6. 8,12,16 7. 4 8. 72 9. 1024 10. 5 11. 8 12. 256 13. 3 14. 56 15. –2 16. 12 17. 32 18. 9/8 19. 10.25 20. 6

Post-Test

1. 34 2. 615 3. 1/5 4. 1/4 5. 12 6. 104,112,120,128,136,144 7. 36 8. 16 9. 55 10. 1300 11. 6 12. 11/9 13. 35/4 14. 1 15. 10 16. 3/2 17. 13/10 18. 22 19. 0,3,6,9 20. 8 21. 24 22. 18 23. 8 24. 12 25. 15 26. 81 27. 13 28. $5\frac{3}{7}$ 29. 1 30. 2592π

BOOK RESOURCES

Bay-Williams, J. M. (2020). Developing the "full package" of procedural fluency. Pearson.

Beckmann, S. (2018). [5th Edition] Mathematics for elementary teachers with activities. Boston: Pearson.

Fuson, Karen C., and Sybilla Beckmann. 2012–2013. "Standard Algorithms in the Common Core State Standards." In National Council of Supervisors of Mathematics Journal of Mathematics Education Leadership: 14–30.

Kilpatrick, Jeremy, Jane Swafford, and Bradford Findell. 2001. Adding It Up: Helping Children Learn Mathematics, edited by Jeremy Kilpatrick, Jane Swafford, and Bradford Findell, Mathematics Learning Study Committee, Center for Education, Division of Behavioral and Social Sciences and Education. Washington, DC: National Academy Press, 2001.

National Council of Teachers of Mathematics. (2014). Principles to actions: Ensuring mathematical success for all. Reston VA: Author.

WEB RESOURCES

https://brilliant.org/

https://illustrativemathematics.org/

https://www.openmiddle.com/

https://www.24game.com/

http://www.kenkenpuzzle.com/

https://www.youcubed.org/

https://mathtopia.com/

Made in the USA
Columbia, SC
16 November 2024